Manila and Santiago

Manila and Santiago

THE NEW STEEL NAVY IN THE
SPANISH-AMERICAN WAR

Jim Leeke

Naval Institute Press
Annapolis, Maryland

Naval Institute Press
291 Wood Road
Annapolis, MD 21402

Library of Congress Cataloging-in-Publication Data

Leeke, Jim, 1949–
    Manila and Santiago : the new steel Navy in the Spanish-American War / Jim Leeke.
        p. cm.
    Includes bibliographical references and index.
    ISBN 978-1-59114-464-9 (alk. paper)
        1. United States. Navy—History—Spanish-American War, 1898. 2. Spanish-American
War, 1898—Naval operations, American. 3. Spanish-American War, 1898—Philippines—
Manila. 4. Spanish-American War, 1898—Cuba—Santiago de Cuba. 5. Warships—United
States—History—19th century. 6. Ships, Iron and steel—United States—History—19th
century. 7. United States—History, Naval—To 1900. I. Title.
    E727.L44 2009
    973.8'945—dc22

                                                                              2009006331

Printed in the United States of America on acid-free paper

        16 15 14 13 12 11 10 09   9 8 7 6 5 4 3 2
                            First printing

For Rainey S. Taylor Jr. and Colonel Al Schalk

*The pleasant thing about fighting with the Spaniards, Mr. Ellis,
is not that they are shy, for they are not, but that
they are never, never ready.*
JACK AUBREY
in *Master and Commander*, by Patrick O'Brian

CONTENTS

AUTHOR NOTE

SOME AMERICAN NAVAL WRITERS adopt the British practice of referring to a warship without using the preceding article. Since George Dewey, Robley Evans, and their contemporaries spoke and wrote of "the *Olympia*" or "the *Iowa*," however, their example is followed here.

A choice must also be made in describing the Spanish naval force at Santiago de Cuba. Writers and even participants have used both "squadron" and "fleet" to describe it (Spaniards generally using the former and Americans the latter). For consistency, "fleet" is used here, except in direct quotations. The American force is also a fleet. At Manila Bay, in contrast, both opposing forces were clearly squadrons.

For reasons having little (but perhaps not nothing) to do with male chauvinism, a writer who himself served in the fleet during the Vietnam era can't easily refer to a warship as "it." The traditional if now politically incorrect "she" is used instead.

PART ONE

Thirty-Three Years
(1865–98)

CHAPTER 1

Fort Fisher

THE NOISE OF THE BOMBARDMENT was splendid and deafening. The fleet of sixty Federal men-of-war, comprising every class and silhouette from side-wheelers to screw sloops to gunboats to squat ugly monitors, stood off from the shore in tidy lines, anchored fore-and-aft, firing shells of every caliber and type into the great sand fortress.[1]

On the wooden deck of the steam frigate USS *Colorado,* Lieutenant George Dewey, the twenty-seven-year-old executive officer, watched dusk darken Smith's Island, a ten-mile sliver of barrier island separating cloudy Cape Fear River from the open Atlantic. At the island's southern tip sprawled Fort Fisher, a bristling rebel stronghold protecting the river approach to Wilmington, North Carolina. In this winter of 1864–65, Wilmington was the South's only open sea-port, the last destination of blockade runners. If Fort Fisher fell, the final door slammed shut to entomb the Confederacy.

As night descended, a breeze lifted a shroud of smoke and dust surrounding the fort. Dewey clearly saw its profile limned against the ebbing daylight. He watched the flash of Federal shells along its battered sand walls. The fleet began to slacken its fire, conserving its energies and ammunition for tomorrow. The bombardment would resume in the morning and continue until the land assault that afternoon. President Abraham Lincoln wanted the fort's capture, and Lieutenant Dewey expected that this time he would get it.[2]

. . .

A short, dark-haired, rather sleepy-eyed man, the youngest son of a Vermont doctor, Dewey was a graduate of the U.S. Naval Academy, Class of 1858. He had fought at New Orleans and in the hard, claustrophobic campaign along the

Mississippi. At Port Hudson, in 1863, he'd had a warship destroyed beneath him. (Ironically, it was the old side-wheeler USS *Mississippi*, Commodore Matthew Perry's former flagship and one of the "black ships" that opened Japan.) Dewey had later served on the sloop *Monongahela*, temporary flagship for David Glasgow Farragut. The great man had once chided Dewey for jumping when a shell screamed past. Dewey later swallowed a smile when the admiral did exactly the same thing. "Why, sir, you can't help it, sir," Farragut had admitted ruefully.[3] Dewey admired his directness and simplicity, which he considered supreme gifts in wartime.[4]

Now in January 1865, the admiral was ill. This fleet sailed under Farragut's foster brother, Rear-Admiral David Dixon Porter, a brilliant, aggressive, and vainglorious leader. Porter craved more than a supporting role for his fleet at Fort Fisher. When the Army charged the sand walls tomorrow, his newly formed naval brigade would attack with it. This was the second Federal expedition to Fort Fisher, and Porter was determined that this one would not end with a whimper.

Porter had reason to worry. Over Christmas, these same ships had approached Smith's Island and landed many of the same eight thousand troops. The fleet had bombarded the looming walls, less forcefully defended than now, and taken casualties doing it. On Dewey's *Colorado*, a 10-inch shot had pierced the starboard side and struck the Number 4 gun, killing one bluejacket and wounding four. The fleet bombardment and an odd scheme endorsed by Porter, a "powder-boat" packed with tons of black powder and exploded close inshore, had failed to silence the fort. Rebel defenders would later say the explosion had succeeded only in waking them in the middle of the night. Dewey thought it was "magnificent and spectacular but not helpful."[5]

The Federal Army commander, pompous and incompetent General Benjamin "Spoons" Butler, afterward had declined to attack. The fleet and not a few soldiers seethed in disgust until Lincoln sacked his reluctant general and ordered the entire expedition back to Fort Fisher. The lesson, it seemed to Dewey, was that the thing to do when the president expected you to attack was to *attack*.[6]

. . .

Normally he would have led the ship's landing force, but Lieutenant Dewey wouldn't be going ashore tomorrow afternoon. His captain was second in seniority to Porter, and if the admiral fell the fleet command would pass to him. *Colorado*'s skipper naturally wanted the executive officer on board to take charge of the ship if that happened. Dewey was disappointed, but understood.

On board the first-class side-wheeler *Powhatan,* Robley Dunglison Evans looked forward to the landing.[7] The eighteen-year-old acting ensign had the stature and grit of a bantam rooster. A shell that had nearly cut him from the rigging during the first expedition hadn't lessened his enthusiasm for the campaign. As the officer of the deck when the order forming the brigade had arrived, Evans had put his name at the top of the volunteers' list. Many others were equally eager. Two of Evans' friends had flipped a penny for one spot in the brigade. He and a former classmate let a superior officer pick between them for a second. The officer had chosen Evans.

Like George Dewey, "Bob" Evans was a doctor's son. Like Dewey, he was an Annapolis graduate—Class of '64, which the war had propelled into the fleet a year early. Also like Dewey, Evans wasn't averse to a scrap. "Shang" Dewey had lunged across an Annapolis mess table at a classmate who had insulted him, and had once threatened to shoot a mutinous bluejacket. Evans' left ankle bore a scar from a Blackfoot arrow, a souvenir of his trek alone to the Utah Territory. Although the two had never met, Dewey and Evans would have enjoyed one another's company. There, however, their similarities ended.

Evans was a Virginian, born in the Blue Ridge Mountains. Doctor Evans had owned slaves, although his son would later recall that he had never mistreated or sold them. After the elder Evans' death, Bob had gone to live with an uncle in Washington, D.C., where he discovered the waterfront and an unexpected passion for the sea. Befriended there by Utah's delegate to Congress, he later headed west to establish the residency that would secure him an appointment to the Naval Academy. Venturing beyond the Mississippi in 1859 meant hard travel, deprivations, and perhaps Indian raids, but thirteen-year-old Bob survived them all with seeming relish.

After a year in Salt Lake City among the Mormons, Evans received his appointment to Annapolis. Returning to the east, he survived a windstorm in Kansas that rivaled any gale he would later encounter at sea. Caught in the open, several trains of "prairie schooners" lived up to their name. The wagons would "run some distance before the wind," he recalled decades later, "and then, as they got canted one way or the other, would capsize and spill out women and children and whatever else happened to be in them."[8] He reached Annapolis safely in August and passed his entrance exams the next month, several weeks before the momentous presidential election of 1860.

Evans soon settled in at the Academy as a midshipman. The following spring, he faced the fundamental question of loyalty that faced every Southern officer, midshipman, and cadet. If civil war came, did he follow Nation or State? The Academy was forced to abandon Annapolis in April 1861, when midshipmen loyal to the Union embarked on the venerable USS *Constitution* after tear-ful farewells to resigning classmates. Heeding the advice of his commandant to "stand by the Old Flag," Evans boarded Old Ironsides with the Yankees. He never regretted his decision. His younger brother, who served in the rebel artillery under John Pelham, never questioned it, either. (Evans said nothing to Federal sentries during the war when he glimpsed his brother in a tavern near Washington.) Their mother, however, was hurt and ashamed. It would be years before Sally Ann Evans forgave her elder son his choice of country over family.[9]

Evans received his commission as an acting ensign on October 1, 1863. A year later, before the Navy's first failed expedition to Wilmington, his brother warned him in a letter sent though the lines, "We will give you a warm recep-tion at Fort Fisher when you get there!"[10] Now it was the night before the sec-ond assault. On board the *Powhatan*, Evans found Seaman James Flannigan waiting to speak with him. The bluejacket asked Evans to take charge of a small box—"it has some little trinkets in it"—and give it to his sister in Philadelphia. Evans asked why he couldn't deliver it himself.

"I am going ashore with you tomorrow," Flannigan said matter-of-factly, "and will be killed."[11]

A veteran of Indian skirmishes and naval engagements, the young ensign tried to tell Flannigan how difficult it was to kill a man. Nothing dissuaded the bluejacket, who seemed to regard his death as a matter of course. Evans finally accepted the box, made a note of it, and stowed it among his personal gear. If he harbored any dark fears about his own fate in the morning, he kept them to himself.

· · ·

January 15, 1865, was a Sunday. It dawned clear and warm, with breezes from the north and west.[12] The North Carolina seascape, so glorious in peacetime, seemed to mock the combatants with its colors—dazzling blues for the Federals who had come from the sea, sandy grays and browns for the Confederates hunched in the fortress along the low barrier island.

The winter sun climbed higher and the fleet came sharply into focus along the horizon. The warships resumed their thunderous bombardment. During the two days, Porter's fleet would expend eighteen thousand shells. But Lord Nelson had declared that "[a] ship's a fool to fight a fort," and even a fleet could-n't capture one. About one o'clock, the *Powhatan* acknowledged the signal, "Land naval brigade." Thirty-five ships contributed men to the force. They had a smooth, sunny beach for the landing. Cheered off by their shipmates, Ensign

Evans and the chosen Powhatans pulled for shore. They aimed for a spot a mile and a half above the fort's northeastern angle, but rebel sharpshooters harassed the landing. The handle of a ball-shattered stroke oar struck Evans sharply across the stomach. The ensign felt broken in two, but reached the beach with no further harm.[13]

The landing parties assembled under their ships' flags. Sixteen hundred blue-jackets and officers plus four hundred Marines comprised the brigade. The plan called for the Marines to dig in near the fort and cover the bluejackets, who at three o'clock would assault the fort's northeastern corner along the seafront. The Army would simultaneously attack the northwestern corner, on the land-front along the Cape Fear River. Like so many grand schemes hatched during the war, the plan went awry almost immediately.

At first, the sailors moved jauntily along the beach under their flags, as if on a lark. The "webfoots" would show the Army how to capture a fort. They got to within about twelve hundred yards of the walls, then lay down in the shelter of dunes. One large rebel gun was still in action. Evans watched its shells ricochet down the beach like jackrabbits.[14] The time was closer to 3:30 than three o'clock when the flagship USS *Malvern* hoisted the signal for the fleet to cease fire.

The Marines weren't ready, the sailors were disorganized, and the soldiers across the island weren't yet in position. None of it mattered. The *Malvern* blew her steam whistle, followed by the whistle of every other ship in the fleet, the signal for attack. The bluejackets rose and started forward amid the thrilling din. On board the *Colorado*, Lieutenant Dewey saw them as clearly as a stage pantomime. With cutlasses and revolvers, the attack reminded him of boarding parties from the War of 1812. Or worse, of the charge of the Light Brigade.[15]

Ensign Evans enjoyed those first moments. He moved forward with his shipmates, following the *Powhatan*'s flag. Then the brigade's three divisions quickly lost cohesion and the charge became a footrace. Defenders appeared on the fort's sandy walls to lay down a murderous fire with Enfield muskets. At eight hundred yards, Seaman Flannigan reeled and fell, a rebel bullet through his heart. Evans stopped and tried to help, but Flannigan smiled and quickly died.

The brigade swept on before stopping suddenly at five hundred yards. The bluejackets dropped to the sand without any signal. By now, none was needed. The officers rallied them, but murderous fire stopped the charge again at three hundred yards. After another rally, Evans was near enough to the walls to hear the rebels yelling. Officers pulled their caps down over their eyes rather than glimpse what Evans later called "the deadly flashing blue line of parapet."[16]

Evans later claimed he'd spotted the Confederate colonel who commanded the fort encouraging his men from atop the wall. The ensign took aim with his Navy Colt. A bullet ripped across his chest and spun him around before he could squeeze off the improbable shot. Evans pulled himself up, bleeding, and went to the head of his company. They moved toward a shell-wracked wooden palisade or stockade that stood in front of the fort. A sharpshooter aimed at the determined young ensign and put a shot through his left leg.

Half a dozen silk handkerchiefs that Evans had carried ashore for the purpose helped stanch the flow of blood. He led a movement around the stockade, hoping to charge the angle of the fort, which now looked impossibly high. The Confederate sharpshooter sent another bullet through Evans' right knee. Behind him, the brigade fell apart. With all the officers at the head of the columns, no one remained behind to steady the shocked bluejackets. They broke for safety.

Seven of the eight men who had made it past the stockade were wounded. Evans and those near him lay trapped almost in the shadow of the walls. Rebel balls spattered in the sand like hail. The sharpshooter kept firing down at the ensign from a hundred feet, cursing as he fired. Hit a fourth time, in the foot, Evans returned the curses. He leveled his big Colt and sent a shot through his tormentor's throat. The Confederate pitched dead over the parapet. A coxswain lying nearby begged, "Mr. Evans, let me crawl over and give that . . . another shot."[17] The furious bluejacket then died, pierced through the lungs.

Evans struggled to survive the afternoon as the fleet resumed its bombardment. Men fell and died all around him. The young ensign watched from a hole as the Army, in action at last, fought magnificently from one rebel battery to another. It was past nightfall when he finally reached a casualty station. There he ducked a rain of embers and shrapnel when a Confederate gunboat fired at the campfire, killing several of the wounded.

The exchange between Federal gunners and the fortress had meanwhile grown heated. The rebels seemed particularly to target Lieutenant Dewey's *Colorado*, which was struck by several shells. Porter ordered the ship to work in closer and continue firing. "We shall be safer in there," Dewey called to his men, "and the works can be taken in fifteen minutes."[18]

Evans soon saw the results of this prophetic bravado. At 9:30, after six hours under fire, with his bloody uniform now cut away and nearly naked except for another officer's cape, he reached the safety of the gunboat USS *Nereus*. As gentle hands lowered him onto a cot, Evans saw a signal torch flash on the parapet of Fort Fisher.

"T-H-E F-O-R-T I-S O-U-R . . ."
Pandemonium erupted before the final letter.[19]

. . .

Rockets arced into the Carolina night and blue lights appeared among the darkened fleet. Bluejackets cheered from the riggings and big guns boomed in victory. Dewey felt mixed emotions as the celebration swept the fleet. He was impressed by the Army's ability when allowed to fight, and proud of the bluejackets who had allowed the soldiers to gain their vital foothold atop the walls. But he would always question the wisdom of ordering the brigade forward.

(Admiral Porter recounted the quixotic adventure of the powder-boat for nearly six pages in his Civil War memoirs, but relegated the second expedition to Fort Fisher to a single paragraph. He omitted any mention of his naval brigade or its cutlasses and Colts.)

The fleet fired its rockets long into the night. More than thirty years later, at the dawn of a new century, when young lieutenants and ensigns had risen to the heights of their service, when a gleaming new steel navy had replaced the canvas and steam of their days under Farragut and Porter, Commodore George Dewey of the Asiatic Squadron and Captain Robley Evans of the battleship USS *Iowa* would again fight a war together. Both would remember what they had learned at Fort Fisher. For now, however, their fight was finished. The land war would drag into another season, but this was the Navy's Appomattox.

The first morning of victory dawned cold and raw beneath a gray drizzle. The casualties' wounds were stiff and sore. American flags flapped at half-mast throughout the fleet. Shortly after daylight, Ensign Evans was transferred to a side-wheel steamer for medical care until he could reach a hospital. Viewed with the hindsight of the coming century, the vessel's name was ironic and eerie.

It was *Santiago de Cuba.*

CHAPTER 2

The Doldrums

ENSIGN EVANS wasn't an ideal patient. Doctors at the naval hospital in Norfolk, Virginia, wanted to amputate his mangled legs. He decided instead to risk slow death from gangrene rather than face life as a double amputee. Evans threatened to use his big Colt revolver on anyone who came through his door "with anything that looked like a case of instruments."[1]

The doctors wisely left him alone for two weeks, during which time he developed a dangerous fever. A surgeon's wife and daughter and a wounded bluejacket named Milligan nursed him through it. Recovery from his wounds took much longer, however, and physicians often expected Evans' death. "I was a skeleton, and nothing more," he recalled.[2] Nonetheless, he was lucky. When his ship called at Norfolk in February, he learned how terribly the naval brigade had been punished at Fort Fisher. Every officer in the *Powhatan*'s landing party had been wounded. Fifty-four of sixty-two men in his company were dead or wounded.[3]

It was June before Evans felt well enough to talk his way out of the hospital. He left on a stretcher in the care of Milligan and joined his uncle in Philadelphia. After a "slow and very tedious convalescence,"[4] he returned to limited duty, assigned first to the Philadelphia navy yard, then to Washington. On crutches and unable to use his right leg, the ensign feared the end of his career. He conceived a desperate solution. He would have his right knee broken again and set "at such an angle that I could walk on it." A prominent Philadelphia surgeon agreed to perform the operation, which was painful but ultimately successful.[5]

After his recovery, Evans faced another hurdle. A medical board had placed him on the retired list, on the grounds that he couldn't perform all of his duties at sea. He was experienced in solving sticky problems like this, however. His

Southern mother had submitted his resignation from the Naval Academy in 1861 without telling him, and Evans had scrambled to get the resignation canceled. Now, as "the only officer in the navy retired for wounds received in battle," he not only got himself reinstated by Congress, he also received a promotion and was advanced thirty numbers on the active list.[6]

The tenacious new lieutenant next set about returning to sea and performing normal duties. By applying directly to her captain, he secured an assignment on the new screw sloop *Piscataqua*, due to depart as flagship for the China station. In October 1867, Evans arrived in Portsmouth, New Hampshire, and within weeks was outbound through snow and ice for South America and the Horn, his career resurrected.

In decades ahead, he would become known as "Fighting Bob" Evans to scores of newspapermen and the American public, and more prosaically as "Old Gimpy" to his seamen. A future president, Theodore Roosevelt, would one day eulogize his "touch of brilliant picturesqueness,"[7] characteristic of great fighting admirals. But that was all in the far distance. Today, nearly three years after Fort Fisher, Lieutenant Evans was content simply to walk a deck, if with a painful corrective device on one leg. Eventually he would toss it into the Indian Ocean as useless.

· · ·

As the long, excruciating ordeal ended for Bob Evans, George Dewey, now a young lieutenant-commander, also began a period of apparent good fortune.

The same month that Evans returned triumphantly to sea, Dewey married Susan Boardman Goodwin. She was the pretty, curly-haired daughter of a former governor of New Hampshire. The couple lived happily for the next three years at the Naval Academy, where Dewey was an instructor, again under Admiral Porter. "There were a great many other young officers and their brides at that station," Dewey recalled fondly.[8] Wags dubbed Annapolis "Porter's Dancing Academy" for the superintendent's social inclinations.

Following brief stints at sea and the Boston navy yard, Dewey next reported to the torpedo station at Newport, Rhode Island. He and his wife looked forward to having their first baby there. Instead, joy arrived almost simultaneously with sorrow. Susan Dewey died on December 28, 1872, five days after the birth of their son, two days after her husband's thirty-fifth birthday.

His great physical courage useless in dealing with domestic tragedy, Dewey nearly crumpled under the blow. He reacted with a kind of emotional flight, hastily resuming his career and avoiding Newport, "which was ever to have sad associations for me."[9] Susan's family agreed to rear his son, also named George, and for many years Dewey would see little of him. In the spring of 1873, newly promoted to commander, he left the East Coast for the Pacific, there to take command of the third-class screw sloop *Narragansett.*

Four decades later, in his 1913 autobiography, Dewey described the birth and death with a brevity that might easily be mistaken for callousness. This was misleading. Dewey took pleasure in young George, and exchanged letters with him as the boy grew up. He also kept a photograph of his late wife tucked inside a gold watch that was inscribed *My Susie.* He said quietly a quarter century after her passing, "My wife goes with me always."[10]

. . .

Just as they were for George Dewey, the 1870s were an era of transition and unhappiness for the Navy. Over a span of a dozen years, the Navy's course had traced a remarkable parabola, from exuberant wartime evolution and growth to the current steep decline. Widower Dewey likely understood the progression.

Advances during the Civil War had sparked interest and competition for the Navy abroad. Peacetime, however, had produced exactly the opposite effect in America. Indeed, reversals began even before the Confederacy's capitulation. Almost overnight, the world's most modern fleet started disintegrating into a rotting, impotent force that would have been hard-pressed to defeat a fifth-rate banana republic. The Navy went backward, a Horatio Alger story in reverse. Its riches-to-rags stagnation led to twenty years of frustration for officers like Evans and Dewey, who nonetheless found the strength to remain in its uniform.

The reasons for this neglect were simple. A century and a quarter later, Captain Edward L. Beach Jr. cited "returning isolationism, the cost of modernizing, and the fact that the nation was mortally tired"[11]—all remarkably like the impulses that had led to the rapid demobilization of the U.S. Army (if not of the Navy) following World War II.

Secretary of the Navy Gideon Welles began selling surplus and unwanted ships after Fort Fisher. By the end of 1865, he had sold off half the fleet, mostly converted merchantmen. He likewise suspended construction of four *Kalamazoo*-class monitors—"the closest that the U.S. Navy ever came to including armored oceangoing 'battleships' until the 1890s," according to a Navy historian.[12] Welles actually *returned* money to the treasury in 1867.[13] By the end of that year, the Navy was down to two hundred thirty-eight vessels from nearly seven hundred at the height of the war, with just fifty-six actually in commission. Construction of the monitors never resumed and reductions continued.

A smaller Navy was understandable and rational. The war was over, after all, and the Navy was large by any peacetime standard. Far more dangerous, however, was the government's parsimony and immobility during a time of rapid technological change. It chose to ignore advances by European navies that expanded upon designs and ideas often introduced and tested in American waters. After the Civil War, Dewey succinctly wrote, the country "allowed Europe to have fifteen years the start on us."[14]

Postwar politicians simply foresaw no foreign entanglements important enough to require ordering powerful squadrons abroad. And if a foreign fleet should menace the East or West Coast, why, monitors alone could counter the threat. Exuberant Americans focused their attention westward, within their own borders, intent on fulfilling the manifest destiny. Thus continued a long, sad period during which, Dewey likewise observed, "the country took no interest in its defences and our ships did little cruising."[15]

The Navy's enfeeblement continued until what became known as the "*Virginius* affair," when the implications became all too apparent.

It began in October 1873, when Cuba was in the midst of a ten-year insurrection against Spain. Joseph Fry, a veteran of both the U.S. and Confederate navies, attempted to run guns to Cuban rebels near Santiago. A Spanish warship stopped his side-wheel steamer, the *Virginius*, and arrested his crew, many of whom were Americans. Local Spanish authorities quickly tried, convicted, and executed as "pirates" fifty-three people, including Captain Fry. Outrage in America was predictably swift and loud. It was also largely irrelevant, since the Navy could have done little in the way of meting out punishment to the Spaniards. Uncle Sam nonetheless rattled his few rusty sabers.

Orders went out in February recalling the Navy's European and South Atlantic fleets. They assembled at Key West, just ninety miles from Havana. This scratch force was nearly everything the Navy possessed. Bob Evans and several of his old Annapolis classmates arrived in the Florida Keys. Evans was now a lieutenant-commander, navigator of the wooden screw sloop *Shenandoah*. He later recalled being "dreadfully mortified" by the scene in Key West. Conditions were pathetic, stores nonexistent, and the fleet laughable.

"We of the navy knew long before this that our so-called naval force was a sham," he wrote in his memoirs, "and that the country was absolutely without sea power." Two modern warships, he added, "would have done us up in thirty minutes."[16]

"Our all was not much at that time," agreed Evans' former classmate, Lieutenant-Commander Charles E. Clark, executive officer of the monitor

Mahopac. The top steaming speed this combined fleet could manage was a miserable four-and-a-half knots. "Nearly all our ships were fitted with spar torpedoes, and these were expected to inflict great damage on the enemy," Clark dryly noted, "always provided he would stay quiet until we got alongside."[17]

The situation looked much different to George Dewey on the continent's opposite shore. Commanding the *Narragansett* on a survey mission in the Gulf of California, Dewey found his officers gathered glumly in the wardroom, all believing they would miss the war that seemed almost inevitable. His response was both immediate and startling.

"On the contrary," Dewey declared, "we shall be very much in it. If war with Spain is declared, the *Narragansett* will take Manila."[18]

He didn't record his officers' reaction. Perhaps they took him at his word. Perhaps, like Clark, they imagined that "the Spaniards were no better off than we, so . . . a fight would have seen us on the winning side."[19] Whatever their emotions, they certainly remembered Dewey's prophetic assertion a quarter-century later.

Despite his confidence, Dewey surely realized the distressing state of the Navy. Probably he did believe he could accomplish something at Manila. But looking back from the perspective of flag rank, he recalled a service that was "the laughing stock of nations," so outdated and tired it represented "a mere waste of money in keeping the relics in commission."[20]

Spain eventually defused the *Virginius* crisis by paying indemnities to the families of the men she had executed. For its part, the United States decided that the steamer had no right to fly an American flag. Otherwise, war might have followed and the long decline of the Navy might have stopped right there— although at what cost to either side is impossible to know.

It would be another decade before the United States finally began reshaping a navy that Admiral Porter once likened to a Chinese fort, painted with dragons to frighten away enemies.[21] Under the prodding of such reformers as Captain Alfred Thayer Mahan, a new steel navy at last began taking shape. But even as late as 1889, although building rapidly, the Navy still ranked a miserable and embarrassing twelfth in the world, lagging even the navies of China and Chile.[22] Visiting admirals sometimes grew misty at the sight of muzzle-loading weapons still in service aboard the Navy's oldest vessels (*"Ah! Capitaine, les vieux canons!"*). [23]

Some American officers called the period that followed the Civil War "the Doldrums." Others marked it down as the "Dark Ages." None who rose to prominence in the decades that followed remembered it with fondness or for a moment mourned its passing.

CHAPTER 3

The Commodore

IN THE LONG YEARS following the *Virginius* affair, George Dewey persevered and reaped what rewards there were.

After the *Narragansett*, he commanded the *Juniata* and *Pensacola*. The *Juniata* was a second-rate sloop of Civil War vintage, which in 1882 he found "as out of date as a stage-coach," good as "something that would float" in peacetime, and to be "murdered in by a few broadsides" during war. The venerable *Pensacola*, which he commanded five years later, was no better. There wasn't "a fourth-rate British cruiser of modern build that could not easily have kept out of range of her battery, torn her to pieces, and set her on fire."[1]

With the *Juniata* in the Mediterranean, Dewey nearly died of complications of typhoid fever and an abscessed liver. As was also true of many of his contemporaries, his health was never perfect afterward. He made captain at age forty-seven. "I was old for a captain who had just been promoted from commander," he later wrote, "and at an age when many English officers receive the grade of rear-admiral."[2]

Coming ashore, he had common but unglamorous duty as a lighthouse inspector. He also served as naval secretary of the Light House Board and chief of the Bureau of Equipment. He reached the rank of commodore in 1896. In the summer of 1897, still ashore, he was apparently nearing the end of his career. His service in the Civil War had been impressive. His peacetime record was impeccable if unremarkable for its slow, steady progression. When Dewey wore dress blues, a Washington wag noted, with his ruddy complexion and hair now gone white, he rather resembled Old Glory.[3]

Now president of the Board of Inspection and Survey, the commodore lived a comfortable bachelor life at the Hotel Everett in Washington. He daily rode a horse named Nancy along Rock Creek, and was considered something of a dandy in the Navy Department, where a pair of his russet-yellow civilian shoes had caused amusement.[4] His son George hadn't followed him to Annapolis, but was beginning his final year at Princeton. The two corresponded and occasionally visited. Although he would celebrate his sixtieth birthday the day after Christmas, Dewey had no thought of retiring before reaching the mandatory retirement age of sixty-two. There was always the chance of further action, he believed, while on the active list.

Although assigned ashore, the commodore considered his duty important. The first vessels of the "new steel navy" were the so-called ABCD ships. These were the protected cruisers *Atlanta, Boston*, and *Chicago*, and the quick little dispatch vessel *Dolphin*. (Dewey had briefly commanded the latter in 1884 before her commissioning.) Next came the capital ships, which were called "coast defense battle-ships,"[5] because neither Congress nor the public still saw much need for a blue-water, offensive fleet. The Board of Inspection and Survey was responsible for certifying that these new battleships all met the Navy's specifications.

Dewey had presided at the sea trials of the *Texas, Maine, Iowa, Indiana*, and *Massachusetts* (although not of the *Oregon*, built on the West Coast), plus those of five cruisers and a number of torpedo boats. If the battleships didn't measure up, Dewey had little doubt that a major political scandal would erupt. "No professional work of any kind," Dewey's Navy historian, Commander Nathan Sargent, would write, "could have been more catholic in its scope or better adapted as preparatory experience for a naval commander-in-chief."[6]

Familiar names from Annapolis now commanded ships and squadrons in the expanding Navy. Four current or future battleship captains were members of the Class of '64. Bob Evans would soon command the *Iowa* and Charles Clark the *Oregon*, while Henry Taylor (now Evans' brother-in-law) already had the *Indiana* and Charles Sigsbee the *Maine*. Like Dewey, all but Clark were veterans of the battle at Fort Fisher.[7] The Navy suddenly resembled a musty old private club that after years of neglect and debate had thrown open its shutters.

He hadn't had sea duty in eight years, but as a new commodore Dewey was entitled to lead a squadron. Although the Asiatic Squadron would soon become available, he doubted he would get the appointment. Dewey considered the man who made the assignments, Rear-Admiral Arent S. Crowninshield, chief of the Bureau of Navigation, a bureaucrat out of step with the majority of capable naval officers of the time. Worse, he knew that an Annapolis classmate, Commodore John A. Howell, was also in line for the squadron.[8]

Fortunately, Dewey had a friend in Theodore Roosevelt, the new assistant secretary of the navy. Roosevelt considered him ideal for the assignment. Young and energetic, a former New York City police superintendent, "Teddy" Roosevelt fervently believed that America would soon be at war with Spain, and that the Navy needed men like Dewey, Evans, and their classmates in key positions to fight it. He was especially struck by an incident in Dewey's service record. In 1891, when a crisis had suddenly bubbled up with Chile in what became known as the *Baltimore* affair, the Navy had required coal to send war-ships around the Horn. Dewey had demanded and received an increased allot-ment. As the story reached Roosevelt, Dewey had then been stuck with it when the affair blew over, and for a time had faced the prospect of a reprimand.[9]

This account wasn't entirely accurate—Roosevelt mistakenly believed Dewey was at sea off Argentina, when in fact he headed the equipment bureau—but Roosevelt was impressed by the display of initiative. He thought Dewey could be "slipped like a wolf-hound from a leash" if war came.[10] The aging commodore and the young assistant secretary met in Washington to dis-cuss their mutual interests.

Roosevelt was the *de facto* navy secretary while the man who actually held the office, John D. Long, took an extended vacation to recover his health. "His ardor," Long later noted, not without admiration, "sometimes went faster than the President or the department approved."[11] Roosevelt disliked officers maneuvering for cushy assignments, but felt that the Asiatic Squadron was an exception. Determined to boost Dewey's candidacy, he had already intercepted and pigeon-holed another senator's letter urging Long to appoint Commodore Howell. Roosevelt felt that Howell was unfit for such responsibility.[12]

"I want you to go," he told Dewey. "You are a man who will be equal to the emergency if one arises. Do you know any senators?"

"Senator [Redfield] Proctor is from my state," the commodore replied, meaning Vermont. "He is an old friend of the family, and my father was of ser-vice to him when he was a young man."[13]

Roosevelt thought Dewey couldn't have a better sponsor, and urged him to speak with Proctor soon. Months later, after Manila, when sudden fame had led to speculation about his own political ambitions, Dewey would sidestep a jour-nalist's question about his party affiliation. A sailor, he said, had no politics. Pointing to his dog, who often accompanied him about the quarterdeck, Dewey added, "I know as much about politics as Bob here."[14]

The quip was disingenuous (if later proven accurate during an ill-advised presidential bid in 1900). Dewey's father had used connections to secure his appointment to Annapolis, his late wife had been the daughter of a powerful governor, and his brothers' political ties in Vermont had helped secure him the earlier Bureau of Equipment posting.[15] Realizing that he held a valuable political string, the commodore promptly pulled it.

Dewey called on Proctor, the senator saw President William McKinley the same day, and Secretary Long returned from vacation to find a White House memorandum recommending Dewey for the Asiatic Squadron. Long dutifully issued the order, in what Roosevelt later called "a fortunate hour for the Nation."[16] (Howell would later command the European Squadron and rise to rear-admiral.) Crowninshield at the Bureau of Navigation was irritated, however. He told Dewey that Long was irate at his political intrigue. The commodore promptly visited Long to set the record straight.

"Mr. Secretary, I understand that you are displeased with me for having used influence to secure command of the Asiatic Squadron," Dewey said. "I did so because it was the only way of offsetting influence that was being exerted on another officer's behalf."

"You are in error, Commodore," Long replied stiffly. "No influence has been brought to bear on behalf of anyone else."

Dewey left the office, no doubt dissatisfied and puzzled by the exchange. A few hours afterward, however, he received a note from Long stating that a letter supporting Howell *had* been received during his absence. Wily Roosevelt had only just brought it to his attention.[17]

Roosevelt then continued his support despite opposition from West Coast politicians, who preferred a favorite son. The assistant secretary dealt brusquely with a delegation protesting Dewey's appointment. "Gentlemen, I can't agree with you," he told them. "We have looked up his record. We have looked him straight in the eyes. He is a fighter. We'll not change now. Pleased to have met you. Good day, gentlemen."[18]

On October 21, Dewey got orders detaching him from duty on the inspection board, effective at the end of November. He was to board a steamer in San Francisco the following month, then report aboard the flagship USS *Olympia* of the Asiatic Squadron. He also paid a price for pulling his one string, however. The Navy customarily gave a commodore commanding the squadron the acting rank of rear-admiral from the moment he hoisted his flag. Dewey would hoist only the broad pennant of a commodore. Secretary Long personally informed him of the decision.[19]

Worse than mere bureaucratic retribution, the snub could have hampered Dewey in dealing with other powers operating in Asia. Had an emergency required international cooperation—as the Boxer Rebellion in China would do just two years later—the commodore would have found himself subordinate to a British, German, or Russian admiral. Dewey had to accept it, however. He took consolation in a friend's observation that the only predecessor who had ever made a name for himself on the station was another commodore—Matthew C. Perry, whose old flagship, the *Mississippi*, Dewey had served to its blazing end on its namesake river.[20]

"I have received what is to me the best gift the president could make," Dewey wrote to a relative, with obviously mixed emotions. "[But] I will not receive my promotion to Rear-Admiral until next summer, a new rule to that effect having been recently made."[21]

. . .

Preparing for what was surely his last assignment after more than four decades wearing a uniform, "Gentleman George Dewey" was respected, liked by his peers, and almost unknown outside the tight little orbit of the Navy. His friends at the Metropolitan Club in Washington threw a farewell dinner for him there in late November. Colonel Archibald Hopkins, clerk of the Court of Claims, proposed a poetic toast that would not only survive, but in time gain some little renown. The first and last of its five stanzas were strangely prophetic:

> *Fill all your glasses full to-night,*
> *The wind is off the shore;*
> *And be it feast or be it fight,*
> *We pledge the Commodore. . . .*

> *And when he takes the homeward tack,*
> *Beneath an Admiral's flag,*
> *We'll hail the day that brings him back,*
> *And have another jag.*

(Hopkins later discreetly changed the lines to read "An Admiral's banner won . . . And laud the duty done.")[22]

The commodore started the long journey to his new command. Traveling by rail for San Francisco, he took with him a pile of books about the Far East. He had already spent the previous month poring over maps and descriptions of the Philippines, which were almost unknown to the U.S. Navy. No American warship had visited the islands in years, and the most recent naval intelligence report Dewey had unearthed was dated 1876.[23] Meticulous as always, he was determined to be prepared for anything that might happen in the region.

At the end of 1897, not one person in ten in official Washington believed that war was brewing with Madrid.[24] Spain was a declining colonial power that had rubbed uneasily against the United States in the Caribbean for decades. Few foresaw much change, but the assistant secretary was influential in the Navy Department among the 10 percent who did. Roosevelt prepared with characteristic energy for war—and, unlike hawkish officials in later administrations, was personally prepared to take up arms and fight it.

Roosevelt believed that national interests such as sugar and tobacco were justification enough for war with Spain. Far more compelling, however, were the conditions in Cuba, where revolt against Spanish rule had long simmered like so much poisoned rice—"so dreadful," he recalled in his autobiography, "as to be a standing disgrace to us for permitting them to exist."[25]

Dewey, however, like any competent officer, was more concerned with preparation and planning. He had long ago determined his course of action against Spain while commanding the *Narragansett*. Bound again for the Pacific, he still intended to take Manila, if and when the orders came.

The commodore's main concern as he rocked westward on the train was ammunition. He had discovered that the Asiatic Squadron hadn't yet received even its peacetime allotment of shells. A shipment had been ordered, Commander Sargent later wrote, but "with the red tape of official conservatism it was suspended like Mahomet's coffin between the upper and nether firmament."[26]

Dewey had tried to hurry it along, only to be told that no steamer or merchant vessel would carry it. The ammo was slated to go out on the cruiser *Charleston*. That ship was undergoing repairs, however, and likely wouldn't sail for another half year. That suited neither Dewey nor Roosevelt. They had arranged for the USS *Concord* to take as much as possible when she left for the Asiatic station from the Mare Island navy yard.

Upon reaching San Francisco Bay in early December, Dewey went to Mare Island and personally urged the yard commandant to load the *Concord* with every bit of ammunition she could carry. He also suggested that the 230-foot gunboat stop at Honolulu and Japan for stores, allowing more room for powder and shells. Aided by her skipper, Dewey saw the little *Concord* crammed with an astonishing thirty-five tons of ammunition—almost half his squadron's allotment. The remaining thirty-seven tons would be shipped later on the elderly sloop *Mohican*. Even if Dewey ever received the full amount, however, his magazines and shell-rooms still would be only 60 percent full.[27]

Having made his arrangements, the commodore then boarded the mail steamer *Gaelic*, accompanied by his flag lieutenant and flag secretary. Various junior officers had declined his tentative invitations to join him in the backwaters of Asia, and Dewey was grateful to the pair that had accepted, Lieutenant Thomas M. Brumby and Ensign Harry H. Caldwell.[28] The party left San Francisco on December 7 and reached Yokohama in time for Christmas. Dewey celebrated his birthday the next day. He relieved Acting Rear-Admiral F. B. McNair on January 3 and hoisted his commodore's pennant over the *Olympia* in Nagasaki harbor.

In addition to the flagship, Dewey's small squadron included the cruiser *Boston* and the gunboats *Petrel* and *Monocacy*. The latter was a Civil War–era side-wheeler of inconsequential value except for river patrol. The crews were mostly long-service men, many of them foreign-born. The flag captain was Charles Vernon Gridley, who had fought at Mobile Bay under Farragut and was an Annapolis classmate of Bob Evans. Liked by his crew, Gridley was also a rarity for the ten years he had served in the "fresh water navy" on the Great Lakes, on the USS *Michigan* out of Erie and in the Tenth Lighthouse District in Buffalo.[29] The commodore soon ordered Gridley to set a course to Yokohama, where the *Olympia* would await the *Concord*.

Settling in to his new command, Dewey studied briefing papers on the German navy's seizure the previous month of Kiau-Chau Bay in China and on official attitudes of Japan. He knew the region was also very concerned about worsening relations between England and Russia. Locally, American relations were often poor with the Japanese, and the *Olympia*'s liberty men had recently fought a huge brawl in Kobe.[30] The Philippines rated only a brief paragraph, which included a reference to newspaper accounts of "a rebellion in progress."[31]

The friction ashore didn't prevent an officially warm welcome for the new commodore in Yokohama. Dewey's most important duty once he arrived was to board a train for the short trip to Tokyo, where on February 4 he met the imperial family. He had requested the audience not only because it was customary, but also for "the perhaps more interested motive of one who might need and whose duty it was to cultivate the good offices of their Government."[32]

Dewey would fondly remember the occasion for the rest of his life. The emperor wore a military uniform and his wife a Parisian dress. Except for the surroundings, Dewey recorded, he might have been in a palace in Berlin or St. Petersburg. What a contrast, he reflected, with Commodore Perry's xenophobic reception forty-four years earlier.[33]

The little *Concord* arrived in Yokohama with its precious cargo five days later. After transferring the ammunition, Dewey steamed for Hong Kong on February 11 to meet the gunboat *Petrel*. Although relations with Spain were tense and Washington had ordered him to retain bluejackets whose enlistments had expired, [34] he headed for the British colony on his own initiative, with no inkling of an imminent crisis. The movement would prove provident, however, because Hong Kong was the logical point at which to concentrate the scattered Asiatic Squadron.

Word of the catastrophic explosions that had sunk the battleship *Maine* reached the colony before the *Olympia* steamed into Hong Kong harbor on February 17. Dewey waited another day before a cable arrived from the Navy Secretary. The cautious stance of Washington was obvious in its wording.

Dewey, Hong Kong:
Maine destroyed at Havana February 15th by accident. The President directs all colors to be half masted until further orders. Inform vessels under your command by telegraph.

Long[35]

The news was devastating to the squadron's officers and bluejackets, many of whom counted friends aboard the lost battleship. To most of them, however, the prospect of war seemed remote. The commodore was less sure. Dewey's thoughts immediately turned southeast, out over the South China Sea toward Manila.

CHAPTER 4

The *Maine*

IN HAVANA, ten thousand miles from China, the night of February 15 had been sultry and overcast, threatening rain.[1] A Marine lieutenant later recalled "the very air held a certain stillness unfelt in northern waters."[2] The *Maine* had been in the harbor for three weeks.

Lieutenant (junior grade) John J. "Jack" Blandin stood the watch this Tuesday night. Nearly twenty years after entering the Naval Academy as a midshipman, Blandin was a veteran of long, hard duty in the fleet. Nine years earlier, he had survived the wreck of the wooden-hulled screw steamer USS *Trenton* during a typhoon at Samoa. Now after an unusually long period of continuous sea duty, the aging lieutenant was disappointed by denials of his requests to be detached from the *Maine*, although he still had hopes. He expected nothing dramatic aboard the battleship this night.[3]

Marine C. H. Newton blew the traditional Taps as Captain Charles D. Sigsbee sat finishing a letter to his wife. Sigsbee occupied the admiral's cabin because the *Maine* wasn't a flagship. Like Bob Evans, he was a graduate of the star-touched Class of 1864. Sigsbee once claimed to have studied just forty-five minutes a day at Annapolis.[4] If no scholar while a midshipman, he had become a fine hydrologist (Sigsbee Deep in the Gulf of Mexico bore his name) and held many patents and foreign decorations. With his wire-rimmed glasses and mild expression, the captain looked more like a professor. He set aside his pen to listen to Newton's mournful bugle, unaware the Marine was playing "his own requiem."[5]

A half hour later, at 9:40 PM, disaster struck the *Maine* without warning.

Up on deck, Blandin heard a "dull, sullen roar."[6] This was followed a heartbeat later by a catastrophic explosion, apparently the *Maine*'s forward magazines. The blast lifted the bow and blew out or peeled back everything forward of the bridge. Bits of the ship rained down on the deck. A piece of concrete struck Blandin's head a glancing blow, knocking him down. Debris showered the steamer *City of Washington*, two hundred yards away, piercing her deck and holing two of her boats.

The *Maine*'s bow sank almost immediately. Wrecked and ablaze, the stern settled more slowly toward the muddy bottom. The harbor was shallow, just thirty-seven and a half feet at high tide. The quarterdeck was soon awash and other wreckage jutted menacingly from the surface. Blandin made his way to the poop, where he found Sigsbee looking "as cool as if at a ball."[7] Boats from the nearby steamer and the Spanish cruiser *Alfonso XII* joined the *Maine*'s two remaining boats in rescuing survivors, at no small hazard to themselves. Captain Sigsbee was the last living man to leave his ship.

Although nothing in the *Maine*'s brief history had foreshadowed such a cataclysm, her past was curious and somewhat unhappy. Laid down in 1888, she hadn't been commissioned until 1895, after delays involving her steel plating. Her original designation was Armored Cruiser No. 1. Early designs had included a sail plan of seven thousand square feet of square-rigged canvas.[8] Reclassified a second-class battleship, shorn of sails, the *Maine* now fit uneasily into any category. She was too lightly armored for a true battleship, but carried heavier guns than any cruiser. Outdated when commissioned, she weighed just 6,682 tons, much less hefty than foreign battleships. She was the Navy's second battleship, the first being the British-designed *Texas*. The arrangement of her guns, which the two ships had in common, was unusual. The forward turret with its big pair of 10-inch guns was mounted to starboard of the centerline, while the matching after turret was to port. The *Maine* also mounted six 6-inch guns and a baker's dozen of smaller guns.

Washington had ordered the ship to Havana in mid-January after rioting in the city. Her mission was to protect American citizens and property. The visit came during the latest incident in a long history of tension between the United States and Spain. Americans were particularly upset by the recent campaigns of a Spaniard with the unlikely name General Valeriano Weyler y Nicolau. Stateside newspapers had dubbed him "The Butcher" for his brutal suppression of Cuban insurgents. Weyler was also the father of a new instrument of population control, the concentration camp, which would see its logical conclusion forty years later in Germany and Poland.

Although Spain had recalled General Weyler the previous October and offered the Cubans limited autonomy, the overture was too late. Cubans wanted self-rule, and the island bubbled with hatreds and internal violence.

Weylerites among the local home-guard volunteers had instigated the January 12 rioting. Into this cauldron steamed the *Maine*, ready but not actually cleared for action.

The battleship reached Havana on January 25 on short notice—so short that Spanish authorities weren't prepared for her arrival. Neither was the American consul general, Fitzhugh Lee, a rotund former Confederate major-general and nephew of Robert E. Lee. A Spanish pilot directed the *Maine* to a buoy in the harbor's man-of-war section. This buoy—it was Number 4 on American charts, although the Spaniards considered it Number 5—was rarely used for warships, according to one report, which would prompt considerable suspicion and speculation later.[9] Sigsbee withheld liberty from his enlisted men during this "goodwill visit" to avoid sparking further violence ashore. Sentries stood watch on deck around the clock.

After three weeks without major incident, the battleship exploded on a perfectly calm night. Because their quarters were located aft, Captain Sigsbee and Executive Officer Richard Wainwright both survived. So did all but two of the twenty-six officers and naval cadets, most of whom were unhurt; Assistant Engineer Darwin R. Merritt and Lieutenant Friend W. Jenkins survived the blasts, but drowned in the sinking.[10] Casualties among the bluejackets and Marines who had strung their hammocks up forward, however, were appalling. Of the *Maine*'s three hundred thirty-five souls, according to official figures, two hundred sixty were killed, drowned, or mortally wounded—three out of every four men on board. [11] (Sigsbee repeatedly referred to three hundred fifty-four officers and men, all but four of whom were on board that night. The source of the discrepancy is unclear.)[12] Only sixteen crewmen escaped uninjured.[13]

Seventy-six-year-old Clara Barton, the Civil War heroine and American Red Cross president, was in Havana to distribute aid to the Cuban *reconcentrados*. She rushed to San Ambrosio Hospital to help her countrymen, and was nearly overcome by the sight. Some casualties were burned beyond recognition. Bodies and bits of bodies were still washing ashore the next afternoon. Recovery of remains from the wreck continued for days. Some missing men were never recovered. Sigsbee reported the ghostly silhouettes of two men on the berth-deck overhead, "mere dust."[14] His own cabin steward, John R. Bell, a much-loved African-American sailor who like his skipper had served since the Civil War, simply disappeared. Nothing was ever recovered of Bell's except his gold watch.[15] The ship's tomcat and the captain's dog Peggy both survived.[16]

Sigsbee immediately and ever afterward believed a mine had destroyed his ship, but his cable to Washington reporting her loss was a masterpiece of brevity and restraint. "Public opinion," he advised, "should be suspended until further report."[17]

This admonition did nothing to subdue the Hearst or Pulitzer newspapers in New York, long locked in a vicious circulation war. "MAINE EXPLOSION CAUSED BY BOMB OR TORPEDO?" Joseph Pulitzer's *World* demanded to know on Thursday, February 17. "DESTRUCTION OF THE WAR SHIP MAINE WAS THE WORK OF AN ENEMY," William Randolph Hearst's *Journal* trumpeted the same day.[18] Nor did Sigsbee's cable restrain such outspoken public figures as Assistant Secretary Roosevelt, who already was deeply antagonistic toward Spain. The initial reaction of the public, however, seemed to be shock rather than a furious assumption that the *Maine* had been destroyed by any hostile act attributable directly or indirectly to Spain.

The cause of her loss, the *New York Times* editorialized two days after the sinking, was "the all-important question, on which the American people have calmly suspended judgment. . . . Of course, nobody is so foolish as to believe that the *Maine* was destroyed by Spaniards with the knowledge and connivance of their Government."

. . .

Into this atmosphere of gloom and suspicion steamed a Spanish warship, the armored cruiser *Vizcaya*. Her visit to New York had been planned to reciprocate for the *Maine*'s call at Havana. Delayed by brutal weather near Bermuda, she didn't arrive until late Friday afternoon, less than seventy-two hours after the explosions. Capitán de Navío Don Antonio Eulate y Fery had no inkling of his terrible timing. He only learned of the American battleship's destruction from newspapermen who located the *Vizcaya* off Sandy Hook. He at first refused to believe the news. Finally convinced it was true, he offered no comment.

Fog and rain plagued most of the visit, mirroring the mood of the city. After shifting from the Hook to the man-of-war anchorage off Tompkinsville, Staten Island, the black-hulled *Vizcaya* lay protected by Navy tugs and police launches ordered by Assistant Secretary Roosevelt. The cruiser's flags flew at half-staff and her crew stayed on board. Eulate went ashore, in civilian clothes and accompanied by heavily armed detectives, to call on Mayor Robert A. Van Wyck. A terse Tammany hack who had uttered just two sentences at his own inauguration, the mayor received him at City Hall with a cold, silent handshake. Boys in the street jeered Spain's consul general, resplendent in his uniform. Crowds gazed at the cruiser from shore during daylight, and searchlights played across her at night. The crew checked coal deliveries for bombs.

Captain Eulate, flattered in the *Times* for his "dark, handsome face, and agreeable manners," remained unruffled and diplomatic. Speaking through interpreters, he expressed pleasure with "the gracious officials I have met," but conceded he was "not in a happy state of mind. I cannot help thinking about the *Maine* disaster, and it fills me with sorrow." At the navy yard, he spoke of the "very sad and much-regretted accident to your gallant battleship. . . . Let me assure you that if the same accident had happened to one of our own ships I could not feel more sorrow."[19]

Navy and police officials nevertheless kept a close watch on the *Vizcaya*. They kept an eye, too, on the new submarine *Holland* at nearby Elizabeth, New Jersey. Builder John Holland repeatedly denied rumors that he had sold the sub to Cubans. When he took it out for the first, very public test dive, the *Times* reported, "Spanish spies watched the *Holland* from docks above and below the shipyards all the morning."[20] Eulate was likely much more concerned about the submarine than Holland was about the black Spanish cruiser.

As the *Vizcaya* lingered off Staten Island, the public's wait-and-see attitude began hardening into something more worrisome. Navy officials fretted that someone might attempt to blow up the ship in retaliation for the *Maine*. The War Department also assured jittery New Yorkers that if the Spanish cruiser should suddenly fire on Manhattan, as was suggested in the yellow press, coastal artillery would put her "very quickly at the bottom of the bay."[21]

The darkening mood wasn't confined to New York City. "ARMY AND NAVY ACTIVITY," headlined a page-one *Times* article from Washington on February 22. "Both Departments Unusually Busy and Cautious in Giving Officials News. NAVAL MEN'S VIEWS CHANGED. The Disaster to the Maine No Longer Attributed to Accident, in the Light of Trustworthy Reports from Havana." On the same day, Washington's Birthday, adjacent headlines proclaimed: "Report that the Officers of the Maine Think the Battleship Was Not Destroyed by Accident" and "WAR SCARE REACHES MADRID."

The *Vizcaya*'s visit ended when she weighed anchor after a long, unhappy week. There had been no arrests or incidents during her stay. The cruiser quickly outpaced a Navy tug and police launch as she steamed for the Narrows. The Spanish flag remained at half-mast until she reached Fort Wadsworth. "There she gracefully dipped and then returned her colors to the truck."[22] With hopes for other port visits long since abandoned, the ship set a course for Cuba.

Eulate later encountered Sigsbee in Havana, where the cruiser arrived on the first of March. The American was wearing civvies, having lost all his uniforms, and the Spaniard didn't immediately recognize him. "Captain Eulate turned in surprise and asked if I was Captain Sigsbee of the *Maine*," Sigsbee recalled. "He took in the situation at once, arose, and, with an exclamation, threw his arms about me and gave expression to his sympathy."[23]

Nearby, the interaction among American officers was less emotional but far more portentous. A Navy court of inquiry was already hearing testimony into the cause of the disaster. Everything depended on its findings.

CHAPTER 5

Inquiry

APPOINTED IN KEY WEST on February 17, the Navy court of inquiry had convened on board the lighthouse tender *Mangrove* in Havana six days after the sinking. The first witness was Captain Sigsbee.

The Navy had moved at flank speed to form the court, appointing as its president Captain William T. Sampson, the honor graduate of the Class of 1861. Formerly the Naval Academy superintendent and chief of the Bureau of Ordnance, Sampson now commanded the battleship *Iowa*. "Nature had been kind to Sampson," Dewey would recall of his old postwar shipmate on the *Colorado*. "Not only had he a most brilliant mind and the qualities of a practical and efficient officer on board ship, but he was . . . one of the handsomest men I have ever seen, with a bearing at once modest and dignified."[1]

Appointed to the court under Sampson was Captain French Ensor Chadwick of the armored cruiser *New York*. A former intelligence officer, Chadwick had also served as chief of the Bureau of Equipment. The Navy had considered him for president before choosing Sampson, senior to both Chadwick and Sigsbee on the navy list. Chadwick's executive officer, Lieutenant-Commander William P. Potter, was appointed to the court for his technical expertise.[2] Named judge advocate was Lieutenant-Commander Adolph T. Marix, a former *Maine* executive officer. Ensign Wilfred V. N. Powelson also assisted, supervising Navy dive teams.

In the tumultuous months ahead, Captain Sampson would become a national figure. For all of his natural gifts, however, he wasn't an easy man to know or to like. Bradley Allen Fiske, a brilliant if often unappreciated lieutenant and inventor, later described Sampson as "always able to get the best work possible out of everybody under him. He was a man extremely cold in manner, the reverse of a politician in every way, and took little trouble to make himself agreeable; but he nevertheless inspired, and always kept, the enthusiastic loyalty of every officer under him, so perfectly loyal was he himself, so straightforward, and so able."[3]

Few reservations would ever be expressed about the court's impartiality with so respected an officer in charge. "In aiming at conclusions the court was ultra-conservative," an Associated Press correspondent later wrote.[4] But however fair-minded the president and its members, any court of inquiry convened during that era would have been hampered (knowingly or otherwise) by ignorance of what today might be called maritime forensics. In the rush to judgment, the Sampson court perhaps further hindered its own investigation by relying only on expertise available at Havana and in the North Atlantic fleet, rather than summoning help from Washington or Annapolis. The Navy's top ordnance expert, for instance, doubted the mine theory, but was not called to testify.

"We know of no instances where the explosion of a torpedo or mine under a ship's bottom has exploded the magazine within," Professor Philip R. Alger of the Naval Academy and Bureau of Ordnance told newspapermen soon after the sinking. The most common cause of shipboard explosions, he added, was "fires in the [coal] bunkers. Many of our ships have been in danger various times from this cause, and not long ago a fire in the *Cincinnati*'s bunkers actually set fire to fittings, wooden boxes, etc., within the magazine, and had it not been discovered at the time it was it would doubtless have resulted in a catastrophe on board that ship similar to the one on the *Maine*."[5]

Alger was hardly alone in doubting the existence of a mine. Most naval officers surveyed by the *Washington Evening Star* thought the ship had been lost through an accident.[6] Several others expressed similar doubts in the *New York Times*.

The Sampson court was determined to establish the source of the explosion. It heard from *Maine* officers and seamen, naval constructors, and other witnesses. Ensign Powelson's divers reported that the battleship's keel was bent into a sharp inverted V between frames 18 and 22, an area almost directly below and abaft the foremast. It was difficult for any witness to imagine that such startling damage could result from an internal force. But if the cause of the first explosion was external, what was its source?

There were several theories. A pre-planted mine, exploded from shore. A magnetic mine, dropped by a passing boat or lighter. A torpedo, launched from ship or shore. But who would have planted or launched such weapons? Again, there were many theories. The Spaniards, although this seemed barely credible to many observers. A lone madman, setting off a prepositioned mine without authority. Perhaps Weylerite reactionaries. Or Cuban insurgents, hoping to shower blame upon their enemies. There was no shortage of conspiracy theories.

As horrifying as these theories were, the notion of an accident was almost worse. An accidental explosion meant that something was wrong with the ship's basic design. Perhaps battleships themselves were inherently unsafe. Indeed, the Navy's most highly acclaimed strategist seemed to caution against embracing exactly such an assumption.

"We should be very cautious in forming hasty conclusions in reference to such things as this disaster," retired captain Alfred Thayer Mahan, author of *The Influence of Sea Power upon History, 1660–1783,* told the Society of Cincinnati at Princeton, New Jersey. "People are liable to jump at conclusions at a great National crisis like this which might involve them seriously. The elements of danger to a modern warship, danger external or danger internal, are not such as can be wholly eliminated."

Mahan warned against "the disposition shown in many quarters to condemn the modern battleship, even as a fighting ship, as a frightful mistake, because it appears that under the circumstances not yet at all understood she may meet with a terrible accident involving many lives. . . . [W]e must wait to learn what really did happen to the *Maine,* or at least, what probably happened, and then view those facts in the light of at least some acquaintance with all the modern multitudinous conditions which a modern ship of war has to satisfy. Above all, remember she exists to meet danger, and that some risk must necessarily be taken."[7]

A catastrophic failure of warship design—if indeed such had destroyed the *Maine*—was not without modern precedent, as Mahan surely knew. Seventeen years earlier, the British sloop-of-war HMS *Doterel* had suddenly exploded and sunk in the Strait of Magellan. There was no suggestion of foreign intrigue, but otherwise the similarities between the two disasters were unsettling. Like the *Maine,* the British vessel had sustained two quick explosions, which had torn off the bow and sent her to the bottom within three minutes, killing all but a dozen of the one hundred twenty men on board. The wreckage was not recoverable. An inquiry focused on the coal bunkers and lack of ventilation in the magazines.

"What caused the loss of the *Doterel* will probably never be determined," the *New York Times* had noted months afterward, "nor can it be shown that the commander or the officers of this ill-fated ship did not exercise due caution in the management of this vessel." The *Times* concluded with a chilling observation from an unnamed "leading authority"—"It is not a matter of shame that the cause of the explosion on board the *Doterel* should remain unknown. What is a matter of shame is that it should be equally unknown whether an omission which might have been a cause of the explosion was or was not made in the construction of the ship."[8]

In Havana, the *Maine* inquiry, too, found no easy answers. The stress of the investigation told on its president. Sampson had been ill when his clerk, now the court stenographer, had reported to him the previous November. The captain's burdens had recently multiplied when, with the court still in session, he was unexpectedly jumped ahead of several senior men to command the North Atlantic fleet. He replaced Rear-Admiral Montgomery Sicard, whose own health was even worse.

On March 21, after a month of testimony, the Sampson court issued its finding. It declared that the USS *Maine* had been destroyed by "the explosion of a mine situated under the bottom of the ship at about frame 18 and somewhat on the port side of the ship." The devastating second blast was "the partial explosion of two or more of the forward magazines" of the *Maine*.[9] The court found no negligence on the part of the ship's crew. Neither did it identify the parties responsible for placing the suspected mine.

Sampson would later conclude, however, that the wrecks of Spanish warships destroyed during the war off Santiago helped to confirm that the *Maine* had been destroyed by an "external agency." The remains of two vessels whose forward magazines had exploded simply didn't match the battleship's twisted hulk. "This is the unanimous opinion," he wrote, "of American officers who have examined these wrecks."[10]

A parallel investigation by Spanish authorities, not surprisingly, set the loss down to an accident. A more thorough investigation funded by Congress in 1910–11 largely agreed with Sampson. The U.S. Army Corps of Engineers built a cofferdam around the *Maine*, allowing the Navy its first detailed examination of the wreckage. The new board agreed that an external explosion had sunk the ship, but placed the source further aft, between frames 28 and 31, or just forward of the bridge. Otherwise, the findings matched the original.[11]

The Navy towed the *Maine*'s hulk out to sea in 1912 for scuttling in six hundred fathoms with full military honors. She slipped quietly beneath the waves, flying a mammoth American flag. Controversy continued to swirl around the ship for years. British writer H. W. Wilson, who had written extensively on naval and military affairs at the turn of the century, called the Sampson court's evidence "far from being absolutely conclusive," and cited several reasons to doubt the presence of a mine—although Wilson himself believed in its "probability."[12]

Doubts gnawed at the American conscience. Three-quarters of a century after the shattering explosions, the finest naval-engineering mind of another generation took up the puzzle of the *Maine*'s destruction. Rear-Admiral Hyman Rickover read an account of the sinking in 1974. He then enlisted as "volunteers" two top Navy Department experts on ship damage and strong-armed the Navy into providing other support. Rickover's experts used government resources that hadn't existed in 1898, including classified data from World War II. After months of investigation, they concluded that the Sampson court had erred.

"What did happen?" Rickover later wrote. "Probably a fire in [coal] bunker A-16. . . . There is no evidence that a mine destroyed the *Maine*."[13] The awesome inverted V, his experts believed, had resulted from conflicting pressures exerted on the keel as the bow and stern flooded and sank separately.

Famously intolerant of any imperfection in Navy nuclear programs he oversaw, the admiral also aimed a few rockets at poor Captain Sigsbee. "From his testimony emerges the portrait of an individual who was unfamiliar with his ship," Rickover wrote. "He might have been a good seaman and a brave man, but perhaps also the victim of the new technology which was transforming the Navy. He might not have understood the complexities of the ship he commanded."[14]

Rickover also commented that President McKinley "was unfortunate in the commanding officer of the *Maine*," adding that although Sigsbee "took proper precautions to protect his ship against harm from external sources, there is no evidence he took more than routine measures in Havana to safeguard his ship from an accident. He knew that spontaneous combustion of coal was an ever-present danger. He must have been aware of bunker fires on other ships. He knew that bunker alarms sounded below the danger point, which was no ground for feeling safe. The important fact was that they were inaccurate. Perhaps it is also significant that the *Kearsarge* and *Texas* while under his command were inspected and found dirty."[15] Rickover did note that the *Kearsarge*'s dirt in 1886 stemmed from "the age of the ship and recent bad weather." He offered no similar explanation for the *Texas* in 1899, but added that it hadn't harmed the captain's career.[16]

Rickover had a point about keeping pace with new technology, but was unfair in isolating Sigsbee for criticism. Even Mahan, after all, had noted that officers of his generation (which included Sigsbee, just five years younger) were "witnesses of one of the most rapid and revolutionary changes that naval science and warfare have ever undergone. It has been said aptly that a naval captain who fought the Invincible Armada would have been more at home in the typical war-ship of 1840, than the average captain of 1840 would have been in the advanced types of the American Civil War. . . . Since that time progress has gone on in accelerating ratio; and if the consequent changes have been less radical in kind, they have been more extensive in scope."[17]

For many historians and critics, Rickover's was the most plausible explanation for the *Maine*'s destruction. But the contentious, acid-tongued admiral engendered considerable controversy himself, and speculation has persisted over the years. One resurrected theory now attributes the first explosion to a small, black-powder mine placed by fanatic Weylerites, who had little notion that they would actually sink the ship. Reaching an irrefutable conclusion is today probably impossible—and may never have been possible at any moment during the intervening century. In 1898, the court's findings were accepted as fact. So, too, were its implications.

The *Maine*'s survivors, meanwhile, returned to the United States or to duty with the fleet. President McKinley himself hosted a reception for her skipper at the National Geographic Society in Washington. With no battleships then available, Captain Sigsbee eventually received command of the *Saint Paul*, a passenger liner converted to an auxiliary cruiser. Lieutenant-Commander Wainwright similarly received the converted yacht *Corsair*, renamed *Gloucester*, which he would command to considerable acclaim off Cuba.

Jack Blandin was promoted at last to full lieutenant and assigned to a shore billet in the U.S. Hydrographic Office at Baltimore. Sadly, the disaster "appeared to affect him greatly," recalled Sigsbee, "and led, doubtless, to the impairment of his health."[18] Blandin died of meningitis on July 16, five months after the sinking. In his deathbed deliriums, he was back on board the battleship, issuing orders and trying to save his shipmates.

PART TWO

Manila

CHAPTER 6

Hong Kong

THE FATES NOW TURNED their gaze from Havana to Hong Kong. In the deep-water harbor beneath Victoria Peak, half the globe and thirty-three years removed from Fort Fisher, George Dewey again prepared for war.

His flagship, the *Olympia*, still wore the distinctive white and buff paint of peacetime. But on February 25, just ten days after the *Maine*'s destruction, the Navy Department took its first overt step toward war, ordering the Asiatic, European, and South Atlantic squadrons to their designated rendezvous points. The cablegram that reached Dewey bore Roosevelt's signature: "Order the squadron, except the *Monocacy*, to Hongkong. Keep full of coal. In the event declaration of war Spain, your duty will be to see that the Spanish squadron does not leave the Asiatic coast, and then offensive operations in Philippine Islands. Keep *Olympia* until further orders."[1]

The gleaming flagship had been due to rotate home, but Roosevelt's cable meant Dewey would keep her. The gunboat *Petrel* had already joined the squadron in the British colony. The cruiser *Raleigh* was en route from the Mediterranean. The commodore ordered the *Boston* and *Concord* to hurry in, too, and the elderly side-wheeler *Monocacy* to lay up in Shanghai. The redundant crew he distributed among the other vessels.

A squadron of five hardly constituted a potent striking force, so Washington dispatched two more ships Dewey's way. One was the new revenue cutter *Hugh McCulloch*. The revenue service, like its successor, the U.S. Coast Guard, operated with the Navy during wartime. Commissioned on the East Coast the previous December, the *McCulloch* was now steaming via the Suez Canal and the Far East for her first duty station in San Francisco. Her captain wouldn't receive the orders to steam to Hong Kong until reaching Singapore in early April.[2]

The second ship ordered to Hong Kong, the USS *Baltimore,* was far more important to the commodore. The protected cruiser not only boosted his fire-power, it was transshipping the remaining ammunition from the *Mohican* in Honolulu. Neither the *McCulloch* nor the *Baltimore* would reach the squadron anytime soon.

Dewey also needed reliable intelligence. Frustrated with the hazy news reports reaching Hong Kong from Cuba and Washington, squadron officers had already chipped in to have an account sent directly out from New York. Within ten days, the editor of the prestigious *Army and Navy Journal* cabled them everything available.[3] More to the point, Dewey cabled the American consul in Manila, Oscar Fitzalan Williams, asking for data on fortifications, mines, and defenses. He also had Williams track the Spanish squadron based in the islands.[4]

The consul would not have been anyone's first choice as an intelligence agent. Although old enough to have served in the Civil War, Williams had no military experience. Instead, he had taught at Rochester Business University in New York for twenty years and served as American consul in Le Havre, France. He had arrived in Manila just the previous month. Now fifty-four, Williams nonetheless proved an energetic agent. He sent Dewey regular reports by letter and cable for the next several weeks, which helped fill the immense gaps in the Navy's knowledge of the Philippines.[5]

The commodore's jury-rigged intelligence network also included an unnamed American employed by a Hong Kong company. This anonymous businessman made periodic trips to Manila, which let him investigate what a Navy historian delicately termed "certain matters upon which special light was desired." Dewey found another amateur spy in Ensign F. B. Upham, who roamed the Hong Kong waterfront impersonating a curious globetrotter and meeting arriving steamers. By piecing together reports from his trio of irregu-lars, according to Sargent, the commodore arrived at "a just estimation of the defensive resources of the port [in Manila] and the strength of the Spanish squadron."[6]

The squadron's final need was high-quality coal for its boilers. With the Hawaiian republic not yet annexed and seven thousand miles between China and the West Coast ports, Dewey was forced to create his own supply line. Since other governments had already bought up the good coal available in Hong Kong, he asked that fuel be sent out from San Francisco. Long instead cabled him authority to contract for five thousand tons of coal directly from Great Britain. The British coal began the long journey out from Cardiff aboard the British freight steamer *Nanshan.* Dewey later requested and received per-mission to buy the ship outright, along with another, the passenger steamer

Zafiro. The pair's English seamen, he later wrote, "welcomed the prospect of an adventurous cruise."[7]

. . .

Although Western diplomatic attention was now focused on Cuba, the international politics of the Far East were hardly less contentious or interesting. As a new century approached, the foreign powers were throwing sharp elbows at China's fat, vulnerable belly—and not incidentally at one another. Great Britain and the Royal Navy were ensconced at Hong Kong and Wei-hai-wei. The Germans had recently snatched Kiau-Chau on the Shantung Peninsula. The colonial French occupied Indochine in the south. The Russian bear had lumbered down into Port Arthur, and the Japanese were watching keenly for any chance to do likewise. Now, unexpectedly, the Americans were flexing newly acquired muscles and gazing hard toward the Philippines and the crumbling Spanish empire.

"And what are you after?" visiting Prince Heinrich of Prussia asked Dewey. "What does your country want?"

"Oh, we need only a bay," the commodore said.[8]

The reply was a masterful twist on sanguine German pronouncements regarding Shantung. It really hadn't occurred to him, Dewey claimed later, that his squadron might soon take permanent possession of Manila Bay. But volatile Asia resembled a Gilbert and Sullivan operetta directed by Joseph Conrad, and the commodore's quip to Prince Heinrich reflected the realpolitik at work. Hong Kong harbor was crowded with Western warships, Dewey recalled, and there was "a feeling of restlessness and uncertainty in the air."[9]

(A rear-admiral in the German imperial navy, Prince Heinrich had also unwittingly caused a flap during a dinner for senior foreign officers on board his flagship, the *Deutschland.* Toasting the heads of the countries represented, he mentioned the president of the United States last, and out of the sequence dictated by protocol. The ship's band compounded the error by playing "Hail, Columbia" instead of "The Star-Spangled Banner." Dewey corrected the prince on the appropriate music, and then pointedly withheld American officers from subsequent functions. Belatedly realizing that he had caused offense, Heinrich called on Dewey and apologized. The two were friendly afterward, but the incident foreshadowed the spiky relationship that would develop between their two navies later in Manila Bay.)[10]

Condolences for the *Maine* had showered on the flagship when the *Olympia* arrived in Hong Kong. By early April, the local newspapers were openly speculating on war between Spain and the United States. On board the *Petrel,* Lieutenant Bradley A. Fiske regarded such articles skeptically. War to him seemed far more likely between Great Britain and Russia. Fiske had even requested duty as a naval observer if it happened. "We held about the same idea regarding the United States getting into war," he later recalled, "that a person holds about dying—a thing possible only to others."[11]

Whatever the opinions in the little gunboat's wardroom, Dewey had a more accurate view from the commodore's quarters aboard the *Olympia*. "War may be declared," Long had warned him on April 5. "Condition very critical."[12]

As April passed, Dewey and his captains planned an attack on their Spanish counterparts in the Philippines. The commodore didn't have a good night's sleep the entire month.[13] Plans were "carefully studied out" on the flagship, he told correspondents later, "and no detail omitted. Any man who had a suggestion to make was heard, and if it was a good one it was adopted."[14] Dewey called this period the hard work of the campaign.

As he laid out his strategy, the commodore recalled all that he had learned from Farragut while under fire on the Mississippi. The key precept he took from the admiral was that combat was decided more by skillful gunnery and excellent weapons than by any other factor.[15] Dewey was determined to take the fight to the enemy, then rely on the quality of his men and equipment once he got there.

The drawback to this approach was that his target was obvious not only to the Spanish navy—it was, observes a modern historian, "one of the worst-kept secrets in Washington"[16]—but even to ink-stained British landsmen. By the middle of April, Hong Kong papers were commenting that the Spanish squadron in the Philippines, together with guns in the fortifications and minefields at the entrance off Corregidor, made Manila Bay nearly impregnable.

Dewey wryly noted that despite apparent sympathy among the British at the Hong Kong Club, "it was not possible to get bets, even at heavy odds, that our expedition would be a success." He later paraphrased sentiments about his squadron expressed at a British regimental dinner: "A fine set of fellows, but unhappily we shall never see them again."[17] None of it deterred the commodore.

"We are still waiting for the declaration of war to begin our work here," Dewey wrote to his sister. "I have seven men-of-war all ready for action, and should war be the word I believe we will make short work of Spanish reign in the Philippines. The insurgents are ready to rise at our first gun, and long before this reaches you we may be masters at Manila and other Philippine cities." Then he revealed the curious duality common to military service. "But, after all, war is a terrible thing," he continued, "and I hope some way out of the dilemma may be found without resorting to it. My health continues good, although it is taxed to the utmost, and my one prayer is that I may be able to hold out until we have finished our work."[18]

. . .

The little *McCulloch* steamed into Hong Kong harbor to join the squadron on April 18, jauntily blowing her whistle as bluejackets on the warships cheered. "Now the squadron is safe," Captain Gridley quipped as he watched the cutter's arrival, flashing what one of his officers called "his queer smile."[19]

The American press suddenly became interested in George Dewey. The journalist in the best position to report on him was a former officer, Joseph Stickney. A graduate of the Naval Academy, Class of 1867, Stickney had served on board Admiral Farragut's flagship *Franklin* after the Civil War. As foreign editor for the *New York Herald*, he had recently gone to Tokyo to observe the British, Russian, and Japanese fleets. Now realizing that the war likely to develop wasn't the one he had envisioned, Stickney secured permission from Secretary Long to join Dewey in Hong Kong, provided the commodore had no objections.

"May I go with you," he cabled Dewey from Japan on April 9, "agreeing not to send while with you any news except when approved by you?" Stickney had his answer the following day. "Yes; come immediately. Dewey."[20] The newsman boarded the steamer *China* the day after that.

Stickney was heartened as he embarked in Yokohama by the arrival of the *Baltimore*. Dewey would stay in Hong Kong until she arrived, he thought. Since the ship had to take on coal before leaving Japan, Stickney was confident of reaching the colony first. (He was wrong at least about the commodore's reliance on the cruiser. Dewey later recalled that although the *Baltimore* was "a most welcome addition . . . without her I had been quite willing to enter Manila Bay.")[21]

The steamer, however, was literally a slow boat to China. Delayed by fog and bad weather that pushed her forty-eight hours behind schedule, Stickney didn't reach Hong Kong until Thursday night, April 21. Together with fellow passenger Commander Benjamin P. Lamberton, who had orders to assume command of the *Boston*, he waited anxiously for the first glimpse of the man-of-war anchorage on Friday morning. When the sun rose, the Americans saw warships still in the harbor. "And simultaneously the same thought flashed through our minds," Stickney recorded later, "and together we cried, 'They're grey! They're grey! This means war!'"[22] Dewey had ordered the ships painted three days earlier.

(Stickney also described the war color as "olive grey." To other observers, it appeared slate. Historian Edgar Stanton Maclay called it "a coat of ugly lead-color paint, which the Russians had found so valuable in eluding the vigilance of their enemies at sea.")[23]

Commander Lamberton's timely arrival in Hong Kong also resolved a sticky personnel problem on the flagship. Dewey had sent the *Olympia*'s ailing executive officer home a month earlier and replaced him with Lieutenant C. P. Rees of the *Monocacy*.[24] Captain Gridley was in no better condition than his exec, however, being "so out of health as to be barely fit for routine duty," let alone what Dewey later called "the rigors of an active campaign."[25] It is generally believed today that he suffered from liver cancer. Unwilling to head home like his exec, Gridley asked permission to stay.

Dewey had another reluctant skipper in the *Boston*'s Captain Frank Wildes, who was due to relinquish his ship to Lamberton. Like Gridley, Dewey noted later, Wildes "was not the sort to give up his command on the eve of an engagement without a protest." The commodore, whose own health had hardly been sterling for years, found a tidy solution by leaving both "gallant Captain Gridley" and Wildes in command, and by making Lamberton his chief of staff. [26]

"The Commodore thus obtained [in Lamberton] the aid of an active and accomplished officer at a time when he greatly felt the need of him," Sargent later wrote, "but he did not realize at the moment to what an extent the sunny, hopeful, and tactful disposition of that officer would sustain him in many anxious days to come."[27]

The *Baltimore* reached Hong Kong late Friday afternoon, a half-day behind the *China*, bringing the long-awaited powder and shells. The voyage from Honolulu had been "a precarious one," one of her officers, Lieutenant John M. Ellicott, later wrote, "for the situation had become so critical that war might have been declared at any moment, in which event it would have been a telling stroke of strategy for the Spanish squadron in the Philippines to intercept this single cruiser in overwhelming numbers and capture or sink her with her invaluable munitions of war."[28] Still wearing peacetime colors, the cruiser immediately began taking on coal and a new coat of gray paint. She was fully prepared for war two days later.

Dewey gave a dinner Friday evening in the Hongkong Hotel to return earlier British hospitality. After dinner and the customary toasts, with his junior officers looking on from a balcony, he delivered a brief talk. Lieutenant Ellicott remembered him saying in conclusion, "We cannot fail. I have captains in whom I have implicit confidence. We will work together with infallible coordination."[29]

Events were already accelerating. In the early morning hours of April 19 in Washington, Congress had passed a joint resolution demanding that "the Government of Spain at once relinquish its authority and government in the island of Cuba, and withdraw its land and naval forces from Cuba and Cuban waters." President McKinley, once described by fiery Roosevelt as having "no more backbone than a chocolate éclair,"[30] signed it shortly before noon on the twentieth. Spain withdrew her ambassador that same day, and the American minister to Madrid asked for his passport the next. Hours before the *Baltimore*'s arrival, Friday morning the twenty-second, Hong Kong time, Dewey received a cable from Washington. "The naval force on the North Atlantic station are [*sic*] blockading Cuba. War has not been declared. War may be declared at any moment. I will inform you. Await orders."[31]

In New York that day, the *Herald* headlines trumpeted: "OUR DOGS OF WAR READY FOR FIGHT. United States Forces Eager to Pounce Upon Their Prey and Successfully Execute the Offensive and Defensive Plans. ATTACK TO BE MADE ON THE PHILIPPINES." The editorial cartoon urged Americans to "RALLY ROUND THE FLAG," upon which was emblazoned a new war cry, "REMEMBER THE MAINE."[32]

On the coast of Asia, the commodore had only a short wait for an announcement of hostilities. The news reached him not from Washington, but through his friend Major-General L. S. Wilsone Black, Hong Kong's military commander and acting governor. An American correspondent later described Black as shrewd but genial, "a typical old Scotsman of the best class."[33] Black informed Dewey in a long, official document on Saturday that "war has unhappily broken out and is existing between the Kingdom of Spain and the United States of America."[34] Since the British government would observe a strict neutrality, Dewey's squadron would have to leave the harbor by four o'clock Monday afternoon. Black added in a private note, "God knows, my dear Commodore, that it breaks my heart to send you this notification."[35]

Neutrality, however, was a flexible commodity. Knowing that he could expect no aid from Britain, Japan, or any other nearby power, Dewey had already prepared to shift the squadron to Mirs Bay, an inlet thirty miles up the coast. Although Chinese territory, supposedly as neutral as the colony itself, the isolated bay was unlikely to draw scrutiny from mainland authorities. The commodore had made secret arrangements to receive coal, provisions, and battle repairs there, all unseen by carefully averted Asian eyes. There was little the Chinese government could have done about such breaches even if anyone had felt inclined. "We appreciated that so loosely organized a national entity as the Chinese Empire," Dewey later wrote, "could not enforce the neutrality laws."[36]

He dutifully reported Governor Black's instructions in a coded cable to the Navy Department. The lieutenant on duty in the cipher room immediately showed it to Rear-Admiral Crowninshield, the commodore's old nemesis, still chief of the Bureau of Navigation. Remarking that there was "no other place for them to go but Manila,"[37] Crowninshield immediately left for the White House. Long and Secretary of State William R. Day joined him there. President McKinley later that day revised and approved a reply to Dewey, which was signed by Long, encoded, and cabled back to Hong Kong. Like all such communications in the days before wireless, it would be some time in reaching its recipient in China.

On Sunday (local time), Dewey sent the *Boston*, *Concord*, *Petrel*, and *McCulloch* to Mirs Bay with the collier *Nanshan* and supply vessel *Zafiro*.[38] At nine o'clock the following morning, Monday the twenty-fifth, the *Olympia*, *Baltimore*, and *Raleigh* also weighed anchor. The crews apparently sensed that they were bound for action in the Philippines and approved of it. The *Olympia* left the harbor missing only three men (two of them Chinese mess men), which may have been a record for the era. [39]

Their bands played the national anthem as the warships stood out of the harbor, a sight that Lieutenant Ellicott recalled as "too much for our Anglo-Saxon kinsmen to look upon unmoved."[40] From British bluejackets on the warships and Tommies lining the cliffs, "cheer after cheer went after the gray, receding ships until they disappeared from sight and the last door of hospitality was closed behind them." The captain of the armored cruiser HMS *Immortalité* shouted to the *Boston*'s skipper, "You will surely win. I have seen too much of your target practice to doubt it."[41] British hospital ships gave the passing *Olympia* three hearty cheers, which the Yankee bluejackets enthusiastically returned. Three steam launches filled with flag-waving Americans paced the warships down the harbor, wishing them all Godspeed.[42] The squadron cleared Hong Kong some six hours ahead of Black's deadline.

Long's cablegram to Dewey finally reached Hong Kong at a quarter past noon. Dewey's flag secretary, Ensign Caldwell, had remained behind to handle such urgent matters. He quickly headed to Mirs Bay with the cable on the chartered tug *Fame*. The squadron was on a war footing and the *Baltimore*'s powder and shells were being distributed. As the tug rushed toward the flagship, the *Olympia*'s gunners mistook her for a Spanish torpedo boat and nearly fired.[43] Tragedy narrowly averted, Dewey at last received his orders. He summoned his captains to the flagship that evening.

On board the *Petrel*, Lieutenant Fiske and his fellow officers anxiously awaited the news, no longer optimistic about the prospects for peace. "At last we heard the call of the sentry and then the splash of oars," Fiske recalled. Captain Edward P. Wood "came over the side with his brisk step, and walked quickly aft on the quarter-deck and, seeing us on the port side, thrust out his hand, in which was a telegram, and said, 'Gentlemen, it is war.'"[44]

Washington's orders to Dewey were direct and concise: "War has commenced between the United States and Spain. Proceed at once to Philippine Islands. Commence operations particularly against the Spanish fleet. You must capture vessels or destroy. Use utmost endeavor."[45]

By one newsman's account, the commodore's reaction was equally blunt: "Thank the Lord, at last I've got the chance and I'll wipe them off the Pacific Ocean."[46] Dewey later merely wrote, in his typically matter-of-fact way, "We were ready to obey."[47]

Despite Dewey's requests, Consul Williams had repeatedly delayed leaving his listening post in Manila. He still hadn't reached China after complying at the last instant, but was expected there in two days on board the steamer *Esmeralda*. Dewey decided to wait for him, since Williams might deliver vital last-minute intelligence from the Philippines.[48] On Wednesday morning, the twenty-seventh, lookouts again spotted the tug *Fame* hustling into the bay. Williams had at last arrived.

Dewey signaled the squadron to light off the boilers and prepare to get under way. He then called his captains to the flagship for a meeting with the consul. Finally, at two o'clock, with the skippers back with their commands and Williams on board the *Baltimore*, the squadron left Mirs Bay.

"We proceeded in two columns," Dewey recalled, "the fighting ships forming one column, the auxiliary vessels another twelve hundred yards in the rear; and with a smooth sea and favoring sky we set our course for the entrance of Manila Bay, six hundred miles away."[49]

CHAPTER 7

Cruisers

THE SQUADRON making for the Philippines wasn't the most powerful force afloat in Asiatic waters, but each of Dewey's sleek steel vessels could easily have sunk the entire American fleet from the Doldrums.

Like all modern warships, the squadron descended from ironclad vessels born in Europe forty years earlier. The French frigate *La Gloire* in 1858 was followed by the British HMS *Warrior* two years later. Ironclads then sprang to lethality in the United States during the Civil War. Briefly, until the Doldrums, America deployed the most fearsome ironclads in the world.

Equally important to the rise of smaller and lighter cruisers like Dewey's was the American screw frigate *Wampanoag*. Conceived during the Civil War, her influence was clearly visible in the Asiatic Squadron. The ship had an "unusually long and tapered" hull, according to the Navy's *Dictionary of American Naval Fighting Ships*, and was "unique for its geared steam engine in which slow-moving machinery coupled to fast-moving propulsion gear."[1] The combination had made the USS *Wampanoag* the fastest ship of her time.

The United States Navy had then quietly moldered for twenty years. But in doing so, it had also avoided the missteps and tragedies that haunt any era of rapid technological change. The experimental British "sea-going turret ship"[2] HMS *Captain*, for example, foundered in an 1870 gale off Cape Finisterre, her heavy masts, spars, and sails proving a disastrous combination with a low freeboard and ironclad hull. American builders learned from such losses, without having to pay the human costs themselves.

In modern terms, the Navy eventually came to resemble a large, troubled industrial concern faced with upgrading an aging computer network after years of neglect. At some point, it simply becomes cheaper and more efficient to build an entirely new network than to continue with the old one. Having spent almost nothing for years to keep pace with the rest of the world, the Navy could forgo costly upgrades and start anew. This reformation had begun in earnest during the 1880s.

The force now steaming resolutely toward the Philippines under Commodore Dewey reflected the change. As the twentieth century approached, the Navy and its Asiatic Squadron were small and ill-assorted, but led by experienced officers who would elicit the most from them. Although the American fleet was not nearly as large or as formidable as its European counterparts, it was nonetheless redeeming a reputation for innovation that it had earned during and immediately after the Civil War.

"We are at least seven or eight years behind," a British correspondent lamented after eyeing the armored cruiser USS *Brooklyn* during Queen Victoria's Diamond Jubilee in 1897. "Her equipment is so admirable that I blush with shame that only one of our British men of war is fitted with electrical shell hoists."[3]

In fact, the *Brooklyn* was an exception, among the newest and best vessels in the expanding fleet. Lieutenant William S. Sims later recalled that the jingoistic American press liked to depict the Navy as "the hottest stuff that ever came down the pike, that every ship that we built was the last expression of naval architecture, and that our personnel was the best in the world." Sims had studied the French, British, and Russian navies as the naval attaché in Paris for a year and a half before the hostilities with Spain. His tart assessment was that "we were not in it at all, either in design or in marksmanship."[4]

Others agreed, if only in hindsight. French E. Chadwick, captain of the armored cruiser USS *New York* during the coming war, later wrote that neither country "had a fleet fitted, as far as material strength was concerned, to meet that of even a second-class naval power. The United States had only just put afloat the nucleus of its splendid fleet" that would eventually follow.[5]

But the U.S. wasn't facing a first- or second-class power, merely Spain. For this, the Navy was amply prepared. The Armada was more than three hundred years in the past. The American star was ascending, while that of the Spanish was clearly in decline—although just how precipitously wasn't apparent to most observers.

. . .

The Asiatic Squadron consisted of the protected cruisers *Olympia* (flagship), *Baltimore*, *Boston*, and *Raleigh*, gunboats *Petrel* and *Concord*, and cutter *McCulloch*. British observer H. W. Wilson believed the flagship was "perhaps the finest unarmored cruiser possessed by the United States."[6] Like the commodore, four of the ships' skippers had fought in the Civil War. Morale was high and discipline good. Ensign W. Pitt Scott of the *Olympia* wrote home: "The thing that we were most afraid of was that the North Atlantic fleet would get in some big engagements before we had a chance."[7]

The Spanish squadron based in the Philippines under Contralmirante (Rear-Admiral) Don Patricio Montojo y Pasarón was larger than Dewey's. It included the cruisers *Reina Cristina* (flagship) and *Castilla*, smaller cruisers *Isla de Cuba*, *Isla de Luzon*, *Don Antonio de Ulloa*, *Don Juan de Austria*, and *Velasco*, gunboats *Marques del Duero*, *General Lezo*, and *El Correo*, and the survey vessel *Argos*. Although armed with modern guns, Montojo's ships were smaller and somewhat older than Dewey's.[8] All of the American vessels were steel; the hull of the *Castilla* was wood.

According to Dewey's later calculations, the American squadron had fifty-three guns above 4-inch caliber to the thirty-one for the Spaniards; fifty-six guns below 4-inch, compared with Montojo's forty-four; and eight torpedo tubes against thirteen. As the commodore later noted in his autobiography, neither squadron had armored ships—the U.S. cruisers were "protected" only by an armored belt—and both sides used brown powder.[9] Excluding small Spanish gunboats, which would never be a factor, Dewey's squadron was somewhat stronger, "superior in weight of metal and in class of vessels," in Commander Sargent's phrase.[10] (Dewey didn't include the *McCulloch* or the *General Lezo*, *Velasco*, *El Correo*, and *Argos* in his postwar calculations, since these vessels were "not engaged" at Manila Bay.)

A similar, roughly equal balance was believed true for the two navies overall. But as Wilson later observed, "the actual readiness or unfitness for sea of many of the Spanish ships was not known." Comparisons of fleet strength were often based on prewar estimates published in America. In reality, Wilson wrote, the Spanish navy "was to a great extent a paper force, whereas the American Navy was generally under- rather than over-estimated, even in America. . . . Yet how enormous was its superiority to the Spanish Navy could not be altogether grasped, even by Americans, without the actual test of battle."[11]

In the Philippines, at least, the Spaniards enjoyed several tactical advantages besides the illusion of strength. As colonial rulers, they had bases and repair facilities in the islands, an arsenal at Cavite, ample coal supplies, undersea mines, and powerful shore batteries. "The fact that we were not armored," Dewey wrote, "made the heavy guns of the Spanish batteries, if they were brought to bear on us, a serious consideration."[12]

Much therefore depended on the character and abilities of Dewey's Spanish counterpart, Admiral Montojo—and in these, Spain was unfortunate.

At age fifty-eight, two years younger than the commodore, Montojo was Dewey's near contemporary. He had first gone to the Philippines thirty-eight years earlier and had spent much of his career there, periodically suppressing native rebellions. Bald and neatly mustachioed, as bedecked with decorations and sashes as a pasha, the admiral held such exalted honors as the grand crosses of Queens María Cristina and Elizabeth the Catholic. Like the commodore, "the fighting Montojo" was highly experienced, but hadn't fought in a big naval battle in more than thirty years—not since "Dos de Mayo" at Callao, Peru, in 1866.[13]

A historically minded observer might have thought it portentous that Callao was a Spanish defeat, strangely similar to the failed first campaign at Fort Fisher just seventeen months earlier.

. . .

Perhaps it made a difference that the United States wasn't yet a world power. Western nations typically didn't dispatch their best ships or officers to the Asiatic Station. Prestige lay closer to home waters. But Assistant Secretary Roosevelt had been right about his man—America was fortunate in having George Dewey.

Compared with their ships, the officers in his little squadron (and not a few of their crewmen) were positively elderly. Indeed, many of Dewey's officers had served in the Navy far longer than any ship in the squadron. Even the *Boston*, one of the ABCD ships, had been commissioned just eleven years earlier.

The Doldrums had done more than retard the advancement of the fleet. With so few ships available, they had brought advancement of the officer corps almost to a halt. Promotion had so stagnated, according to Commander Sargent, "that grey-haired lieutenants of fifty years of age were doing duties which, in the British and German services, were performed by young men of thirty."[14]

Bradley Fiske, one of the Navy's brightest minds, had once considered resigning to join the staff of the *Scientific American*, believing that he had "no chance . . . of having any sort of career of any kind."[15] Now he was almost forty-four and still a lieutenant. Thomas Brumby, Dewey's flag lieutenant, was only a few months younger. The *Olympia* navigator, Carlos G. Calkins, was nearing fifty.

The executive officer of one of the Atlantic battleships had served twenty-one years as a lieutenant—officially a "young officer." During that span, he recalled, "I could have married, had a son, got him appointed to the Naval Academy, and have seen him graduate and come out into the service and relieve me on midwatch."[16]

Many capable young officers, such as newspaperman Stickney, had given up and left the Navy to pursue other careers. A tough, determined few—among them Fiske, Brumby, and Calkins—had stuck it out. By 1898, the logjam was broken. Although advancement was still frustratingly slow, the lifelong service of its "junior" officers was about to pay handsome—and perhaps undeserved—dividends for the Navy in the Philippines.

CHAPTER 8

"God of Victories"

THE GHOSTS OF JOHN PAUL JONES and Stephen Decatur might have been smiling as Dewey's squadron approached its destiny in the Philippines. If so, they weren't the only ghosts to accompany the squadron. A graying seaman named Purdy was dealing with darker shades.

Purdy lingered on the *Olympia*'s upper deck as the flagship neared the islands. He was a "privileged character," according to Stickney, but he wasn't where he belonged while on duty. When Dewey asked if something was on his mind, Purdy delivered a salute and spoke up.

"I hope, sir," he said, "that ye don't intend to fight on the third of May."

Dewey asked why.

"Ye see, sir," came the reply, "I got licked the last time I fought on the third of May." That was the date of the battle at Chancellorsville, Virginia, thirty-five years earlier, when Purdy had been a Union soldier serving under General "Fighting Joe" Hooker.

Dewey assured the seaman that he wouldn't fight on the third. He had already confided to Stickney, in fact, that he expected the battle to come on May first. The commodore told Purdy that when the squadron did fight, "you'll have another kind of May anniversary to think about."[1]

. . .

Ghosts and shades seemed to wander about the cruisers almost as if conceived by Dickens or Shakespeare, whispering into the ear of Purdy and any sailor old enough to remember the Mississippi, Mobile Bay, or Fort Fisher. The most powerful and benevolent spirit belonged to Dewey's old hero, David Glasgow Farragut.

The admiral was everywhere on the *Olympia*, unseen but definitely felt. Many of the senior squadron officers had revered him in their dangerous youth. Dewey had known Farragut on the Mississippi. Gridley and the *Baltimore*'s chief engineer had fought beside him at Mobile Bay. The *Baltimore* and *Boston* skippers had served in his West Gulf Blockading Squadron. After the war, correspondent Stickney had been a midshipman on his flagship, USS *Franklin*.

No crisis had permitted another to rise and displace Farragut in the Navy's regard during the long years of the Doldrums. Not even his foster brother, Admiral Porter, had equaled his stature. There was still only Farragut. Almost to a man, the Navy's senior generation clung to him. Dewey held him in particular esteem, with good reason. The parallels and similarities between the admiral and the commodore were numerous and uncanny.

Alfred Thayer Mahan once described Farragut as "not above medium size— about five feet six and a half inches high, upright in carriage, well proportioned, alert and graceful in his movements. In early and middle life he was rather slight than heavy in frame: it was not until the war, with the prolonged physical inactivity entailed by the river and blockade service, that he took on flesh. Up to that time his weight was not over one hundred and fifty pounds. He was very expert in all physical exercises, and retained his activity to the verge of old age." Author Murat Halstead later observed that this description "needs only the name changed to fit Dewey."[2]

Farragut and Dewey had both seen combat early and late in their careers. Farragut had fought the War of 1812 as a twelve-year-old midshipman, seen no action while on blockade duty in the Mexican War, then fought again in the Civil War. Dewey's peace had extended from 1865 to the present day. A senior officer had remarked early in the Civil War that Farragut, then a captain, was "a bold, impetuous man, of a great deal of courage, and energy, but his capabilities and power to command a squadron was a subject only to be determined by trial."[3] Much the same could be said now of Dewey.

The parallels extended even to small details of their respective lives. Farragut's birthday was the day after the Fourth of July, Dewey's the day after Christmas. Each was sixty years old at the beginning of the war that made him famous. Farragut's first wife died on December 27, Dewey's on December 28, thirty-two years later. Each man was a notably devoted husband. Farragut's tender ministrations to his wife during sixteen years of illness had earned widespread admiration, although he had soon remarried and Dewey had not. (In at least one crucial matter, the admiral had more in common with Bob Evans than with Dewey. Like Evans, Tennessee-born Farragut had chosen to "stick to the

Admiral George Dewey and Bob (from Dewey, *Autobiography*).

Lieutenant-Commander
Dewey, 1867 (from
Dewey, *Autobiography*).

Susan Goodwin Dewey
(from Stickney, *War in the
Philippines*).

Admiral David Farragut (from Dewey, *Autobiography*).

Commander Robley Evans, ca. 1880s (from "War Time Snap Shots," *Munsey's*).

Admiral "Fighting Bob" Evans, ca. 1907 (from Matthews, *With the Battle Fleet*).

Capitan Antonio Eulate, from a drawing (from Goode, *With Sampson*).

Captain Charles Sigsbee (from
Everett, *Exciting Experiences*).

Chief Yeoman George Ellis,
from a drawing (from Graham,
Schley and Santiago).

Captain Charles V. Gridley
(from Dewey, *Autobiography*).

Commodore Winfield Scott
Schley (from Watterson, *History
of the Spanish-American War*).

Admiral William T. Sampson (from Everett, *Exciting Experiences*).

Captain "Jack" Philip (from Everett, *Exciting Experiences*).

Naval-Constructor Richmond Hobson (from Watterson, *History of the Spanish-American War*).

Admiral Patricio Montojo y Pasarón (from Watterson, *History of the Spanish-American War*).

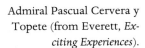

Admiral Pascual Cervera y Topete (from Everett, *Exciting Experiences*).

flag" during the Civil War, despite family upsets, Southern scorn, and short-lived suspicion among Northern superiors.)[4]

"Farragut has always been my ideal of the naval officer, urbane, decisive, indomitable," Dewey wrote in his autobiography. "Whenever I have been in a difficult situation, or in the midst of such a confusion of details that the simple and right thing to do seemed hazy, I have often asked myself, 'What would Farragut do?' . . . I confess that I was thinking of him the night we entered [Manila] Bay, and with the conviction that I was doing precisely what he would have done. Valuable as the training of Annapolis was, it was poor schooling beside that of serving under Farragut in time of war."[5]

. . .

The squadron approached the Philippines at just eight knots to conserve the Welsh coal carried by the merchantmen. On board the *Olympia*, Charles Kindleberger, the flagship's junior surgeon, noted that the slow pace annoyed the crew, "who were keyed up to fighting tension and suffered under the enforced idleness."[6]

Dewey kept his bluejackets as busy as possible with drills and battle preparations. The men draped sheet chains to shield the ships' vulnerable sides and ammunition hoists and erected canvas-and-iron barricades to add protection for the gun crews.[7] They also ruthlessly stripped woodwork from bulkheads and decks, and sought out anything else flammable—rails, planks, chairs, tables, chests, personal possessions—and tossed it all overboard.

"It was hard on the lovers of curios," Kindleberger observed, "but nothing escaped the vigilance of the officers whose orders were to guard against splinters, more deadly on the gun-deck of the modern man-of-war than solid shot."[8] The *Baltimore*'s assistant engineer, Edward L. Beach Sr.—later father of Captain "Ned" Beach, famed submariner and naval historian—long remembered "the grief displayed by our chaplain when he saw his pulpit heaved overboard."[9] His shipmate Lieutenant Ellicott recalled seeing the sea "strewn for fifty leagues with jettisoned woodwork."[10]

A crewman on the flagship wrote that the *Olympia*, at least, merely covered her wooden paneling with canvas and splinter nets.[11] Still, the squadron tossed so much material over the side that the crew of a passing vessel reported finding no survivors amid what they mistook for the aftermath of a terrible wreck or battle.[12]

. . .

As if his crews weren't sufficiently energized, Dewey received a motivational weapon from the Spaniards themselves. The governor-general in the Philippines, Basilio Augustin y Dávila, had announced the war to his people with the florid, overwrought prose common to blinkered authority. He might as well have printed it on cards for pinning directly on Yankee bulletin boards. It became the "Mother of All Battles" speech of the Spanish War.

"The struggle will be short and decisive," Augustin declared, with what later must have struck even the governor-general as horrendous accuracy. "The God of victories will give us one as brilliant and complete as the righteousness and justice of our cause demand. . . . A squadron manned by foreigners, possessing neither instruction nor discipline, is preparing to come to this archipelago with the ruffianly intention of robbing us of all that means life, honor, and liberty. . . .

"The aggressors shall not profane the tombs of your fathers, they shall not gratify their lustful passions at the cost of your wives' and daughters' honor, or appropriate the property that your industry has accumulated for your old age. . . . [T]o the calls of our enemies, let us oppose with the decision of the Christian and the patriot the cry of '¡Viva España!' "[13]

Copies of the Spanish and Filipino newspapers in which the proclamation had appeared quickly fell into the hands of the Americans, who recognized a public-relations bonanza when they saw one. Augustin's proclamation (actually written by the Archbishop of Manila)[14] was read all around the American squadron bound for the Philippines. Captain Nehemiah Mayo Dyer read it to the *Baltimore* crew the second day out of Mirs Bay. The men's nicknames for Dyer included "Hot Foot" and "Snarlyowl," both apparently apt; it was said that he had once pitched an ill-mannered apprentice boy overboard through a gun port.[15]

(Nicknames like "Snarlyowl" abounded in the fleet, often bestowed by naval cadets on officers at the Naval Academy. Captain Wood of the *Petrel* was "Tangle-foot," while Captain Walker of the *Concord* was "Little Sally." An officer with "a lean and hungry look" who would distinguish himself at Manila Bay was called "Polly," because "it occurred to generations of cadets that he must certainly want a cracker.")[16]

Assistant Engineer Beach remembered Dyer's performance on the *Baltimore* that day for the rest of his life.

"This is what the Spanish governor general of the Philippine Islands had published," the skipper told his assembled crew. "And this means me, and you, and you! and you! *and you!*" As he began reading the proclamation aloud, Beach recalled, the captain "became possessed of a mad fury that constantly augmented. His wonderful voice rolled over the deck and reached and roused every heart. With the last words he had become a mass of passion. He lost control of himself, threw the paper on the deck, jumped on it, threw his hat at it, cursed it, then broke into a most beautiful, though violent, statement about the soul of America, past and present."

The *Baltimore* men let out a wild cry, moved "in a way I had never before seen men stirred," Beach marveled. Dyer restored order by raising an arm, then ordering the divisions marched to their quarters. His crew was primed for the fight.[17]

. . .

Early on April 30, three days after leaving Mirs Bay, the squadron made landfall at Cape Bolinao, the westernmost point of Luzon.

The first task for Dewey was to find the enemy squadron. He originally had hoped to engage it at Manila, but in China Consul Williams had told him that Montojo instead had steamed around to Subig Bay. (Few contemporary accounts used the more modern spelling "Subic.") Subig is a fine, protected anchorage at the top of the Bataan Peninsula, the eastern coast of which forms the western shore of Manila Bay. "Thus Admiral Montojo at the last moment seemed to have realized the strategic advantage of Subig over Manila, which we had hoped he would fail to do," Dewey wrote.[18]

Subig lay along his course southward to Manila. The commodore ordered the *Boston* and *Concord* to surge ahead and peek into the bay. When officers thought they heard big guns firing in the distance, he sent the larger *Baltimore* up to support them. With the rest of the squadron and the colliers, Dewey steamed slowly behind, keeping three or four miles off the coastline.

At 3:30 in the afternoon, his lookouts sighted the scouts at the entrance to the bay. After waiting "very anxiously" for a signal, Dewey was deeply relieved to learn that the trio had found no enemy warships inside Subig. The commodore said to Commander Lamberton, his chief of staff, "Now we have them."[19]

The Spaniards had indeed been at Subig, exactly as Williams had reported. If the Americans had arrived just a day earlier, Lieutenant Ellicott wrote, Dewey "would have found there nearly the whole Spanish fleet."[20] But Montojo had since returned to Manila Bay. Specifically, he had taken his squadron to Cavite, "the miserable station under the guns at Sangley Point," in the words of Lieutenant Calkins, the *Olympia*'s navigator.[21]

Montojo reported several reasons for his surprising move. The mounting of four big guns ashore to guard Subig's entrance was six weeks behind schedule.

(According to Commander Sargent, they were just lying on the beach and could have been mounted by competent hands in twenty-four hours.)[22] The wooden *Castilla* was leaking so badly that she was merely "a floating battery, incapable of maneuver." The Spanish consul at Hong Kong had reported via cable that Dewey was heading directly for Subig. And a council of the squadron's captains thought the position at Subig was therefore "insupportable."[23]

What later most astounded American officers, however, was the admiral's conclusion that Dewey could have destroyed all the Spanish ships at Subig, and that the crews couldn't have been saved because of the forty meters of water under their keels—an "amazing and unseamanlike notion," to Calkins' way of thinking.[24] His colleagues generally shared the navigator's low opinion of Montojo's command abilities. "What a singular lack of morale," Dewey exclaimed with a rare burst of emotion in his autobiography, "and what a strange conclusion for a naval officer!"[25]

He didn't speculate on what might have happened at Subig if he hadn't decided to wait for Consul Williams at Mirs Bay, thus unknowingly providing Admiral Montojo the time to make his fateful decision to retire to Cavite.

. . .

The American squadron re-formed near the entrance to Subig at sunset. Dewey called the skippers into a conference on board the flagship. Lieutenant Ellicott remembered the scene as deeply impressive, "nine ships, dark as the clouds of a gathering storm, resting against a background of bright green hills and graceful waving palms." The ships' bands all struck up an evening concert, playing "There'll Be a Hot Time in the Old Town Tonight."[26]

The captains returned to their commands and the squadron set a southeasterly course. "It was quickly known," Ellicott recorded, "almost without the telling, that Commodore Dewey was going to run past the forts into Manila Bay that night and engage the enemy as soon as the morning."[27] His ships steamed into the gathering night in single file, the *Olympia* leading and the colliers bringing up the rear.

"As darkness slowly descended," Lieutenant Fiske wrote twenty-one years later, "the scene took on a character at once soothing and disturbing—soothing, because everything was so calm; disturbing, because of the grim preparations evident." On board the lieutenant's *Petrel*, the guns were all manned and ready, with "considerable ammunition" nearby on deck.[28]

Dewey proceeded slowly, conserving both time and fuel. Awaiting him thirty miles beyond Subig were the fortified islands that guarded the entrance to Manila Bay.

CHAPTER 9

Magistrate and Monk

THE SQUADRON STEAMED steadily southeast, each ship showing only a single shielded stern light to guide the ship behind. The night was clear and calm but for a shower that passed over the column about eleven o'clock. Luzon was faintly visible two or three miles to port.

From the *Olympia*, correspondent Stickney reported, only "a faint suggestion of a ghostly shape [was visible] where the *Baltimore* grimly held her course on our port quarter, while the *Raleigh*, somewhat farther away on our starboard quarter, could be seen by only the sharpest eyes when the moon was wholly unobscured by clouds."[1]

Copper-colored lightning flickering over Luzon silhouetted the headlands as the squadron approached Manila Bay. In the distance lay Corregidor, the largest of five islands strung like sentries across the bay's entrance. Corregidor rose in the darkness, Lieutenant Ellicott remembered, "like a huge, ill-moulded grave."[2]

The bay opened to the southwest, its entrance ten nautical miles across. Two shipping channels led inside. Like everything associated with Manila, both had colorful Spanish names. The more heavily used channel, Boca Chica (literally, "Little Mouth"), passed between Corregidor (Chief Magistrate) and the Bataan Peninsula. The second channel, Boca Grande (Large Mouth), went between Caballo (Horse) Island near the center and a tiny fortified rock called El Fraile (the Friar or Monk) off the eastern shore. There was no practical middle passage between Corregidor and Caballo. A fourth island, Carabao (Water Buffalo), rose near the Bataan headland and a fifth island, La Monja (the Nun), near the western headland. All but the Nun later became American forts.

Manila Bay itself was thirty nautical miles wide and relatively shallow. The city was below the horizon on the eastern shore. Its position there was marked by "domes and spires of public buildings and churches," correspondent John Barrett later wrote, a busy waterfront along the Pasig River, and the "long, low, frowning walls of old Manila." Behind these were "pretty hills, which gradually grow into high mountains."[3] The landscape would remind Dewey of his native Vermont. To Bradley Fiske, Manila would seem "the most beautiful city we had ever seen."[4] Tonight, however, the islands commanded their attention.

Forty-four years on, tadpole-shaped Corregidor would become a symbol of Yankee resistance as it held out for months against the Japanese bombing and invasion of the Philippines. Tonight, in Spanish hands and not nearly so well fortified as later, the Magistrate threatened the approaching U.S. squadron. Corregidor stood guard over Boca Chica, while the Horse and the Monk protected Boca Grande. Big guns hastily and belatedly mounted on these islands were capable of delivering what Dewey would call "a very unpleasant quarter of an hour . . . provided the gunners had been enterprising and watchful."[5]

The squadron's other great concern was naval mines. Consul Williams had informed Dewey at Mirs Bay that the Spaniards had heavily mined Boca Grande. The American consul-general at Singapore had reported the same. With shore batteries and mines protecting the channels, Lieutenant Ellicott wrote, "it must be conceded that the apparent odds were not in the favor of the United States squadron."[6]

The key word was *apparent*. Dewey largely dismissed the danger from mines, considering it "negligible."[7] He intended using Boca Grande, which was so deep that only true experts could usefully plant mines there. The commodore also believed that contact and electrical mines were both likely to deteriorate rapidly in the warm tropical water. Finally, the public Spanish warnings and fuss about mines were so great that Dewey believed the whole thing a "specious bluff."[8] He later cited the example of an Italian warship that had reopened the Suez Canal during the Orabi Pasha revolt in 1882, despite fears of mining by the Egyptians.

Still, his decision to force Boca Grande was no small gamble. Dewey's old hero, Admiral Farragut, had famously damned the torpedoes (as mines were then called) during the battle of Mobile Bay in 1864. But Farragut had actually seen the Confederate torpedoes and been able to judge their effect. Dewey was damning the *likelihood* that the Spaniards could effectively deploy their weapons. According to an account by Lieutenant Ellicott, written during World War II, the commodore had promised his captains at Subig that "if there are any mines in our path the flagship will clear them away for you."[9]

Lieutenant Calkins, the *Olympia*'s navigator, was not alone in marveling at what in hindsight he described as Dewey's "unflinching readiness to act in ignorance—ignorance of the enemy's batteries, of his mine fields, of the stations, and even of the numbers of his fighting ships."[10]

Dewey's memories of the murderous Mississippi and Fort Fisher campaigns had never dulled. He surely understood the wisdom behind Lord Nelson's admonition against attacking forts with ships. But Farragut had damned the torpedoes, and Nelson had advised his Band of Brothers before Trafalgar that no captain could do very wrong by placing his ship alongside that of the enemy. To get to the Spaniards' ships, Dewey first had to pass the armed islands.

"It was thirty-six years since, as executive officer of the *Mississippi*, I was first under fire in the passage of Forts Jackson and St. Philip under Farragut," he recalled in his autobiography, "and thirty-five years since, as executive officer, I had lost my ship in the attempted passage of the batteries of Port Hudson. Then, as now, we were dependent upon the screen of darkness to get by successfully, but then I was subordinate and now the supreme responsibility was mine."[11]

Dewey had given his captains one simple order in the meeting at Subig Bay—"follow the motions and movements of the flagship, which will lead."[12] Now, at about 11:30 PM on this last day of April, he led the squadron toward Boca Grande.

. . .

Although less used than the other channel, Boca Grande was farther from the dangerous big batteries on Corregidor. The Spaniards had extinguished all the navigation lights on the island, and on Caballo and the San Nicholas Shoals inside the bay. Perhaps, Dewey later speculated, they thought these steps would be enough—that with neither pilots nor any knowledge of the channel, he wouldn't "be guilty of such a foolhardy attempt as entering an unlighted channel at midnight."[13]

Despite the covering darkness, the Spaniards clearly saw the squadron approaching and later told Dewey as much. He was still ten miles from Boca Grande when lights began flashing ashore.

About 11:30 PM, the *McCulloch*'s stack suddenly emitted a shower of flame and sparks, frightening half the squadron. "Well," said an officer on the flagship, "if some one don't see that, the whole island must be asleep."[14] When a signal rocket soared above the Magistrate, the commodore remarked, "We ought to have a shot from Corregidor very soon now."[15]

The *Olympia* could easily have upped her speed to fifteen knots and the other warships to at least twelve. But Dewey increased the squadron's speed to only eight knots so his colliers could keep up. Corregidor and Caballo still withheld their fire. No good explanation why has ever been offered.

Perhaps the Spanish chain of command was so rigid that no one in authority could give a timely order. Perhaps the batteries were badly positioned or manned. Perhaps the gunners were more afraid of return fire from the Americans than they were of their own superiors. Or perhaps it was simply that Montojo and many of his officers were ashore at a ball in Manila when the Americans forced the entrance. Beach of the *Baltimore* reported as much in a letter home,[16] as did Dewey fifteen years later in his autobiography, although their evidence appears anecdotal. The commodore also wrote that the El Fraile crews were ashore and "could not get off to their guns in time after they heard of the squadron's approach."[17]

Whatever the reason, Corregidor fired only its signal rocket and Caballo nothing at all.

The *Olympia* steamed past both silent sentinels and to within a half mile of El Fraile. When the Monk was due south, the flagship changed course to northeast-by-north, directly into the dark bay. One by one, the other ships matched her turn. On board the *Baltimore*, Assistant Engineer Beach was amidships in the starboard waist. At a quarter past midnight, the Monk awoke.

"Suddenly, in the direction I was looking," Beach recalled, "there was a vivid streak of fire, the reverberating roar of a great gun, and a violent rush of wind."[18] As Ellicott dryly recalled, "That the Spaniards would have a battery on this isolated and tiny island was not expected."[19]

The Monk's shell passed between the *Petrel* and the *Raleigh* near the rear of the column. It "cleared up the situation at once," Lieutenant Fiske remembered, "and gave everybody a definite idea of where he was and what he was trying to do."[20]

The *Raleigh* was first to return fire, followed by the *Concord*, *McCulloch*, and *Boston*. Fiske watched the latter steer straight for the tiny island, firing everything she could bring to bear. From the *Petrel*, the gunboat looked like "a wargod fighting with thunder and lightning."[21] El Fraile fired just twice more before falling silent. With that, the squadron was quickly through the channel and into the bay.

With no further need for stealth or concealment, a vertical row of red and white lights rose on the flagship, the signal for "speed four knots."[22] This the other ships answered with blazing lights of their own. The "chagrined and astounded Spaniards on Corregidor," Ellicott recalled, "must have thought the Americans were holding a water carnival."[23]

The anxiety over Spanish mines, however, lessened only slightly. As he passed through the *Petrel*'s darkened wardroom, it occurred to Fiske that "the ship might at any moment explode a torpedo." (He apparently used "torpedo" in the old-fashioned sense, meaning a mine.) The idea lingered as he tried to sleep. "The deck above my head was distant about two feet," he wrote, "and I thought how very flat I would be squashed out against that deck if a torpedo exploded under the ship."[24] The fearsome explosion never came, and thoughtful officers like Fiske would forever puzzle over this failure.

To navigator Calkins, the lack of mines was the "unfathomed mystery."[25] Spanish officers would believably declare that they had indeed sown them. Ellicott later wrote in a naval journal that if they were contact mines, "they had become innocuous from barnacles and seaweed or badly adjusted moorings; if they were electro-controlled, the firing devices had not been installed or were defective."[26] Decades later and long retired, Ellicott speculated that perhaps very few mines had ever been laid; he finally concluded that "by passing close to El Fraile our squadron found a gate through the mine field."[27] He subsequently quoted a remark by Captain Dyer that Dewey was "an old hand at crossing mine fields and figured that if there was a gate through this it would be close to that rock."[28]

Dewey recorded that indeed there *had* been explosions, which few others in the squadron would have been positioned to see. "As we moved past Corregidor, the *Olympia* being in advance, suddenly, not fifty yards to the right, there was a muffled roar, and a column of water shot upward thirty or forty feet high," he wrote to a friend a few weeks later. "In a moment another to my left. 'So the place is mined,' I said to Lamberton."[29]

However they had accomplished it, Dewey's ships and colliers were all inside Manila Bay, utterly undamaged. Officers and crews snatched a few hours of sleep as the commodore patiently awaited the dawn.

CHAPTER 10

"Perfect Line of Battle"

THE SHARP EXCHANGE with El Fraile helped settle American nerves. Before the firing, according to Junior Surgeon Kindleberger, the *Olympia* crewmen were "nervous and overwrought." After it, "they dropped down in the warm tropical night beside their guns or wherever they had been stationed, and were soon sound asleep."[1] Sailors not on watch did the same on Dewey's other warships.

The squadron steamed slowly on toward Manila in the early hours of Sunday, the first of May. Fiske recalled "a silence that was unbroken by any warlike sound."[2] The first hints of daylight appeared a little before five. The seamen stirred, stretched, and looked around for coffee and crackers. "In the early dawn," Ellicott wrote, "Manila Bay was like a sheet of silver."[3]

As in wars before and since, reams of nonsense would be published later— on each side of the Atlantic—about how men in both squadrons had eagerly anticipated this conflict. Edward Beach Sr., while not immune to this syndrome (being "wild with delight"[4] while under fire off El Fraile), also described a distraught junior officer on the *Baltimore*, newly appointed to the Navy from civilian life, who wrongly suspected that others considered him a coward. Frantic and "sick at heart" over the approaching horrors, the man repeatedly sought solace and brotherly advice from Beach. This "gentle, timid, retiring" fellow later performed well under fire at Manila, assisting the *Baltimore*'s surgeon. Weeks afterward, however, he committed suicide on his way Stateside. "He had received a mortal wound in his first and only battle," Beach recalled, "but not the sort of injury any of us had any idea how to handle."[5]

Ellicott recalled that the *Baltimore* chaplain also dreaded whatever horrors the day would bring. "Brace up, Chaplain," Beach had told him Saturday night. "Remember that you represent God in this ship. If you fear all that, go to your room and pray for us." For his part, Ellicott stoutly reassured a *Baltimore* blue-jacket that "[w]e'll all be together after it's over." Privately, "I didn't feel so sure about it."[6]

As the gray warships appeared through the morning mist "in perfect line of battle," *El Diario de Manila* reported, "gloom and surprise were general among the people of Manila."[7] Spaniards and Filipinos began gathering on every high wall, tower, or rooftop with a view of the bay to watch the battle develop.

In the rising light, American lookouts spotted a tangle of masts and hulls off the city. Dewey looked in vain for the Spanish squadron, "which I had rather expected would be at the anchorage."[8] He instead found only sixteen merchant-men. Believing that anchoring off Manila would "provoke the enemy to bombard the plaza, which doubtless would have been demolished,"[9] Montojo had shifted his force seven miles southwest, around the curve of the bay to the arsenal at Cavite.

At five minutes past five, the *Olympia* hoisted "prepare for general action." The signal flags "flew out fairly well," Fiske recalled. (Later they would hang "up and down like rags; and although the ships were well closed up, it was impossible to read them.")[10] In response to the flagship's signal, an American flag appeared in the breeze from every staff and masthead in the squadron, twenty-six altogether. Each was "the largest regulation ensign," according to correspondent Stickney.[11]

With full daylight, lookouts at last sighted Montojo. Almost simultaneously, two mines exploded two miles ahead of the squadron on the bearing toward Cavite. "Evidently, the Spaniards are already rattled," Dewey said to Lamberton, puzzled by the distance.[12] The Spaniards later said they were only clearing room to maneuver.

Three batteries in the city opened fire at ranges of five to seven miles, with what *El Diario* termed "more courage and valor than effect."[13] The *Boston* and *Concord* replied by firing twice apiece into the Luneta battery, the only one of the trio situated where the old walled city wasn't in danger if American shells overshot. The squadron's other ships withheld fire to conserve their ammunition.

Fiske reported to the *Petrel*'s bridge as the action heated up. "The Spanish fleet is over there," Captain Wood said, pointing to starboard. Fiske's duty this morning was to estimate ranges for the gunners. He began clambering to the ship's foretop toting his stadimeter, an instrument he had designed for measuring distances. Although the fire from Manila was inaccurate, one shell sent up a geyser that drenched Fiske and his assistant, now forty-five feet off the deck. The bluejacket said solemnly, "That was pretty close, sir."[14]

Montojo had arrayed his squadron in what Dewey described as an "irregular crescent" in front of Cavite.[15] His western flank was protected by Sangley Point and its battery, his eastern flank by shoal waters. The admiral's line of battle consisted of the flagship *Reina Cristina*, *Castilla*, *Don Juan de Austria*, *Don Antonio de Ulloa*, *Isla de Luzon*, *Isla de Cuba*, and *Marques del Duero*. (The transport *Isla de Mindanao*, on the right of the line, was quickly beached once the fight began. Two gunboats in the lee of Cavite Point, the *Velasco* and *Lezo*, played no role in the fight.)

Heavy iron lighters filled with stone protected the wooden-hulled *Castilla*, which was moored head and stern and still wore her jaunty cream peacetime paint. "Some of the vessels in the Spanish battle-line were under way," Dewey wrote, "and others were moored so as to bring their broadside batteries to bear to the best advantage."[16] To Fiske, the disposition suggested the French fleet's at the battle of the Nile, while Dewey's column suggested Nelson's—"a pleasant augury."[17]

The Spaniards had lowered and sent ashore most of their topmasts and spars to reduce the danger from deadly splinters in the battle. Consequently, Ellicott reported, "no flags flew at their mastheads except on the *Castilla*, and the Admiral's flag on the *Cristina*."[18] The bold, red-and-gold colors of Spain—sometimes called "blood-and-pus" through the country's long and bloody history—flew instead from gaffs and flagstaffs. In his old age, Ellicott would recall that as the Americans approached, "I had a curious feeling that it was almost a sacrilege to cause those beautiful flags of a 400-year-old nation to flutter down in defeat."[19]

Dewey sent his two unarmed colliers, *Nanshan* and *Zafiro*, into the middle of the bay, escorted by the revenue cutter *Hugh McCulloch*. Lieutenant W. P. Elliott, executive officer of the *Baltimore*, commanded the three auxiliaries. He was "the most disappointed man in the fleet" upon being ordered off, according to an observer.[20] (The *McCulloch* would stand in close to the fighting with hawsers on her deck, ready to pull off any disabled vessel, but her assistance wasn't needed.)

The commodore's line now comprised the *Olympia*, *Baltimore*, *Raleigh*, *Petrel*, *Concord*, and *Boston*. Steaming at eight knots, he turned to close with the Spaniards and reduced the interval between his ships from four hundred to two hundred yards. His guns stayed trained on the Spanish vessels as a leadsman continually took soundings in the unfamiliar waters.

At 5:15 AM, "a puff of very white cloud rose from a clump of bushes on shore," newspaperman Stickney reported. "It was a pretty sight, for the smoke floated away in fantastic shapes above the red clay shore and the bright green foliage."[21] The Spanish squadron soon joined the bombardment, though with no greater effect than the batteries at Manila or Sangley Point. The fire from Manila remained so inaccurate that an artillery colonel fired a bullet through his head that night—the only intended target he hit all day.

The Americans approached Montojo obliquely, "keeping him on our starboard bow," Dewey wrote. "[O]ur converging course and ever-varying position must have confused the Spanish gunners. My assumption that the Spanish fire would be hasty and inaccurate proved correct."[22]

Spanish fire grew more frantic, if no more true, as the squadron swept closer. Dewey still withheld his fire, conserving powder and shells until he judged he was within effective range. His uniform cap had been misplaced or accidentally discarded as the flagship cleared for action. He stood now on the *Olympia's* bridge wearing baggy white ducks and a soft gray traveling cap (some accounts describe it as a golf cap). In the awful physical and mental heat of the coming hours, when seamen stripped to their trousers or less, Dewey was "the most dressed man in the battle."[23]

During their approach to Manila, Captain Gridley was noticeably ill. Dewey had offered to relieve him, and so spare him the strain of conning the *Olympia* in action. The flagship skipper had politely refused, saying that "she is my ship and I will fight her."[24] Gridley would later concede on his deathbed, "Going to Manila killed me, but I would do it again if necessary."[25]

Almost miraculously, after twenty minutes under fire from Montojo and Sangley Point, neither the *Olympia* nor any other ship in Dewey's squadron had sustained any damage. At 5:41 AM, within five thousand yards of the Spaniards, the commodore again turned to his ailing captain. "You may fire when you are ready, Gridley." (A slightly streamlined quotation caught the popular imagination, but this is how Dewey recorded it in his autobiography.)[26]

Gridley went into the armored conning tower below the bridge, his duty station throughout the battle, and relayed this now-famous order. An 8-inch gun in the *Olympia's* forward turret bellowed first. "Almost instantly—it seemed to me like an echo—came the sound of the guns of the other ships," Kindleberger recalled.[27]

The warships' starboard batteries fired until they neared the 5-fathom curve. There, Dewey changed course to westward, allowing the port batteries to bear. The squadron would steam opposite the Spanish line alternating broadsides throughout the early morning, two runs to the east and three to the west.

The displays of grace under pressure in both squadrons off Cavite required no embellishment later. But aside from the two commanders, the man whose performance proved most crucial to the outcome was Carlos Calkins. The navigator stood near the commodore on the *Olympia's* exposed forward bridge, constantly under fire during the firing runs, using inaccurate charts and verifying his position within the bay through cross-bearings and depths called out by the leadsman. Dewey would especially commend Calkins in his report to Washington and colleagues would recount his feat with awe.

"When one thinks of how much disaster might have followed a mistake of Calkins," Fiske wrote, "or a mistaken order of the commodore relative to the course alone . . . one can appreciate what the responsibilities of their positions were, and what was the necessity for coolness and clearness of head."[28]

In the first hour, the Spaniards apparently tried to attack the flagship with a makeshift vessel that Dewey called a "torpedo-launch." The flag secretary, Ensign Caldwell, was temporarily on duty with the 5-inch guns, so Annapolis grad Stickney was serving as Dewey's volunteer aide on the *Olympia*'s bridge. The correspondent directed the commodore's attention to the launch as it appeared around Sangley Point.

"You look after her," Dewey snapped. "I have no time to bother with torpedo boats. Let me know when you've finished her."[29]

Deep-sixing his journalistic detachment with an alacrity that modern "embeds" might envy, Stickney rushed to notify a secondary battery. Whoever commanded the launch seemed to Stickney either "ignorant of modern guns or utterly indifferent to death."[30] Peppering gunfire quickly drove the little craft ashore. (According to Calkins, it was a "humble market boat" whose movements were misinterpreted as an attack. He also dismissed numerous accounts of a second torpedo boat sunk by gunfire. "Had there been half a dozen real torpedo-boats in Manila Bay in the hands of fearless and skilled officers," Calkins added, "the whole situation would have been transformed.")[31] Along with many regular officers, Stickney, too, later received Dewey's praise in the official report.

As the Americans fired on his ships, Montojo reported, "The battle became general. We slipped the springs and our cables and started ahead with the engines, so as not to be involved by the enemy. The Americans fired most rapidly. There came upon us numberless projectiles, as the three cruisers at the head of the line devoted themselves almost entirely to fight the *Cristina*, my flagship."[32]

Rapid fire at short range was precisely what Dewey had wanted. When Calkins reported that the bay was deeper than indicated on his charts, Dewey ordered him to plot courses even nearer the Spaniards, at times closing to less than two thousand yards. At such short distances, shells from the troublesome Sangley Point battery passed harmlessly overhead. A post-battle inspection revealed that the guns couldn't be laid for targets so unimaginably close—the muzzles hit the sill of the embrasure.[33]

Dewey's gunners naturally concentrated on the biggest and most threatening targets, the *Reina Cristina* and the *Castilla*. The concentration of fire was "smothering," according to the commodore, although "in the early part of the action our firing was not what I should have liked it to be."[34] Fiske, too, was disappointed by American gunnery, and believed it could be better directed with specific orders. "Our practice was evidently much better than that of the Spaniards," he would write, "but it did not seem to me that it was at all good."[35]

Counterbalancing the gunnery was discipline. "It was evident that Dewey's watchful eye was upon us," Ellicott wrote. "From time to time a vessel's call letter would be displayed with the brief signal: 'Close up.'"[36] An officer on the *Olympia* likewise recalled a volcanic, profane tirade from the commodore when the *Baltimore* swung too wide during one of her turns, which was followed by the signal Ellicott remembered;[37] Dewey later claimed no memory of the incident.

Dewey carefully deployed his line so that "no ship ever got between any other and the enemy," Fiske recalled.[38] Speed and direction also kept the gun crews free of the obscuring smoke from their own weapons. Command and control among the Spaniards, in contrast, was pitiable. The Spanish ships, Calkins wrote, "steamed about in an aimless fashion, often masking their comrades' fire, occasionally dodging back to the shelter of the arsenal and now and then making isolated and ineffectual rushes in advance."[39]

Like other American officers, Calkins shuddered at such useless machismo. "'To breed men and waste them,'" he ruefully observed, "is the awful tradition of the ancient Kingdom of Castile."[40]

The *Don Juan de Austria* and the *Reina Cristina* made what Dewey termed "brave and desperate attempts" to charge the *Olympia*.[41] Each was severely repulsed. Montojo reported that a single shell wrecked the *Cristina*'s forecastle, took out everyone manning four rapid-fire cannon, splintered the foremast, and wounded the helmsman on the bridge. (A lieutenant took over the wheel "with a coolness worthy of the greatest commendation," Montojo reported, and steered until the end of the fight.)[42] Another shell started a fire in the orlop that the crew managed to control. Dewey's ships, the admiral continued, then bore in and "covered us with a rain of rapid-fire projectiles."[43] Montojo's flagship and squadron were literally shot to bits.

In the *Baltimore*'s after engine room, Beach saw nothing of the battle except the soles of Ensign Noble Irwin's shoes on a hatch grating overhead. Stokers

and boiler-men throughout the squadron saw even less as they worked to pros-
tration in enclosed spaces. The temperature, measured at 116°F below decks
on the *Boston*,[44] was improbably estimated at 170°F in the *Baltimore*'s forward
fireroom.[45] To keep up morale, Beach began inventing a vivid commentary on
the fight, which he relayed forward via a speaking tube.

Beach asked an officer who had served under Farragut in the Civil War
whether this was "a real battle."

"Yes, this is a real fight," Chief Engineer John D. Ford said, "and a big one,
too."[46]

. . .

The Spanish squadron was coming apart. According to Montojo's report to
Madrid, the flagship had sustained heavy damage and the *Austria* was on fire.
The *Ulloa* and *Luzon* were both damaged and one of the *Duero*'s engines was
useless. The wooden *Castilla*, Dewey recalled, had "fared little better than the
Reina Cristina"; she was ablaze and soon to be abandoned. [47]

Conditions were appalling on the *Cristina*. A shell destroyed her steering
gear; another exploded on the poop; a third shot away the mizzen masthead,
bringing down the Spanish flag and Montojo's ensign, "which were immediately replaced";[48] a fourth exploded in the officers' cabin and wrecked the hospital; and a fifth hit the after ammunition room, filling the ship with smoke and
making steering by hand impossible.

"As it was impossible to control the fire, I had to flood the magazine when
the cartridges were beginning to explode," Montojo reported. As more shells
smashed the flagship, putting half the crew out of action, he gave the inevitable
order to sink her. "I abandoned the *Cristina*, directing beforehand to secure her
flag, and accompanied by my staff, and with great sorrow, I hoisted my flag on
the cruiser *Isla de Cuba*."[49] The *Cristina*'s captain was killed directing rescue
efforts.

The captain of the British steamer *Dalcairne* watched as the admiral shifted
his flag under fire in a small boat. "During that perilous passage of a mile or
more," the skipper recalled, "[Montojo] stood upright in the stern perfectly
unmoved, although splashes of water flew repeatedly over the little craft. . . . It
was an example of unparalleled heroism."[50]

Very little of this was apparent to Dewey. As his ships began their fifth firing
run, to the west, the pall of smoke over the Spanish squadron made battle-
damage assessment impossible. "Victory was already ours," Dewey wrote,
"though we did not know it." With the *Olympia* opposite the center of the Spanish line, Gridley sent a report up to the bridge that shocked the commodore—

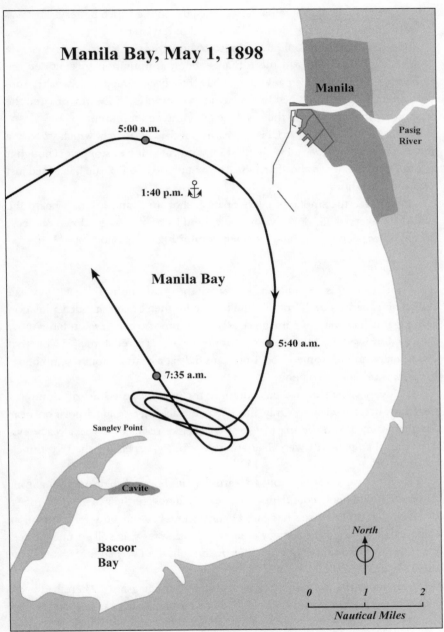

Track of Dewey's squadron in Manila Bay. (Map by Tina Bozzuto)

only fifteen rounds apiece remained for the guns in the 5-inch battery. This was a "most anxious moment for me," Dewey admitted later.[51]

Indeed, as far as he could tell, Montojo's force was as intact as his own. He believed the Spaniards had more than enough ammunition to continue the fight, even if they rarely hit anything, while the *Olympia*'s apparently paltry supply of 5-inch shells could be "shot away in five minutes."[52] Dewey ordered the squadron to withdraw into the bay to redistribute his ammunition.

In the foretop of the *Petrel*, Fiske wearily checked his watch, which stood at a few minutes past 7:30 AM. He thought for a moment it had stopped. Though it felt to Fiske like two in the afternoon, the first phase of the battle had lasted just two and a half hours.

"I could see the smoke of every Spanish shot fired, and I think I heard the whistle of every shell," Fiske wrote later, "and I was glad to get down on deck, where other people were, and feel their comforting companionship."[53]

· · ·

The American press would later popularize the quaint notion that Dewey had pulled his squadron back from Cavite to give his men breakfast. Such adulation was too much even for the image-conscious commodore; in his autobiography, Dewey dismissed the "nonchalance that had never occurred to me."[54] Nonetheless, Calkins noted, "some 1,700 Americans did eat a hearty, though scrambling, breakfast during the next hour."[55]

As Dewey's line steamed back out into the bay, the true state of Montojo's squadron became clearer. Only the *Ulloa* still held her original position near Sangley Point. From the mast of the *Petrel*, Fiske recalled, it was already evident that the Spaniards were "suffering very badly, especially the two principal ships."[56]

The Americans were anxious to learn the condition of their own squadron. Although individually confident of the seaworthiness of their own ships, many believed that other vessels had fared badly. Some had indeed seen companion ships struck by shellfire. Dewey's order to withdraw was still so unexpected that the executive officer of the *Baltimore* thought the *Olympia* must have been suddenly disabled.[57]

Once out in the bay, the captains reported to the flagship. "There had been such a heavy flight of shells over us," Dewey recalled, "that each captain, when he arrived, was convinced that no other ship had had such good luck as his own in being missed by the enemy's fire, and expected the others to have both casualties and damages to report."[58] To general astonishment, there were few instances of either.

True, the *Baltimore* had been hit at least five times, but only one shell had caused casualties. (Ricocheting wildly through several compartments and groups of men, this shell was "perhaps the most remarkable in the annals of naval warfare," Ellicott wrote;[59] Ensign Irwin was one of eight men it slightly wounded.) The *Boston* had been struck four times and was briefly afire; the *Petrel* had been hit once without grave damage or injuries. The *Boston*'s wooden boats had been shattered not by Spanish fire, but by concussion from her own guns. The same thing happened to two of the *Baltimore*'s boats. The *Olympia*, in contrast, had put her boats over the side before the battle.

The flagship was hulled five times and her rigging cut, with shells passing both above and below where Dewey had stood on the exposed bridge. Although tales of dented plates, punctures, and close calls abounded, the squadron hadn't suffered a single combat fatality. The only American who died was Chief Engineer Frank B. Randall of the *Hugh McCulloch*. He had suffered "apoplectic convulsions" during the firing off El Fraile and died two hours later. [60]

(Although navy histories generally blame heat and stress, Ellicott reported that Randall was so mortified by the flare from the *McCulloch*'s stack off Corregidor that he "had a heart stroke and died."[61] Beach Sr. uncharacteristically repeated the perhaps cruel squadron gossip that the engineer had been killed by "John Barleycorn . . . with neatness and dispatch."[62] Regardless of the clinical or emotional cause of death, the cutter's crew lowered Randall's body into the bay with "an impressive ceremony" late on Sunday afternoon.)[63]

No captain could conceal "his satisfaction at the condition of his ship and crew," Stickney reported, but each was "desirous that this should be understood to be no proof that he had not been in danger."[64]

Dewey was also relieved to learn that the *Olympia* was not, in fact, low on 5-inch ammunition. "How Gridley became confused . . . is not clear at this distance in time," states a modern biographer.[65] The captain was ill and under pressure. The conning tower was hot, crowded, and noisy. Communications within the ship were iffy. Somehow, somewhere, information had gotten garbled, and Gridley had passed it along to Dewey. The only lasting effect of the mistake was the widespread misimpression that the squadron had hauled off for breakfast, which only enhanced Dewey's reputation among the American public.

After three and a half hours, his crews refreshed in body and spirit, and his concerns about ammunition allayed, the commodore steamed back toward Cavite.

. . .

Spanish authorities had convinced themselves that the Americans hadn't with-
drawn but retreated, and had cabled as much to Madrid. Montojo, however,
shared no such optimism. As soon as Dewey steamed away, the admiral had
ordered his surviving ships to "take positions in the bottom of the Roads at
Bacoor," below Cavite. They were to resist "to the last moment," and then be
sunk before surrendering.[66] Only the *Ulloa* remained off Sangley Point.

By 11:16 AM, when the Americans returned, the *Reina Cristina* was abandoned, partially submerged, and afire, with her superstructure aglow from the
heat; the wooden-hulled *Castilla* had burned to the waterline and was smolder-
ing.[67] All that was really left to oppose Dewey were the shore batteries and
what the commodore later called "the gallant little *Ulloa*."[68] With the major
work done, he ordered the *Baltimore* and *Petrel* in to mop up.

The battery at Sangley Point was "well served," Dewey recalled, and "several times reopened fire."[69] The limitations of the embrasure's construction
proved fatal, however. The *Baltimore* rushed in and pounded the guns into
silence. "The beach seemed to be torn up with the impact of her shells," Fiske
wrote, "and the air there to be filled with clouds of sand and the smoke and the
flames of burning powder."[70] An improvised white flag appeared over the
ruined parapet.

Like the battery, the *Ulloa* "defended herself firmly."[71] Ellicott reported that
her captain disobeyed a signal to scuttle and abandon her.[72] Instead, the
Spaniards opened fire as soon as the *Baltimore* cleared Sangley Point. The American cruiser stopped engines and delivered "a point-blank broadside."[73] The
Ulloa heeled from the blast, righted herself, heeled the other way, and then
began sinking as her surviving crewmen swam for shore. Her masts and stack
were still visible once she settled upright in the shallow bay.

Forty-five years afterwards, Ellicott still recalled that on the *Baltimore* "we
stood in awestruck silence as if witnessing an execution." Captain Dyer refused
an officer's request to retrieve the Spanish ensign from the *Ulloa*'s gaff as a prize.
"Let it fly," he said. "She has made the most gallant fight of all."[74] (In contrast to
this and similar accounts, however, Fiske recalled that the *Ulloa* had been abandoned, and that "we fired on her a long time without seeming to do much damage or eliciting any reply."[75] The *Baltimore* likely already had silenced her before
the *Petrel* cleared Sangley Point and began firing, too.)

When the Cavite arsenal also hoisted a white flag, the *Olympia* signaled:
"*Petrel* pass inside."[76] Another signal followed, ordering her to burn the remaining Spanish ships. The gunboat's executive officer set off to accomplish the task

with seven crewmen in a whaleboat. This party set fire to the *Austria*, *Cuba*, *Luzon*, *Lezo*, *El Correo*, and *Duero*, all of which, Dewey recorded, "had been abandoned in shallow water and left scuttled by their crews."[77]

While the *Concord* went in to destroy the transport *Mindanao*, beached near Bacoor, the *Petrel* kept at her tasks until early evening. She eventually rejoined the squadron "towing a long string of tugs and launches, to be greeted by volleys of cheers from every ship."[78] The beached, undamaged steamer *Manila* was also spared and eventually taken over by the U.S. Navy.

Montojo, meanwhile, assured Madrid that his crews had taken care "to save the flag, the distinguishing pennant, the money in the safe, the portable arms, and the breech plugs of the guns, and the signal codes" of the scuttled vessels.[79] After coming ashore, the admiral himself went to the Convent of Santo Domingo de Cavite, where he received treatment for a leg wound.

. . .

As soon as Sangley Point and the *Ulloa* were quiet, Dewey started the *Olympia*, *Baltimore*, and *Raleigh* for the anchorage off Manila. The city's batteries, too, had now fallen silent. Consul Williams crossed to a British ship in the Pasig River to arrange for a message to be sent to Governor-General Augustin, issuer of the disastrous "God of victories" proclamation (Dewey called him captain-general, a literal translation). As the commodore recalled, the note stated that if the Spanish artillery resumed fire "we should destroy the city."[80] This message was delivered through the British consul.

Dewey received assurances by mid-afternoon that the forts wouldn't open fire unless he deployed with the apparent intention of bombarding the city. This was enough, and the squadron dropped anchor for the first time since entering the bay. Without any troops except his handful of Marines, Dewey had no way of actually taking possession of Manila or its garrison, which had not officially surrendered. Nor could he compel the surrender of the Philippines. All that would have to await the arrival of the Army.

At sunset, crowds gathered along the waterfront to gaze at the American warships. The *Olympia*'s band played "La Paloma" and other Spanish airs.[81]

. . .

Montojo reported 381 total casualties from his ships and the arsenal. Later American figures showed 320 Spanish dead and almost 300 wounded.[82]

"The shrieks and groans of the wounded were appalling," wrote surgeon Kindleberger, who visited the Cavite hospital. "I could not stay to hear them, though my profession is calculated to harden one against such scenes."[83] When the flagship *Reina Cristina* was raised in 1903, Dewey wrote, "eighty skeletons were found in the sickbay and fifteen shot holes in the hull."[84]

Except for the captured boats and launches and the occasional wandering steamers taken by the Americans, the Spanish squadron was destroyed. The commodore with his superior ships and equipment had fully expected to trounce the Spaniards, but no realistic naval officer anywhere could have expected to do so at so insignificant a cost.

The Spaniards *had* tried to fight. As Fiske recalled, "the sea between us and the Spaniards had been covered with spouts of water thrown up by their falling shell, and so had the sea beyond us."[85] The poorly trained gunners simply hadn't fired the correct distances. If the American fire had been mediocre, especially in the battle's early moments, Spanish fire had been atrocious. The difference proved fatal. Compounding the poor gunnery were innumerable other failures by the Spanish military commanders and civil authorities.

Whether attributable to sins of omission, commission, negligence, incompetence, or mere pessimism, the catalog of Spanish calamity seemed to Dewey "almost incomprehensible."[86]

Spanish possession of the islands was now all but finished. The only remaining issues were when Spain would lose them, and to whom. "Manila had close in front of it a powerful, victorious fleet," Fiske wrote, "and behind it and in it, and all around it tens of thousands of bitterly hostile Filipinos, partly organized and armed, waiting for revenge."[87]

The outside world didn't learn the outcome of the battle for several days; Dewey had cut the undersea telegraphic cables to halt misleading Spanish communiqués to Madrid. ("Our fleet engaged the enemy in brilliant combat, protected by the Cavite and Manila forts," read one cable. "They obliged the enemy with heavy loss to maneuver repeatedly.")[88] On Wednesday, May 4, the commodore finally dispatched the *McCulloch* to Hong Kong with his own terse but accurate reports for Washington. "The squadron arrived at Manila daybreak this morning. Immediately engaged the enemy and destroyed the following Spanish vessels. . . . The squadron is uninjured."[89]

As Americans cheered the news, Commodore Dewey awaited orders and troops, Filipinos pressed their revolution, and the rest of the world looked across the globe toward Cuba and the Caribbean.

PART THREE

Santiago

CHAPTER 11

"Fighting Bob"

IN THE WINTER of 1891–92—summer in the Southern Hemisphere—civil war had swept Chile. As was often the case during such foreign unrest, the United States and several European countries sent warships to protect their nationals and financial interests. Among those vessels was the *Baltimore*.

The ship's captain was Winfield Scott Schley, a veteran of the tough Mississippi campaign under Admiral Farragut. Schley (pronounced "sly") was already a public figure, having stepped confidently into the national spotlight in 1884. That year the Greely expedition, an Army-sponsored polar exploration, had gone tragically wrong, its boats crushed by ice, its men stranded in northern Greenland. Under extreme conditions, Schley led the rescue of six survivors by the USS *Thetis*.

"He did not spare himself from the cold, discomfort, and long hours, and his example inspired his crew," a biographer has written. "The rescue of Greely and his men was the high point of Schley's professional career."[1] Flamboyant and quotable, Schley became the newspapers' darling and something of a nineteenth-century media star. President Chester A. Arthur personally greeted the relief expedition in New York, this during an era when the Navy had very little else to celebrate.

Five years later, now a national figure, Schley became the new *Baltimore's* first commanding officer. In 1890, the cruiser conveyed the body of USS *Monitor* designer John Ericsson back to his native Sweden for burial. When war erupted the following year between the Chilean government and its congress, Schley suggested shifting the ship from the Mediterranean to South America. Navy Secretary Benjamin Tracy quickly agreed. The *Baltimore* arrived at the hilly port city of Valparaiso in April 1891.

For various and often complex reasons, including American seizure of a steamer that had transshipped arms for the insurgents, feelings soon ran high against the United States. Many Chileans suspected, rightly or wrongly, that the country was choosing sides in their war. Tensions and misunderstandings persisted for months. A congressional army captured Valparaiso in late August, an event quickly followed by the arrival of the insurgent Chilean navy.

Six weeks later, on October 16, Schley perhaps unwisely allowed 115 of the *Baltimore*'s crew to step ashore on liberty. "A long interval had elapsed since the *Baltimore*'s crew were granted leave," he recalled, "and . . . every foreign man-of-war in Valparaiso at this time gave their men liberty."[2]

At about six o'clock that evening, mobs began attacking the *Baltimore* men at several points around the city. An American merchant skipper reported the violence to Schley and urged him to shell the city. Schley refused to fire and endanger civilians. Some Chileans, in fact, had aided his sailors, including an artillery officer who drew his sword to defend them. Schley soon received word that the rioting had subsided, making any immediate retaliation unnecessary. The fighting had left one of his bluejackets dead, another mortally wounded, and several injured. Schley's men also charged complicity by the city police, some of whom had clearly done little or nothing to protect them.

Schley took no action that night, later citing an old French proverb that "sleep brings counsel."[3] The following day, he established a three-man court of inquiry and began lengthy, earnest correspondence with Chilean naval and civil authorities. Reaction at home, however, was louder and angrier. More American warships were dispatched toward Chile. One of them was the USS *Yorktown*, a gunboat commanded by Bob Evans.

. . .

Evans had advanced but hardly mellowed in the years since the Doldrums. He was now a commander. It was not surprising that Schley's measured, diplomatic approach to resolving the crisis didn't appeal to so volatile an officer as Evans. He later noted with dry disdain that Schley had conducted his correspondence with the Chilean *intendente* "in the most perfect Castilian."[4]

Furthermore, the captain's almost spinsterish insistence that the *Baltimore* liberty parties had all been sober during the violence in Valparaiso struck the feisty *Yorktown* skipper as absurd. Evans believed that American sailors drunk on "Chilean rum paid for with good United States money . . . were more entitled to protection than if they had been sober."[5] And he heartily disapproved when the Navy ordered the *Baltimore* home, feeling that Schley "should remain until the trouble about his men had been settled."[6]

The coolness—and perhaps distrust, at least on Evans' part—that developed between the two men in Valparaiso would linger for the remainder of their careers. It certainly colored later operations off Cuba, although it probably didn't affect the outcome at Santiago. Years later, their personalities and temperaments were evident in their respective memoirs. Schley frequently referred to himself in the third person as "the commander" and titled one of his chapters on Valparaiso "Adjustment of the Chilean Difficulty." Evans used a colorful, first-person narrative and titled one of his chapters "Chilean Hostility."

After the *Baltimore*'s departure, the *Yorktown* was the only U.S. warship in Valparaiso harbor for much of December and January. The crisis continued to simmer, prompting Dewey to buy the additional coal that later caught Theodore Roosevelt's attention. Although the affair "may not have merited the attention that United States and Chilean officials devoted to it,"[7] according to a modern historian, for many weeks war appeared not only possible, but likely. "Evans cut a dramatic figure in Valparaiso harbor, and before long he turned nasty, which was not difficult for him."[8]

Evans demanded every courtesy from the Chilean navy, and dealt immediately with any slight, real or perceived. During the New Year's Eve celebrations, a rocket fired by a Chilean warship barely missed the *Yorktown*. Evans turned a searchlight on his flag and manned his guns, and no more rockets flew his way.[9] After civilians threw stones at his gig crew, Evans threatened to "arm my boats and shoot any and every man who insulted me or my men or my flag in any way."[10]

When torpedo boats repeatedly darted toward his ship, apparently conducting target practice, Evans assumed it was more than bad manners. "I went to quarters at once and gave orders, if one of them even scratched the paint on the *Yorktown,* to blow the boat out of the water and kill every man in her, so that there could be no question of an accidental collision."[11] (This incident is "perhaps apocryphal," according to a modern history of the affair.)[12] When finally the *Yorktown* departed Valparaiso, ferrying political refugees, Evans warned the Chilean admiral that if any ship followed his gunboat to sea "I would regard it as an act of gross discourtesy and insult to my flag, and would resent it on the spot."[13]

From Davy Crockett to George Patton to Tommy Franks, a tough, aggressive stance has always appealed to the American public. For the reviving Navy, Evans became a new Stephen Decatur. His bluejackets might still call him Old Gimpy because of his leg wound from Fort Fisher, but newspapers back home began hailing him as "Fighting Bob," the only hero of a war the United States hadn't fought.

Evans only halfheartedly objected to the colorful sobriquet. Despite his disclaimers, a modern biographer noted, he "discovered the benefits of a favorable press—and was not adverse to exploiting it to his own interests. 'Fighting Bob' Evans he had become, and 'Fighting Bob' Evans he would remain."[14]

Under tremendous international pressure, Chile finally defused the *Baltimore* crisis by paying a $75,000 indemnity to the injured sailors and the families of the dead. Evans wrote that although he could have "stirred up a war" at Valparaiso, he couldn't have justified it to himself.

Instead, Evans had struggled—almost against his very nature—to maintain what he later called a "dignified and resolute position." But had the Chilean navy provoked a naval fight at Valparaiso, he added, "I should have engaged their nine ships without hesitation, and the chances would not have favored my getting the *Yorktown* out of their harbor."[15]

. . .

The six years following the *Baltimore* affair, if not exactly the "Gay Nineties" for the Navy, were nonetheless a vast improvement over most comparable periods since the Civil War. The ships of the new steel Navy continued emerging from shipyards on both coasts. Able officers long stuck in low pay grades began to assume posts worthy of their talent, experience, and ambition.

Schley and Evans both moved on to larger, more important commands. Schley's actions at Valparaiso were reviewed by a second inquiry at Mare Island, California, and personally approved by President Benjamin Harrison. When he left the *Baltimore* in February 1892, Schley's crew presented him with a gold-headed cane, a "precious gift [that] has a high place in the heart of the recipient."[16] Duty followed with the Lighthouse Board, during which Schley several times accompanied yet another president, Grover Cleveland, on trips to and from his summer home in a lighthouse tender.[17]

After briefly serving with the Board of Inspection in 1895, Schley next assumed command of the big armored cruiser USS *New York* in the Atlantic fleet. (Ironically, he relieved Evans, which neither man later mentioned in his memoirs.) Following two years with the cruiser, Schley next became chairman of the Lighthouse Board. Finally, after forty-two years in the Navy, and three weeks after the *Maine*'s destruction in Havana Harbor, Schley received a promotion to commodore.

On March 24, 1898, with just sixteen days at flag rank, and with the country headed toward war, Commodore Schley received orders from Secretary Long to proceed to Hampton Roads and take command of a new "Flying

Squadron," which might be used anywhere from the Atlantic Seaboard to the coast of Spain.

The Flying Squadron comprised the cruisers *Brooklyn* (flagship), *Columbia*, and *Minneapolis*, "and such other vessels as may be directed to report to you."[18] Aside from noting in his memoirs that President William McKinley had selected him for the command, Schley offered no details later about what he had thought or felt upon receiving this vital assignment. "The squadron was held in readiness for any movement or service," he wrote, "so far as coal and other supplies were concerned."[19] The Flying Squadron would remain held for almost two months.

. . .

Evans, too, had advanced since Valparaiso. After departing Chile, he and the *Yorktown* had led a small squadron of Navy vessels and revenue cutters to enforce a ban on pelagic seal hunting in the Bering Sea. For this, Evans was cited in the Navy secretary's annual report for his "judgment, energy, and skill."[20] After leaving the *Yorktown*, he then briefly served with the Lighthouse Board in Washington before being promoted to captain in 1893 and subsequently taking over the *New York*.

The cruiser participated in the opening of the Kiel Canal in Germany the next summer. "The *New York* was about the newest thing in the way of a cruiser," Evans recalled, "and everybody wanted to see her."[21] During the celebrations, he became friends with Germany's Prince Henry and his wife, Princess Irene, "two of the most delightful people I ever met."[22] (In hindsight, this description might have surprised George Dewey, at least as it pertained to the Kaiser's only brother, as this was the same Prince Heinrich who bedeviled him at Hong Kong and Manila.) Evans admired the seagoing prince's perfect English, willingness to speak his mind, and "sharp professional talk."[23]

Evans was a good if traditional commander, little interested in innovators like Bradley Fiske. (He had declined, for example, to use Fiske's inventions in either the *Yorktown* or the *New York*, although in time they were widely adopted.) As his nickname indicated, Evans preferred missions to experiments or diplomacy. During his time in command, the *New York* carried the flag for three admirals, a distinction that he thought few captains would have cared to share. "Flagship duty," he noted, "is not considered desirable as a general rule."[24]

After the *New York*, Evans went to Philadelphia to fit out and command the new battleship *Indiana*, "a real machine shop from top to bottom . . . a magnificent command."[25] Dewey and his inspection board then "took us to sea and gave us a thorough overhauling,"[26] which they followed with a favorable report. In the fall of 1896, Evans reported to the Lighthouse Board. He was also detailed to the Personnel Board, where he became a confidant of Assistant Secretary Roosevelt—who, like Evans, believed that war was brewing in Cuba.

Evans was on an inspection tour through the Deep South when the *Maine* made her last voyage to Havana. "I could see, from the set faces of those Southern chaps," he remembered, "and the quiet, determined way in which they spoke, that somebody was going to get whipped because the *Maine* had blown up."[27]

Evans was in Secretary Long's office with Roosevelt when Long gave the directions relieving ailing Admiral Sicard from command of the North Atlantic Fleet. After issuing the orders that promoted Captain Sampson over numerous senior captains (including Schley) to replace Sicard, the secretary turned to Evans.

"Now, captain, I have a surprise for you," Long said. "I am going to order you to relieve Sampson in command of the *Iowa*. How soon can you start?"[28]

Evans had believed until this moment that all key seagoing commands were already filled. He had hoped only for the *Saint Paul*, a merchant cruiser armed and newly taken into the Navy. (That command went instead to Captain Sigsbee.) Unlike Schley, Evans later recorded exactly what he had felt: "I was therefore much gratified to command the finest battle ship in the navy."[29]

The captain left Washington immediately by train to join the *Iowa* at Key West. He was "Fighting Bob" Evans once more.

CHAPTER 12

Cervera

THE STRATEGIC SITUATION in the Atlantic and West Indies wasn't as simple as it had been in the western Pacific. Dewey had set out to locate and destroy the opposing squadron in the Philippines. This he had quickly achieved, if greatly aided by the Spaniards themselves. Closer to home, however, the United States initially found itself on the defensive.

Much of Spain's fleet operated from her Atlantic and Mediterranean ports. She maintained only a few outdated vessels at Cuba, but routinely sent warships to call at Havana, just ninety miles from Key West. The Spanish navy also enjoyed access to other fine Cuban harbors and to Puerto Rico. The American fleet, in contrast, had no similar staging point anywhere near the Iberian Peninsula. At first glance, the Spaniards seemed much more likely to attack American targets than the *Yanquis* were to bombard Cádiz or Barcelona.

Indeed, early in the war, a sort of bombardment hysteria swept like influenza through the U.S. coastal states. The "timid among the inhabitants of our seaboard," as Secretary Long later categorized them, all sensed marauding Spanish squadrons lurking just beyond the horizon. Mayors, governors, legislators, Chamber of Commerce members, and other influential bigwigs all pressed their "insistent demand for protection."[1] A prominent Boston banker was astonished when a businessman postponed a deal until "after the bombardment. . . . The Spanish Fleet will be here in a few days."[2]

Once the clamor reached the White House, the Navy was forced to respond. Long would have preferred to concentrate the North Atlantic forces in the Florida Keys. Instead, he created the Flying Squadron at Hampton Roads, "a thousand miles from Key West, but within reach of that point and of Porto Rico, yet within easy striking distance of . . . New York, upon which particularly it was apprehended that an attack might be made."[3]

The Navy also seemingly bowed to political pressures to dispatch individual vessels to the defense of key port cities. Assistant Secretary Roosevelt was still on the job, though soon to resign to form what would become his famous "Rough Riders" regiment. T. R. considered the whole affair ludicrous, but also dangerous if it diverted his warships. "I was bound that, as long as a ship had to be sent," he later wrote, "it should not be a ship worth anything."[4]

Thirteen Civil War monitors, each armed with a single, smooth-bore turret, were brought out of mothballs. Manned by naval militia, these relics were distributed among a dozen Atlantic ports and Mare Island, California. Roosevelt would quip that they couldn't have threatened anything more modern than "the galleys of Alcibiades."[5]

Admiral Sampson was burdened at Key West with the newer monitors *Amphitrite* and *Terror* (also the name of a Spanish vessel), two decades under construction and now largely unwanted. They were "manifestly unsuited" for coastal defense, according to Long, and equally unsuited for offensive operations, but the Navy needed every ship. "Never," Sampson wrote, "was a commander-in-chief more harassed by any ships under his command."[6] But if nothing else, all the monitors helped calm public fears.

The Spanish navy in fact had no serious plans for commerce raiding, although the idea was discussed. Madrid actually had few military plans of any sort. Many Spanish officers hoped for what people along the Atlantic seaboard would have cheered—long-range American naval operations against the Iberian coasts. These would have stretched American supply lines and perhaps affected the tide of popular opinion in Europe, already running high in favor of Spain.

"History shows that Spain has been always courageous in defense," Long noted. Had seagoing officers determined her naval strategy, he believed, rather than ministers and politicians, "they would have endeavored to shift the burden of offense to the shoulders of the United States."[7] Some sentiment for commerce raids by the Spanish navy would, in fact, surface later—if only in hindsight—as a tactic for relieving American pressures on Cuba.

The U.S. *did* plan to take the offense, but would not venture more than three thousand ocean miles to do so. The Navy would operate instead within a few hundred miles of Key West. By the beginning of the war, Long recalled, the Navy had decided to concentrate its Atlantic forces "upon Cuba particularly, and Porto Rico incidentally." Given the geography, this "must have been apparent to Spain and to other naval and military nations."[8]

This decision forced the Spaniards toward their own difficult choice. To maintain a defensive stance in home waters, Captain Mahan pointed out, "was to abandon Cuba in accordance with our demand."[9] Militarily, this was a wise if bitter course. Politically, it was nearly impossible. With a Hapsburg queen regent (the widow María Cristina) and a boy king (her son, twelve-year-old Alphonso XIII), the Spanish monarchy was weak and unstable. Most real power resided in the hands of a council of ministers, which insisted on carrying on a naval war off the island possessions.

"While on our part not the least preparations were being made," Capitán de Navío Víctor M. Concas y Palau, the commanding officer of the armored cruiser *Infanta María Teresa*, later wrote, "the United States was not neglecting the smallest details, as though the war they were anticipating was to be fought against the most powerful nation."[10]

· · ·

The Spanish War, like so many others, was colored by the racism and jingoism of its day. Its language reflected the beliefs and prejudices on each side. American officers might harmlessly refer to the Spaniards as "the Dons"; just as often, however, even officers like Jack Philip, the sincere, pious captain of the *Texas*, spoke unthinkingly of "dagos." Captain Chadwick of the *New York* was notoriously suspicious of Jews. Bob Evans' views of African-Americans, while common at the time, are indefensible today.

Consider a description of the U.S. Army in World War II by military historian Carlo D'Este: The officer corps of 1942 was "strongly upper middle-class, overwhelmingly white Anglo-Saxon Protestant, conservative in its political views, and tainted by racial bias and institutional anti-Semitism." While such men as General Dwight D. Eisenhower didn't necessarily dislike minorities, they "simply found them different and therefore suspect . . . and would have been surprised had they been informed that they were using racist epithets."[11] The passage applies equally well to the Navy of forty-five years earlier.

The Spaniards were no different. Their naval officers typically came from the upper class or aristocracy—hence the title "Don"—and exhibited a strong national and racial pride. Many sneered at what they considered the mongrel mix of American seamen, many of whom were foreign-born—witness Augustin's "God of Victories" proclamation. Attitudes in both countries toward the Filipinos and Cubans they squabbled over were even more deplorable, if hardly unique among nineteenth- or even twentieth-century Western powers. They ranged from the Spaniards' long history of often brutal repression to the Americans' smug patronization of people they would call their "little brown brothers."

Despite such endemic prejudices, one man would emerge from the war with the admiration and respect of both Spaniards and Americans. This was

Contralmirante Don Pascual Cervera y Topete, an almost quixotic figure whom Commodore Schley later called "the knightly Cervera."[12] As war approached, Cervera unhappily commanded a small Spanish fleet.

. . .

Admiral Cervera had entered the Spanish naval college at age thirteen, son of a Spanish army officer who had fought Napoleon. Now fifty-nine, Cervera looked less like a senior naval officer than someone's successful, benevolent uncle. Despite his dress uniform, in official photographs he was often smiling slightly, as if he has just told a funny story to the photographer.

Cervera's military record was as exemplary and varied as George Dewey's. Highly respected within both the navy and the government, he had commanded several ships and held several important posts. These included naval adjutant to the queen regent, chief of the Naval Commission in London, and, very briefly, minister of marine, which was an appointed military post in Spain.[13]

His tragedy was that Cervera served the Spanish navy. He knew its true condition, which at the beginning of 1898 was worse than the United States suspected, and far more appalling than the international community—especially the Europeans and particularly the Spaniards themselves—believed it to be. "At a last banquet for Spanish naval officers, a serious affair where duty was the keynote," an American naval writer noted years later, "the archbishop himself proposed a toast to their assault upon the city of Washington!"[14]

A month before the destruction of the *Maine* at Havana, Cervera had confided his fears to a kinsman. "The relative military positions of Spain and the United States has grown worse for us," he wrote, "because we are extenuated, absolutely penniless, and they are very rich, and also because we have increased our naval power only with the [armored cruiser] *Colón* and the torpedo destroyers, and they have increased theirs much more."[15]

The following month, still days before the *Maine* disaster, he wrote to someone identified only as "a high official personage" that the Spanish navy had "no charts of the American seas, although I suppose that they have been ordered."[16] In another letter, he noted that the "eight principal vessels of the Havana station have no military value whatever, and, besides, are badly worn out, therefore they can be of little use."[17]

In mid-March, with war now clearly in the offing, Cervera suggested that there shouldn't be "the least doubt that the war will simply lead us to a terrible disaster, followed by a humiliating peace and most frightful ruin." He thought Spain should try to resolve the issue of Cuban independence through arbitration or mediation, and wrote that the country would be ill-advised to defend "an island which was ours but belongs to us no more, . . . what is now no more than a romantic ideal."[18]

If Cuba was to be lost either way, war with the United States made little sense to the admiral. He certainly didn't think the government should divide the navy and deploy a fleet all the way to the West Indies. Despite his cogent arguments and pleas, all delivered either privately or confidentially, Cervera couldn't divert Madrid to a sounder course.

"There was infinite tragedy," British observer and historian H. W. Wilson wrote not long afterward, "in the spectacle of a people going to certain defeat, because national pride would not permit it to abandon its colonies at the dictate of a stronger Power. . . . With her medieval organization and eighteenth-century methods, Spain was, indeed, bound to succumb."[19]

.   .   .

Admiral Cervera steamed from the historic port city of Cádiz, on Spain's southern Atlantic coast, on April 8, with his flagship *Infanta María Teresa* and the *Cristóbal Colón*. Remarkably, he had no instructions except to reach St. Vincent in the Cape Verde Islands. Orders were to follow him there by collier.

Madrid had already dispatched a flotilla of three torpedo boats and three torpedo-boat destroyers ahead to St. Vincent, where they were delayed. The United States had little experience with the latter class of vessels. The Royal Navy had begun developing what it called torpedo-boat "catchers, hunters, or destroyers"[20] in the mid-1880s, but for most navies they were still novelties. Confusingly, officers often referred to these ships as torpedo boats, from which they had evolved. Eventually, they were simply called destroyers.

While Cervera was still en route, a former minister of marine told the *Heraldo* newspaper that "the squadron [sic] detained at Cape de Verde, and particularly the destroyers, should have and could have continued the voyage to Cuba, since they have nothing to fear from the American fleet. In this class of ships we are on a much higher level than the United States."[21] (While this was perhaps true, the destroyers likely would have met much larger American warships.) According to Captain Concas of the *María Teresa*, however, Cervera apparently believed that he was going to St. Vincent only to escort the flotilla back home, because the little torpedo boats couldn't have crossed the Atlantic once war was declared.[22]

Cervera and his two cruisers reached the Cape Verdes, off the broad shoulder of northwestern Africa, six days later, on April 14. There the admiral learned that Captain Eulate's *Vizcaya* and the cruiser *Almirante Oquendo* were steaming east from Puerto Rico to join him, which they did on the nineteenth.

The presence of four big Spanish warships at St. Vincent worried the United States. The Cape Verdes were controlled by the Portuguese, the Spaniards' Iberian neighbors. "It had been rumored that Portugal would throw in her fortune with Spain," Long recalled later, "and this report was important, because the attitude of the Lisbon government would determine the length of time Cervera would remain at St. Vincent."²³

Events were now moving swiftly. On Tuesday, April 19, the U.S. Congress passed a joint resolution with three important provisions. These recognized the independence of Cuba, demanded that Spain surrender its authority and government of the island, and authorized President McKinley to use military force to carry out the resolution. There was no likelihood that Spain would meet the American demands.

In the meantime, Cervera had received instructions via the promised collier. He was to take his fleet and defend Puerto Rico, although he was also authorized to go to Cuba. Cervera said a few days later, "It is impossible for me to give an idea of the surprise and astonishment experienced by all on the receipt of the order to sail."²⁴

While Cervera's crews coaled their ships and prepared to depart, McKinley signed the congressional resolution into law on April 20. That same day, the admiral called a council of war on board the *Colón*. It lasted four hours. Afterwards, Cervera sent a cable to Madrid reporting that he, his second-in-command, and the captains all unanimously favored taking the fleet to the Canaries, the Spanish islands midway between the Cape Verdes and the Iberian Peninsula. "Canaries would be protected from a rapid descent of the enemy," he cabled, "and all the forces would be in a position, if necessary, to hasten to the defense of the mother country."²⁵

Cervera didn't stop there. He continued resisting his orders and the following day cabled again. "The more I think about it the more I am convinced that to continue voyage to Puerto Rico would be disastrous. The captains of the ships are of the same opinion as I, some more emphatically."²⁶

Despite belated debate within the government, a council of admirals, which included both active and retired officers, voted fourteen to four for the fleet to depart St. Vincent.²⁷ Cervera's unhappy captains discussed "returning to Spain contrary to instructions"—an act that could have been viewed as treason, almost certainly as rebellion. They concluded, however, that ignorance of the navy's plight was so pervasive that, in Concas' words, "we should not only be punished, but ridiculed."²⁸

Mahan thought the decision to order the fleet to the West Indies indicated "uninstructed popular and political pressure, of the same kind that in our country sought to force the division of our fleet among our ports."[29] The insurmountable problem for the Spaniards was that, unlike the Americans, they had very little except public outcry to support them.

CHAPTER 13

Battleships

By the third week of April, the North Atlantic fleet at Key West had been awaiting the start of the war for more than a month. Newspapermen and correspondents gathered like seagulls on the verandah of a local hotel, waiting there with the officers.

"They had waited while the President's message had been postponed once," author and journalist Richard Harding Davis later wrote of the scene, "and three times while Representatives and Senators moved and amended and referred, while foreign powers had offered services more or less friendly, and while all the machinery of diplomacy had been put in motion to avert or to delay the inevitable end."[1]

The fleet now assembled at Key West comprised twenty-six vessels, ranging from monitors to cruisers, yachts to battleships. The flagship *New York* lay anchored with the other big ships off Sand Key light, eight miles from Key West. Correspondent W. A. M. Goode of the Associated Press considered the force "powerful, though mixed and slow."[2]

As events accelerated in Washington, Secretary Long on April 21 notified Captain Sampson that he now held the rank appropriate for the commander of the North Atlantic fleet. "Hoist the flag of a rear-admiral immediately," Long cabled.[3] Having shown him this carrot, Long that evening sent Sampson another dispatch: "Blockade coast of Cuba immediately from Cardenas to Bahia Honda. Blockade Cienfuegos, if it is considered advisable. Issue a proclamation of blockade covering blockaded ports. Permit neutrals now loading to come out. Do not bombard, according to terms of my letter of April 6."[4]

This short message, Goode wrote, "set the war machinery of the United States in action."[5]

(Bob Evans, on the *Iowa*, remembered the war's beginning differently and somewhat less accurately. His memoir says the captains were summoned that evening into a conference on board the flagship. Afterwards, Sampson asked them to linger. "Just before midnight," Evans recalled, "a naval cadet came to the cabin and reported a torpedo boat coming out at high speed, and in a few minutes a staff officer handed the admiral a telegram from President McKinley, which he immediately read to his assembled commanders. It said: 'War declared; proceed to blockade the coast of Cuba,' etc., etc.—Then, with serious, thoughtful faces, we said good-night to the admiral and each other, and returned to our ships.")[6]

The blockade areas included stretches of the long northwestern ("Cardenas to Bahia Honda") and south-central ("Cienfuegos") coasts of Cuba. The former was much closer to Key West and encompassed Havana, just a few hours steaming to the south-southwest.

Sampson didn't favor the blockade. He had unsuccessfully lobbied Long with a plan for steaming directly to Havana and bombarding its fortifications. Evans and other captains agreed. "I have always thought that we could have captured or destroyed Havana in two days after the declaration of war," Evans later wrote, "and it is my belief that this of itself would have ended the struggle in a very short time, and that Cervera's fleet would not have crossed the Atlantic."[7]

But the Navy was sticking to the strategy outlined in Long's April 6 letter, in which the secretary had detailed the fleet's orders in the event of war. It had effectively (if not expressly) prohibited Sampson from exposing his vessels to fire from the batteries at Havana, Santiago de Cuba, or other fortified positions, "unless the more formidable Spanish vessels should take refuge within those harbors." (The crucial sentence began, "The Department does not wish . . ." rather than "You will not. . . .")[8]

Long gave two reasons for this decision. First, no troops were available to occupy captured strongholds (which was also Dewey's problem at Manila). Second, lack of Navy docking facilities "makes it particularly desirable that our vessels should not be crippled before the capture or destruction of Spain's most formidable vessels."[9]

Captain Mahan, the consummate naval strategist, agreed with Long's thinking and had no doubt influenced it. "[T]he country could not at that time, under the political conditions which then obtained, afford to risk the loss or disablement of a single battleship . . . ," Mahan later explained. "If we lost ten thousand men, the country could replace them; if we lost a battleship, it could not be replaced."[10]

. . .

After the loss of the *Maine*, the Navy possessed just five battleships, but these few already formed the backbone of the fleet. The first hours of the war marked their ascendancy in the U.S. Navy—ironically, through the decision not to endanger them until absolutely necessary. The battlewagons would maintain their primacy for more than four decades, until supplanted by naval aviation during World War II.

Every American battleship in 1898 was new. The first two, the *Texas* and the *Maine*, had been commissioned just three years earlier. The Navy considered them the first armored warships since the Civil War that were the equals of their European counterparts.[11] This was hardly surprising, since the *Texas*, the first under construction, was built to plans purchased from an English company. The *Texas* and *Maine* were alike in having the forward turret mounted to starboard of the centerline, the after turret to port.

Until the *Maine* exploded in Havana harbor, the *Texas* was considered the luckless one. Early accidents and mishaps—"some the result of faults in the original design," according to a navy historian[12]—had reflected badly on both the *Texas* and the Navy Department. She had a reputation as a "hoodoo" or unlucky ship. Her watertight integrity was so poor that she had once sunk at dry dock. Her captain had recently signaled that a grounding on uncharted coral in the Dry Tortugas was the "luck of H," her call letter.[13] Whether he had meant hell, *Texas*, or hoodoo, no one was quite sure.

The "coast-line battleships" *Indiana*, *Massachusetts*, and *Oregon* soon followed the *Texas* and *Maine*. All three were laid down in 1891 and commissioned in the middle of the decade. All had 13-inch gun turrets, plus secondary batteries. They were well-armored and fast for their type; the *Massachusetts* topped 16 knots in speed trials, and the *Oregon* hit nearly 17 knots.[14]

When the *Iowa* was commissioned in 1897, the American battleship took another step forward. Her sisters had the squat, low profile of their ancestor, the Civil War monitor. The *Iowa* had an additional deck forward, which increased her seaworthiness and gave her a more modern appearance. Her armament was slightly less formidable, 12-inch rather than 13-inch turrets, and 4-inch, quick-firing secondary guns instead of 6-inchers. But her armor protection was somewhat improved and she was fast, capable of making better than seventeen knots.[15]

Sampson's flagship could almost have been counted as the sixth American battleship. The *New York* was a popular, well-known vessel, and although an armored cruiser, carried the state name of the bigger ships.[16] With her 8-inch gun turrets and armor protection, naval historian Wilson noted, she "verges on the battleship."[17] Lieutenant Winston Churchill, who visited the big cruiser in

1895, came away impressed by her crew, praising "their intelligence, their good looks and civility, and their general businesslike appearance."[18]

Commodore Schley's flagship in the Flying Squadron was in many ways comparable to the cruiser. The *Brooklyn* was slightly younger and larger than the *New York*, and notable for the extreme tumble home (upward curve) of her hull amidships, which gave her side turrets clearance to fire both fore and aft.

When the war began, Sampson had the *Indiana*, *Iowa*, and *New York* in the North Atlantic fleet. The *Massachusetts*, *Texas*, and *Brooklyn* were with Schley, awaiting orders at Hampton Roads to descend on phantom Spanish raiders. The Navy's fifth battleship was meanwhile making an historic voyage to join them all in the Atlantic.

The *Oregon* was the only member of her class built on the West Coast, in San Francisco. Her new skipper, Captain Charles E. Clark, assumed command just two days before the battleship steamed out through the Golden Gate on March 19, bound for the opposite coast. With the Panama Canal still only a failed French ditch, Clark and his crew faced sailing around the entire length of South America—although some of his men wagered that the *Oregon* would return to San Francisco after reaching Callao, Peru.[19]

Shifting the *Oregon* to the East Coast was "so essential," Clark wrote, "that the government felt the risks of the long voyage, till then untested by a vessel of her class, must be undertaken, even though they included a possibility of meeting with the enemy's fleet."[20] Clark pushed his men and machinery to their limits to reach Sampson quickly. The *Oregon* had rounded the tip of South America and was approaching Rio de Janeiro when the war began, her progress of great interest to the nation's newspapers and the world's navies.

.   .   .

The fleets were now stirring. Admiral Cervera was at St. Vincent, still under orders to lead his cruisers and destroyers into the West Indies. But Admiral Sampson and the North Atlantic fleet beat him to sea, standing out from Key West with eleven ships and four torpedo boats early on the morning of April 22.

"There was no pageantry nor pomp, no fluttering of pennons nor playing of bands, no cheering, no bystanders," wrote Lieutenant A. S. Staunton, Sampson's assistant chief of staff. "The sun rose upon fifteen gray masses, large and small, steadily moving south, the smoke pouring in black clouds from their funnels."[21]

Evans of the *Iowa* later commented, "Fortunately for the country, we were in much better shape than people thought we were."[22] Unfortunately for Cervera, the Spaniards were in much worse.

The decision to send Cervera with four cruisers and three destroyers against the American forces marshaling in the West Indies can hardly be defended, but proud Spain had left herself few options. Captain Concas of the *María Teresa* noted bitterly that "while it was recognized at Madrid that we should have to lose the island of Cuba, it was said that this could not take place without *a second Trafalgar* to justify so painful a loss."[23] (The damning italics are Concas'.)

An intelligence report from Madrid on April 16 only slightly contradicted this theory. Routed on to Washington, it also provided further insight into Spanish motivations. The government and intelligentsia there dreaded the prospect of war, the report stated, and were willing "to do anything they can to avoid it without revolution." But both groups in Spain would accept war if they felt that it was forced upon them, "and the lower classes ardently desire it."

Newspaper reports on the superiority of the Spanish navy, the agent added, accounted in large measure "for the determination to fight us. This opinion is shared also by many intelligent persons, in fact, I believe, by all Spaniards."[24] (Lieutenant Sims, among others, was running a network of agents from his post in Paris. The identity of this particular agent, whose report was forwarded to Sampson on April 30, was withheld in official publications.)

Having chosen to fight a hopeless battle on the American side of the Atlantic, the Spanish government should have deployed a reasonably large and effective naval force. That it wasn't able to do so stemmed from Madrid's multiple failures of materials, imagination, and planning, all of which were eerily reminiscent of American failings during the Doldrums. The *Yanquis* had learned and grown during the preceding quarter-century. The Spaniards had not.

Secretary Long thought that sending the cruisers and destroyers to the Cape Verdes was a "sagacious" first move by Spain.[25] But he had also expected that she would send her only battleship, the *Pelayo*, and an armored cruiser, the *Emperador Carlos V*, to follow them. This would have made some tactical sense.

The French-built *Pelayo*, according to Wilson, was "decidedly superior to the *Texas*, and just as decidedly inferior to the *Indiana* class." The *Carlos V* he dismissed as "large but feebly armed and ill-protected."[26] Whatever their relative assets or limitations, these ships would certainly have strengthened Cervera's force. Unfortunately for Spain, neither vessel was remotely ready for sea at the start of the war.

The immobile pair had numerous compatriots at Cádiz and other ports. These included the cruisers *Alphonso XIII*, *Lepanto*, and *Cataluña*—all unfinished after several years under construction (the *Cataluña* without even her hull completed)²⁷—and various lesser vessels. Like Spain's lone battleship, whose mordant nickname was *El Solitario*, none was in any condition to join the fleet when its presence might have counted.

This poverty left the Italian-built armored cruiser *Cristóbal Colón* as Spain's most fearsome warship. Wilson considered her superior to any American cruiser, including the *New York* and *Brooklyn*. Her 10-inch guns, however, had never been mounted and she had sailed from Cádiz without them. "Virtually she was a small battleship of exceptionally powerful type," Wilson wrote, "and though wanting her heaviest guns, her splendid battery of [6-inch] quick-firers was quite capable of making her an awkward antagonist for the *Indiana* and her sisters."²⁸

The cruisers *Infanta María Teresa*, *Almirante Oquendo*, and *Vizcaya* were sister ships, built in Bilbao by the British and launched at the start of the decade. But these, too, were all less than they appeared to be. Despite her fine paintwork and gleaming brass topside, for example, the *Vizcaya* hadn't had her hull scraped in nearly a year. The bottom of Captain Eulate's beautiful cruiser was so foul that she could "no longer steam, and . . . is only a boil on the body of the fleet," Cervera wrote from St. Vincent. Days later, he dismissed her again as "nothing but a buoy," but added, "I can not abandon her."²⁹

Before the war, indeed before he had even assumed command of the fleet, Cervera had observed that the only way to avoid another Trafalgar was by "allowing me to expend beforehand fifty thousand tons of coal in evolutions and ten thousand projectiles in target practice."³⁰ This foresight was entirely ignored. The support he did receive was pitiful. "The Spanish navy," declares a modern expert on naval logistics, "was desperately short on everything needed to wage war at sea—supplies, ammunition, coal and provisions."³¹

Cervera's ships also lacked trained mechanics and gunners. The minuscule supply of ammunition, the quality of which was suspect, would have appalled even Dewey, who had dared steam to Manila with magazines nearly half empty. If mounted at all, some Spanish guns were in such poor condition that Cervera rightly feared they might be more harmful to his gunners than Sampson's. "The list of ordnance faults of the ships sounds like a nightmare," an American naval historian noted later.³²

The list of woes was almost unending. The fleet had no opportunity to maneuver together before leaving the Cape Verdes. The cruisers were rich only in decorative woodwork, which although dangerous in combat was never removed. The modern torpedo-boat destroyers might have offered Cervera some hope—the U.S. had none of this type vessel, which, "its possibilities unknown, was greatly feared by experts and laymen," according to Long[33]—but these, too, worried the admiral.

"As for the *Furor* and *Terror*," Cervera wrote at St. Vincent, "their bow plates give as soon as they are in a sea way, and some of their frames have been broken. The *Plutón* had an accident of this kind when coming from England, and had her bows strengthened at Ferrol."[34]

Despite everything, including skepticism in various quarters on the continent, the terrible poverty of Admiral Cervera's fleet remained largely invisible outside the Spanish navy.

"European opinion, and largely, American, gave the Spanish the superior force," Captain Chadwick of the *New York* noted in his two-volume history of the war.[35] Long likewise recalled, "To the department and to the world, Spain possessed a fleet composed of vessels of tactical and strategic value, and properly handled it would have a chance of obtaining control of the sea. We know now how misleading was our information."[36]

. . .

On April 25, McKinley formally declared that a state of war had existed between the United States and Spain since the twenty-first. When Portugal's king declared his country's neutrality three days later, Cervera ran out of options and time. Neither the admiral nor his captains were willing to disobey their terrible orders to sail. Cervera had voiced his objections from first to last, on every level, but the Spanish public wouldn't learn of his warnings until after the war had ended.

"I insist no more," he had written from St. Vincent. "The act has been done, and I will try to find the best way out of this direful enterprise."[37] The four armored cruisers and the torpedo-boat destroyers *Plutón*, *Furor*, and *Terror* got up steam on April 29. At ten o'clock that morning, Concas recalled, "we lost the Portuguese islands from view to the eastward."[38]

Emotion was now steering strategy in both countries. Fear of bombardment kept the American squadrons near their home ports. Ancient national pride propelled the Spanish fleet into the Atlantic. Winston Churchill, then a young newspaper correspondent, rumbled that "Cervera was turned loose by his government quite as pitilessly as his fellow countrymen are in the habit of pushing a bull into the ring."[39]

Although soon aware of his departure, the Americans had no precise information on Cervera's route, timetable, or destination. His command became a "fleet in being"—an inferior force whose great, dangerous asset was its momentary cloak of invisibility. Although more than two hundred years old, the concept was as valid under steam as in the days of sail.

Mahan called a fleet-in-being "a perpetual menace to the various more or less exposed interests of the enemy, who cannot tell when a blow may fall, and who is therefore compelled to restrict his operations, otherwise possible, until that fleet can be destroyed or neutralized." Mahan also observed that it was "difficult to estimate too highly the possibilities open to such a body of ships."[40]

Admiral Cervera was now moving, likely in the very direction American planners had hoped. But the Navy still had to locate him and bring his fleet to action. "For almost two weeks," Secretary Long recalled, "the Navy Department floundered in a sea of ignorance as to his whereabouts."[41]

CHAPTER 14

The Crossing

ADMIRAL SAMPSON got word of the Spanish fleet's departure from St. Vincent the following day, April 30, on the blockade line off Havana. He rightly surmised that Cervera was bound for Puerto Rico. "There he would be at home; only there could he hope to make repairs; and there he could be sure of more coal, so necessary to enable him to reach a port in Cuba."[1]

Sampson steamed eastward to intercept on May 4. His force comprised the *New York, Iowa,* and *Indiana,* two cruisers, two monitors, a torpedo boat, and a tug. He hoped to see San Juan in four days, but received a mistaken report putting Cervera off Martinique on May 7. Sampson tried to confirm this at Haiti, delaying arrival at San Juan until May 12. This was four days past the earliest date the Navy calculated Cervera might arrive. "A glance," Sampson recalled, "was sufficient to show that Cervera's ships were not in port."[2]

The Americans had no way of determining if they had missed Cervera, or indeed whether he had been in the port at all. He seemed maddeningly elusive. Before steaming off, Sampson shelled the Spanish batteries near the Morro. The return fire seemed to Evans "the best shooting I saw the Spanish artillery do during the war."[3] The squadron's casualties were one sailor dead and seven wounded; most of them had come topside against orders to watch the action.

San Juan might easily have fallen right then. But as at Manila and Havana, no troops were available to take possession; also, the big ships weren't to be endangered until Cervera was located. The value of the exchange, Sampson wrote, "lay not a little in the practice it gave the men under fire, and which, no doubt, had its effect in the battle of Santiago."[4]

Sampson concluded that the Spanish fleet had reached some other anchorage in the West Indies. He lingered offshore until nightfall, then turned westward. He wanted to position his squadron to intercept if Cervera steamed toward Havana, which seemed a probable destination if the Spaniards had found coal elsewhere.

The American public, however, was perplexed by the whole affair. "With Dewey's achievement fresh in its memory, it looked for fresh victories in the Atlantic," Lieutenant Staunton recalled, "and was disappointed at what seemed to be a successful defence against its best fleet, especially as this fleet withdrew uninjured."[5] The public wasn't alone in its doubts. Mahan considered the expedition "an eccentric movement," while Secretary Long regarded it as "rather a failure."[6]

.   .   .

Had even a single circumstance favored him, Cervera might have reached Puerto Rico in a week. The trial speed of his cruisers was twenty-one knots, extremely fast for the era. The Navy Department had assumed that the top speed he could maintain on a transatlantic voyage was 16 knots, the average perhaps 12 knots.[7] But a fleet was only as fast as its slowest vessel and the foul-bottomed *Vizcaya* was slow indeed. Cervera made fewer than 200 nautical miles most days of the crossing, averaging just 6.5 knots.[8] He averaged 12 knots only once, and that barely.

The lack of colliers or auxiliary vessels compounded his problems. Once the fleet left St. Vincent, Cervera could refuel his destroyers only by transferring coal from the cruisers. This was no small or easy feat, especially on open seas in any sort of breeze. So he towed the destroyers instead, saving coal and sparing the engines.

As with so much else, however, no one had foreseen this possibility in Madrid. The fleet had none of the custom bridles that would have allowed efficient towing on the long voyage. Consequently, Concas wrote, "it became extremely difficult to tow the destroyers, especially as their small size and their large screws caused them to yaw considerably, so that the towlines parted frequently and much valuable time was lost." Still, he added, "this was better than coaling them at sea."[9]

Mahan later wrote that Cervera's fleet took so long in reaching the West Indies that within the Navy Department "ready credence was given to an apparently authentic report that it had returned to Spain." It seemed possible that Madrid might belatedly have recognized what was always blazingly apparent to Mahan, Cervera, and others—that it was "incorrect to adventure an important detachment so far from home, without the reinforcement it might have received in Cádiz."[10]

But if Cervera *was* still steaming westward, it seemed likely that he would touch first at Martinique in the Windward Islands, on the eastern arc of the island groups enclosing the Caribbean Sea. As Sampson recalled, "the general impression among Americans was that France was decidedly favorable to the cause of Spain, and might permit the fleet to receive coal at that island."[11]

On April 29, the day Cervera left St. Vincent, Long had sent the *Harvard* and *St. Louis* to sea with sealed orders to scout for the fleet on the eastern approaches to Martinique. Both were passenger steamers that had undergone quick wartime conversion into auxiliary cruisers. (Many such vessels were rechristened for U.S. cities or Ivy League colleges. Dewey mischievously suggested renaming a captured gunboat the USS *Massachusetts Institute of Technology*. Long kept the name *Callao*, but seamen called her the *Calamity Jane*.)[12]

"It is very important that you should, if possible, make 336 miles per day on the passage from New York to your cruising ground," Long told the *Harvard* and *St. Louis* captains.[13] Such haste ensured that these scouts reached the West Indies long before Cervera.

. . .

The battleship *Oregon* had meanwhile reached Rio de Janeiro on April 30. There Captain Clark learned that the war had begun.

"Four Spanish cruisers heavy and fast, three torpedo-boats [destroyers], deep-sea class, sailed April 29th from Cape Verde Islands to the west," a cable from Washington warned him on May 1. "Destination unknown. Must be left to your discretion entirely to avoid this fleet and to reach the United States or the West Indies."[14]

The Spaniards actually had no intention of waylaying the battleship. Their intelligence reports were so deficient, in fact, that Cervera believed she was still in the Pacific. American concern over Cervera's whereabouts was nonetheless legitimate (and proof of the fleet-in-being concept, whether or not he had consciously employed it). Sampson wrote that if Cervera had "stopped the career of the *Oregon*, he would have been amply repaid for crossing the Atlantic."[15]

The May 1 cable authorized Clark to take his ship where he thought best; as a last resort, he could also seek Brazilian protection "under plea of repairs." The gunboat *Marietta* and auxiliary cruiser *Nictheroy*—later renamed *Buffalo*—were also subject to his orders. (The latter, newly purchased from Brazil although built in America, was "almost worthless," according to Clark. He soon left both vessels behind.) Other cables followed, issuing and countermanding orders. Washington couldn't seem to make up its mind what it wanted Clark to do or whether he should leave Rio. On May 3, he received another cable. "Inform Department of your plans. Spanish fleet in Philippines annihilated by our naval force on the Asiatic station."[16]

Although he appreciated that the department was leaving important decisions to him, the man on the scene, Clark later wrote that "one would have much preferred to be backed by positive orders."[17] He didn't think the Spaniards would steam all the way to Rio just to confront the *Oregon*, however. And if they did, Clark decided he would order full speed and try to engage the four cruisers singly.

On May 4, the battleship left Rio and returned to sea. Off the mouth of the Amazon, she encountered the tiny sloop *Spray*. Her captain, New England merchant skipper Joshua Slocum, was making a solo voyage around the world. The battleship hoisted a signal, "Are there enemy ships near?"[18] This was the yachtsman's first news of the war.

"My signal, 'Let us keep together for mutual protection,' Captain Clark did not seem to regard as necessary," Slocum puckishly recalled.[19] The *Oregon* didn't see his hoist, but dipped her colors and rushed on.

. . .

The commander of Cervera's three destroyers was Capitán de Navío Don Fernando Villaamil Fernandez-Cueto. An experienced and popular officer, Villaamil had helped to develop the torpedo-boat destroyer concept with a ship called the *Destructor*.[20] He might have returned to Spain once Cervera had assumed command at St. Vincent, but chose to remain with the fleet.

On May 10, the admiral ordered Villaamil to dash ahead to Martinique with the *Furor* and *Terror*. Cervera wanted both coal and news. The destroyers started out at 20 knots, but the *Terror* soon broke down. Villaamil left her behind, knowing the fleet would soon catch up. He continued on to Fort-de-France with the *Furor* and arrived the next afternoon.

Spain's consular officer in Martinique, a French national, was off in the country when Villaamil arrived. Had the man received "the least intimation" that the fleet was nearby, Concas later wrote, "he would unquestionably have been in the city to lend his cooperation in favor of Spain."[21] As it was, the island's governor received Villaamil coolly, maintained French neutrality, and provided no coal. Just as bad for Cervera, a promised collier was not in the harbor.

Villaamil did receive some useful information from the captain of the Spanish hospital steamer *Alicante*. Mostly gleaned from press reports, it included news of Montojo's defeat at Manila Bay, the blockade of Cuba, the *Harvard* and

St. Louis, and the presence of Sampson's fleet off Puerto Rico. The *Furor* slipped secretly out of Fort-de-France at midnight, then raced off at 20 knots to rendezvous with the fleet three hours later.

Cervera was in an unenviable position. "[W]e were right on the scene of war," Concas wrote, "and . . . the enemy had gained control of it, without any opposition whatever, having preceded us there by a number of days."[22] The Spaniards rightly believed that their presence off Martinique had already been reported. (At nearby St. Pierre, when the *Furor* touched at Fort-de-France, the *Harvard* had quickly cabled Washington.) The coal in their holds was still dwindling.

Cervera sent the *Terror* into Fort-de-France for repairs to her crippled boilers, perhaps suspecting that she would never return to him. (The *Terror* later reached San Juan, where on June 22 she engaged Captain Sigsbee's *Saint Paul*. Damaged in the fight, the destroyer was beached to avoid sinking.)

While his two remaining destroyers refueled at sea, Cervera held a conference with his captains off the west coast of Martinique. The result was a decision to steam southwest to Curaçao, off Venezuela in the Dutch Antilles. There Cervera hoped finally to locate his collier. In assuming this new course, however, the admiral unknowingly sealed his fate.

Madrid knew that the fleet had reached the Windwards, but was unaware that only the destroyers *Furor* and *Terror* had actually docked or that the *Furor* had already left. The absence of a consul likely abetted the confusion. The government tried to cable Cervera at Martinique.

"Situation changed since your departure. Your instructions amplified so that if you do not believe that your squadron can operate there successfully, may return to Peninsula, choosing route and destination, preferably Cádiz. Acknowledge receipt and indicate decision."[23]

Cervera never entered Fort-de-France to receive this reprieve. Additional instructions from Madrid also shifted the destination of his collier to Martinique from Curaçao, ensuring the coal would never reach him.[24] Concas later concluded that it was already too late to return to Spain without a collier;[25] in another week, a new minister of marine would revoke permission to do so. In a war "riddled with ironies," historian David Trask has observed, the missed opportunity was "perhaps the most striking."[26]

· · ·

The Spanish fleet found neither a collier nor a warm welcome at Curaçao. The Dutch governor maintained strict neutrality, permitting only two ships to enter the port and just for forty-eight hours. It was also a holiday, so the island could supply only a trifling 400 tons of coal and some provisions.

Cervera sent the *María Teresa* and *Vizcaya* into port. His other four ships remained at sea. That night, May 14, Concas recalled, "we interpreted every noise we heard as an attack on our comrades, and we could not even go to their assistance, for the harbor . . . is completely cut off from the outside at sunset."[27] The pair of cruisers steamed out before the next sunset, having little to show for their stay at Curaçao.

The fleet's destination was no longer Puerto Rico. Cervera's orders clearly gave him some leeway, and with the Americans blockading and waiting for him, both San Juan and Havana seemed too risky. Cienfuegos, near the center of Cuba's southern shore, was a possibility. But that port was "a veritable rat trap," in Concas' view, "very easy to blockade, and from which escape is more difficult than from any other harbor of the island."[28]

The best alternative was therefore Santiago de Cuba, at the base of the island's broad southeastern foot. Concas supposed it was "well supplied with provisions and artillery." Moreover, it offered "chances of sortie on stormy days and an open sea for operations, after we had refitted and made repairs."[29] This almost desperate optimism was out of character for the flag captain. But by now, Cervera and his officers had little else in which to believe.

The fleet headed northwest across the Caribbean. The pace remained slow, due in part to nearly empty bunkers on the *Colón* and *Oquendo*; each would have less than 100 tons of coal remaining at the end of the voyage. The fleet slipped through the Jamaica Channel on the night of May 18–19 and arrived off Santiago at daybreak. There wasn't an American ship in sight.

"The destroyers therefore made a reconnaissance of the coast," Concas wrote, "while the large ships entered the harbor, where they cast anchor in complete security at 8 o'clock AM of that day." He considered the fleet's safe arrival a miracle, but also knew that nothing lay ahead now "but to suffer the consequences of its departure from Cape Verde."[30]

CHAPTER 15

Cienfuegos

THE *New York* WAS WAITING for dispatches off Haiti early on May 15 when the torpedo boat *Porter* brought out "a great budget of news."[1] ("We had no despatch boats, properly speaking, and these delicate torpedo boats had to be used for that purpose," Evans wrote of the days before wireless radio. "It was like ploughing a stumpy field with a carefully groomed and trained thoroughbred horse.")[2] Cervera's fleet had been sighted at Curaçao; the destroyer *Terror* was at Martinique; Commodore Schley had finally been released from Hampton Roads and was steaming south with the Flying Squadron; and Sampson was ordered to Key West. Later dispatches provided the names of all six Spanish warships at Curaçao.

The flagship hurried for Key West alone, the other ships following as quickly as they were able. Sampson now believed that Cervera's destination was either San Juan or Santiago. The admiral also thought that if he was wrong, he still had time to refuel and return before Cervera could round Cuba via the Windward Passage and reach Havana.

The hunt was far from clear-cut, however. On May 17, while the *New York* was in the Bahama Channel off northern Cuba, Sampson received another report. This one stated, incorrectly, that Cervera was carrying munitions that were badly needed in Havana, and that he had orders to reach either that city or a port connected to it by railway. This seemed to narrow the destination to Matanzas on the northern coast or Cienfuegos on the southern.

The *New York* reached Key West on May 18, the same day as the Flying Squadron. They were followed in that night by the *Iowa*, which had orders to join Schley. The battleship immediately began coaling. Evans was fortunate she didn't also need a new skipper; he had been struck and injured hours earlier by a falling battle hatch. Though it had very nearly killed him, the freak mishap didn't remove Old Gimpy from command.

The Flying Squadron, comprising the flagship *Brooklyn*, battleships *Texas* and *Massachusetts*, and converted yacht *Scorpion*, left early the next morning for Cienfuegos. The route was around the western tip of Cuba via the Yucatan Channel. Bandaged and bound, Evans left with the *Iowa* at midday to catch up. Various scouts, auxiliaries, and the collier *Merrimac* followed later.

. . .

Sampson was the antithesis of a Dewey-type commander. He was quiet and reserved, rarely given to temper, and bore a workload that might have crushed a man twenty years his junior. Now with the blockade and the quest to intercept Cervera affecting his already precarious health, the admiral increasingly looked drawn and tired.

During their conference together on board the *New York*, Schley recalled, Sampson seemed "much worn and apparently anxious; in fact, his appearance was that of a sick man."[3] The commodore wasn't an impartial observer when it came to the admiral, but the description matches those offered by others.

Ship's Writer Fred Buenzle wrote that in the days following San Juan, Sampson and Captain Chadwick routinely worked past midnight. Every morning, Buenzle found a stack of memoranda in Sampson's hand ready to be turned into letters. "It was a wonder to me how the old man's enfeebled physique could stand such a strain."[4]

During the coming months, Sampson would sometimes become confused or forgetful; once he repeatedly gave the name of the wrong ship while issuing orders.[5] His symptoms multiplied as he entered a long, progressive decline; by autumn he would often take to his cabin unable to work, his subordinates taking up the slack. Calling on an intervening century of medical insight and on his own family history—his retired father had similarly faded mentally before his death in 1943—historian Captain Ned Beach later wrote: "Today it would be guessed he was suffering from Alzheimer's disease, or something very like it in its effects on memory and general mental condition."[6]

For the most part, the dreadful days were still ahead. Through the campaign's next six critical weeks, at least, Sampson remained reasonably alert and competent. He was able to rely, as Dewey had done, on talented, experienced officers. Evans, Clark, Chadwick, and other captains would all serve Sampson well in tracking and confronting the Spanish fleet.

In Commodore Schley, however, the admiral encountered difficulties he neither needed nor deserved. Schley was among the senior officers he had leapfrogged when selected to command the fleet. Schley seemed to resent the appointment, and to hold a grudge not against the Navy or the secretary, but against Sampson himself.

The fleet chain of command should have been clear. Long had told Schley at the outset that although the Flying Squadron might for a time operate independently, it was nonetheless part of Sampson's fleet. Long had added that if their forces merged, Schley would be subordinate. (Long later clarified the situation in a one-line cable: "Till further orders the flying squadron is under the orders of Sampson, commander in chief North Atlantic Station." Sent May 24, the message was probably delivered two or three days later off southern Cuba.)[7]

"To this condition he cheerfully agreed," the secretary recalled, "and expressed his cordial readiness for cooperation and service."[8] But once in command of the Flying Squadron, Schley's acceptance of the arrangement proved questionable.

. . .

Cervera reached Santiago on May 19, a beautiful tropical morning. A Spanish lieutenant later remembered that "not the slightest breeze rippled the surface of the water; not the least cloud was to be seen in the deep blue sky, and still, . . . very few were the people who came down to witness the arrival of the ships."[9]

The Spaniards were lucky no Americans witnessed the arrival. The *St. Louis* and tug *Wampatuck* had been off the harbor entrance the day before, cutting the submerged telegraphic cable between Santiago and Jamaica. They had then steamed together for Guantanamo Bay to attempt cutting another cable there. On the clear, beautiful morning, the Americans missed sighting the Spanish fleet by one hour.[10]

About the time Cervera dropped anchor in Santiago, Schley steamed from Key West. The Flying Squadron neared Cienfuegos two days later on the afternoon of May 21. From the bridge of the *Brooklyn*, while still some forty miles away,[11] Schley heard "a number of guns . . . apparently with the cadence of a salute."[12] He supposed they signaled Cienfuegos' welcome for Cervera.

The topography of the harbor entrance prevented the Flying Squadron peering inside. Schley lingered nearby that night, then stood in to blockade the following morning. The *Iowa* arrived on May 22. The following night, May 23, lookouts reported three white lights on the shore. Bob Evans knew this was a signal that Cuban insurgents wanted to communicate. Evans took it for granted that the commodore "understood this signal as well as I did, otherwise I should have informed him of its significance."[13]

Schley later declared, however, that despite a discussion with Sampson at Key West about signals, he hadn't known about this one. He also later criticized Evans (without naming him) for not speaking up. "It was fortunate for this officer," the commodore wrote, "that the commander of the Flying Squadron did not know at that time, 1898, that this officer knew and withheld information. . . ."[14]

The cruiser *Marblehead* had helped cut the Cienfuegos telegraphic cable in a celebrated action on May 11. She now arrived off the harbor again on the morning of May 24. The *Marblehead*'s skipper, Commander Bowman McCalla, also knew what the signal meant. He ran in to communicate with the insurgents and learned from them that Cervera wasn't in the harbor. Schley consequently started the squadron that night for Santiago.

The Flying Squadron steamed slowly eastward along the underbelly of Cuba for the next two days, the pace allowing the converted yacht *Eagle* to keep up with the bigger ships in rough seas (although Evans thought he could have towed her faster).[15] Late on the afternoon of May 26, the squadron met the *Saint Paul, Yale,* and *Minneapolis* some thirty miles south of Santiago. The mountains behind the port were visible from the rendezvous. "No attempt was made, so far as I know, to determine whether the Spanish fleet was in the harbour or not," Evans wrote.[16]

Schley's officers expected to investigate the harbor that night or the next morning, but the commodore had other plans. The *Brooklyn* signaled by red-and-white Ardois lights that the squadron would retire to Key West at 9 knots via the Yucatan Channel.

The quickest route to the Keys was via the Windward Passage; using the Yucatan Channel, at the western tip of Cuba, added 300 miles to the trip and would take the squadron back past Cienfuegos. To a *New York Evening Sun* correspondent on board the *Texas*, Schley's signal was "the most remarkable thing of the naval campaign."[17]

Evans hailed Captain John Philip of the *Texas*, who had served longer under Schley.

"Say, Jack," he called, "what the devil does it mean?"

"Beats me," Philip replied. "What do you think?"

"Damned if I know," Fighting Bob bellowed back. "But I know one thing—I'm the most disgusted man afloat."[18]

Despite feeling reasonably sure that Cervera was in Santiago, Evans concluded that Schley possessed better information than he did. Maybe the Spaniards had left the harbor to steam westward. "This inference was completely wrong," he wrote, "for after two hours we stopped again and drifted about until noon the following day, while some of the vessels took coal from the collier."[19]

Both Sampson and Long had been sending Schley anxious messages about reports that Cervera was indeed at Santiago. These messages went via cable and in written dispatches relayed by torpedo boats or converted yachts. Schley regarded the reports as inconclusive—which, taken individually, they were. ("At first, they were looked upon with suspicion," Lieutenant Staunton recalled, "but they were repeatedly confirmed, and were finally believed.")[20]

The commodore also received a report from Captain Sigsbee that the *Saint Paul* had seen nothing of Cervera's fleet, although she had captured a Spanish collier. "It is surprising," notes a modern historian, "that none of the American cruisers ordered stationed off Santiago de Cuba established Cervera's presence there."[21]

On the morning of May 27, Schley received another dispatch from Long via the *Harvard*. The secretary repeated that the department's information strongly indicated Cervera's presence at Santiago. He ordered Schley to report the situation there "without delay."[22] The commodore, however, sidestepped these orders.

"Much to be regretted, can not obey orders of Department," Schley replied. "Have striven earnestly; forced to proceed for coal to Key West, by way of the Yucatan passage. Can not ascertain anything respecting enemy positive."[23]

The commodore later provided a complicated defense of his actions, citing several factors. The dispatches he received about Cervera's location were all characterized by uncertainty. The collier *Merrimac* was experiencing problems with her engines. The weather had worsened as the squadron arrived off Santiago. All of his ships were low on coal, there was no convenient harbor in which to refuel (nearby Guantanamo Bay wasn't seized by Marines until mid-June), and to attempt it at sea was to invite disaster.

Schley's response to Long's cable reached Washington the next day. Mahan, a former seagoing officer, later observed that while there was no "known reason to censure the decision of the officer on the spot, . . . he was mistaken, and each succeeding hour made the mistake more palpable and more serious to those in Washington."[24] Long took an even harsher view, characterizing May 28 as "the darkest day of the war."[25]

The secretary shot back the sort of message that usually ends a naval officer's career. Sent via three different cable stations to assure arrival, it read in its entirety, "It is your duty to ascertain if the Spanish fleet is in Santiago and report. Would be discreditable to the navy if that fact were not ascertained immediately. All military and naval movements depend upon that point."[26]

Schley apparently was already reconsidering his tactics, if perhaps not his motives. The *Merrimac* engines were repaired, the bad weather abated, and those ships most in need coaled at sea. After first starting west again, the squadron stopped and finally turned east toward Santiago. It arrived there on the evening of May 28.

Evans and the other captains were "completely bewildered as to what this particular manoeuvring might mean."[27] Some thought uncomfortably of Admiral Byng, a Royal Navy officer court-martialed and shot in 1756 for retiring before a superior French fleet.[28] The Spaniards were equally perplexed, Captain Concas later writing that "the manoeuvres of the hostile squadron up to the 29th were incomprehensible to us."[29]

Long later conceded that his department might fairly be criticized for not immediately relieving the commodore and ordering an inquiry.[30] But to Schley, the whole affair was a "tempest in a teapot."[31]

. . .

At first light on May 29, ten days after Cervera's arrival, the Flying Squadron at last stood in to investigate the harbor of Santiago de Cuba. Evans stood on the *Iowa*'s bridge, straining to see up the narrow channel. His executive officer exclaimed, "Captain, there's the *Cristóbal Colón!*"[32]

The *Iowa* quickly flagged the discovery to the *Brooklyn*. The flagship replied, "I understand." When the *Iowa* reported another ship and a destroyer (Evans wrote "torpedo boat" in his memoirs, the term he and many other officers still used for destroyers), the reply was the same.[33] The position of the rest of the Spanish fleet was obscured by the land's contours—the channel turns ninety degrees and broadens into the harbor.

Evans called general quarters, but no action ensued. The squadron simply steamed back and forth off the entrance until Schley called a captains' conference on board the flagship. There, Evans recalled, the commodore "was at last satisfied that Cervera's fleet was in Santiago Harbour and not in Cienfuegos." The Flying Squadron continued steaming back and forth for the next two days, "while the *Colón*, with fires hauled and awnings spread, lay in plain sight, quietly watching us."[34]

On May 31, Schley ordered a firing run at 10 knots by the *Iowa, Massachusetts*, and cruiser *New Orleans*. Although, like Sampson, he was under orders not to expose his ships unnecessarily to shore batteries, Schley in this instance was trying to engage Cervera's best cruiser. The announced range for what the commodore called the "reconnaissance"[35] was 7,000 yards, an estimate Schley later conceded was inexact.

"The harbour entrance was so narrow and our speed so great we could only fire a few shots before the Spanish ship was shut out by the land," Evans wrote.[36] The *Iowa* kept elevating her 12-inch guns until she was firing at 11,000 yards, with the rounds still falling short.

Although lacking her 10-inch guns, the *Colón* returned fire. The Spanish shore batteries fired, too. In an action lasting more than an hour, neither side hit anything. (The captain of the *Colón* later told Evans that shrapnel from the *Iowa*'s last shell pierced his cabin.)[37] Admiral Cervera then withdrew his big cruiser into the shelter of the harbor.[38]

During the previous days, Sampson had hurried east along Cuba's northern coast and down through the Windward Passage, believing that Schley in his quest for coal had left Santiago uncovered. The admiral arrived off the harbor on June 1 with the *New York* and the *Oregon*, which had joined him after completing her nearly 15,000-mile voyage from San Francisco in sixty-eight days. (The battleship had reached Jupiter Inlet, Florida, late on May 24, having swung up and around the island chains from South America and touched briefly at Barbados. Long had then ordered Captain Clark on to Key West, adding, "The Department congratulates you on your safe arrival, which has been reported to the President.")[39]

Although he had exhibited toward Schley "a spirit of forbearance so generous as to be called gentle,"[40] according to correspondent Goode, Sampson was unhappy with what he found off Santiago. Schley's ships were bunched ten miles offshore, rather than in any sort of formation.[41] The blockade, the admiral wrote, "can hardly be described as a close one, of the sort desired and expected by both the Navy Department and myself."[42]

Sampson immediately directed the *New York* in near the entrance, and signaled the others, "Come closer." The commodore's days of independent command were over. From that hour onward, Evans remembered with evident satisfaction, "the blockade of Santiago was so maintained that it was not possible for any vessel to escape."[43]

CHAPTER 16

The *Merrimac*

HAVING SAFELY REACHED CUBA, Admiral Cervera was little better off than he had been at the Cape Verdes, Martinique, or the Dutch Antilles.

Captain Concas later railed against the "disastrous conditions" he found at Santiago and the "stupendous ignorance" of the Spaniards there who seemed already to have accepted defeat. The regular Spanish troops in the region, Concas also discovered, were hungry, "completely exhausted by three years of warfare in that horrible climate," and had been unpaid for more than a year.[1]

Santiago could provide the fleet with only a paltry 2,400 tons of coal.[2] "Everything which was required for rapid coaling—lighters, tugs, and even baskets—was lacking," Concas later wrote, "and we had to use the sacks which we had brought to Cape Verde for use on the destroyers, but which were insufficient for the larger vessels."[3]

Santiago's only other naval asset was a ship that was sitting in the harbor when Cervera arrived. The *Reina Mercedes* never really counted as the fleet's seventh vessel, however. The unprotected cruiser was outdated and practically immobile, one of the station ships that the admiral had earlier discounted as having "no military value whatever."[4] She served now as a "stationary torpedoship," her guns removed and sent ashore to the army.[5]

As crews coaled their ships, bag by inadequate bag, Cervera seriously considered renewing his voyage. He was hampered, however, by his one great failing as a commander. Namely, he saw too clearly the awfulness of his situation. He knew he couldn't prevail in a fleet engagement with the Americans. In his despair, he was slow to react and hesitant to pursue desperate or daring tactics that might have led to something different. The courtly Spaniard lacked the soul of a high-stakes gambler.

"If early in the campaign he had attempted a bold policy," Sampson observed, "he might have accomplished something important, and might have prolonged the war; certainly the consequences would have been less disastrous to Spain."[6]

(Sixteen years later, during the opening months of World War I, German Admiral Maximilian Graf von Spee would demonstrate what Cervera might have achieved if he hadn't hesitated at Santiago. Spee vanished with his cruiser squadron from his base in colonial China. Reappearing across the Pacific weeks later, he sank two British cruisers off Chile and sent two others fleeing. A detached raider, Karl von Müller's light cruiser *Emden*, destroyed a Russian cruiser at Penang, paralyzed shipping in Australasia, and occupied Allied navies for months in the Pacific and Indian oceans.)

Cervera's options once at Santiago, however, were severely limited. With Schley off Cienfuegos and Sampson off Havana, Concas wrote, "there was no other course but to remain where we were or to go to San Juan." But once at Puerto Rico, the fleet could no more have remained safely in port than at Santiago. The sole object in going would only have been to "coal more rapidly and put to sea before the arrival of the enemy, in order to make an attempt to go to Habana or return to Europe."[7]

During those crucial, early days, before the Americans had determined his whereabouts, Cervera dithered. He made and abandoned various plans in consultation with his captains. Lieutenant-General Arsenio Linares y Pombo, the army commander in the region, reported on May 24 that Cervera had "decided to remain here until assured that he will not be pursued by the Americans when he endeavors to leave port."[8]

But Cervera was still considering a sortie two days later, according to Concas. He abandoned the idea when the same bad weather that had chased Schley away to coal the Flying Squadron also sent heavy swells into the harbor entrance. Cervera judged it too risky to venture out with the *Colón*, which had a deep draft. With only eight feet of water under her keel in the narrow channel, he feared, she might ground or be irreparably damaged.

Although he had supported a sortie, Concas thought Cervera was wise to "remain at Santiago in expectation of whatever opportunity fortune might offer us."[9] But fortune was a miser. Schley soon reappeared, followed by Sampson. Now the Spanish cruisers and destroyers were ships in a bottle. Having tightened his grip on the neck, Admiral Sampson next tried inserting a stopper.

· · ·

Sampson's fear was that Cervera might slip out of Santiago "under cover of a blustery night"[10] and escape, at least temporarily, by using what the department mistakenly believed was his superior speed. So Sampson had developed a plan to prevent this while hurrying around the eastern tip of Cuba.

The original scheme was for Schley to seal the harbor by scuttling two schooners loaded with ballast at the channel's narrowest point. If the tactic succeeded, Sampson wrote, "the idea was to leave one or two ships to prevent any attempt at removal, and employ the [flying] squadron for other service."[11] A cruiser captain then suggested scuttling the collier *Merrimac* instead of the schooners. The admiral endorsed the refinement and sent Schley instructions to sink her across the channel. The order went out, but the text mistakenly named the smaller *Sterling* instead of the *Merrimac*. (This was the instance when Sampson repeatedly confused the names.)

When he thought Schley had left Santiago uncovered—and mistakenly assumed he had started east (not west) to reach Key West—Sampson decided to implement the plan himself. He asked a young assistant naval constructor on the *New York* for opinions on how best to sink the collier. Richmond P. Hobson quickly concluded that simply opening the sea-valves would not swiftly sink her. He withdrew to ponder what Sampson conceded was a curious problem.

On May 30, as the *New York* steamed toward Santiago, the constructor "came into the cabin with his plan, quite perfected, involving the use of ten torpedoes," Sampson recalled. "To improvise so many torpedoes seemed to me to be a difficult task, but Mr. Hobson was confident of success. He had thought out every detail, even to the smallest point."[12]

Hobson's audacity clearly lifted the admiral's spirits. Once the flagship was off the harbor and the Spaniards were finally within sight, "there was a great change in the admiral," clerk Buenzle wrote. "The worries of the previous week seemed to drop from his shoulders. He entered into the *Merrimac* scheme with the enthusiasm of a boy, and perfected the plans and details which had been hurriedly outlined the day before."[13]

Sampson invested his faith in a formal, grave, and beautifully handsome young officer. Hobson was a brilliant and unbending ideologue, just twenty-seven, the sort most people can't abide until he suddenly achieves something quite spectacular. At Annapolis, from which he graduated at age eighteen, Hobson was once cast into "Coventry"—ostracized and enveloped in silence by classmates—for "meticulously reporting, as duty required, their misdemeanors."[14] (Hobson, in turn, refused to speak to *them* once they resumed speaking to him.) Becoming a constructor rather than a line officer only emphasized his stubborn independence. Hobson was teaching a postgraduate course in naval construction at the Academy when the war began.[15]

Sampson may have recognized something of his younger self in this difficult officer. He certainly respected Hobson, writing that "I was greatly impressed with the faith and the absolute fearlessness which Mr. Hobson displayed."[16] Since the constructor had devised the plan and knew it better than anyone else, the admiral granted his request to command the scuttling mission.

Sampson convinced the *Merrimac*'s skipper to step aside, reporting to Secretary Long that Commander J. M. Miller "relinquished his command with the very greatest reluctance."[17] Hobson, too, recognized Miller's disappointment, and wrote that the commander was "foremost in cordiality and expressions of kindness."[18] Schley later questioned replacing Miller, a "skillful, intelligent, and gallant" officer.[19] The commodore wasn't alone in considering Hobson a curious choice.

Hobson had finished preparing his torpedoes and fuses by the time the *New York* reached Santiago. Crewmen working aloft on the flagship could see the military tops of the *Vizcaya* and *Colón* in the harbor beyond the cliffs.[20] Hobson immediately began readying the *Merrimac* for destruction. His plan was to arrange all ten torpedoes down the port side, about 12 feet beneath the waterline, "abreast the bulkheads and the cargo hatches so as to give the maximum sinking effect to a breach opened up by each."[21]

The port side would be forward as the ship turned in the channel, increasing the inrush of water on that side. Exploding all the torpedoes on one side would also cause a list, which in turn would cause the water to rise inside more quickly.

The "torpedoes" were actually improvised mines assembled by the gunner's gang on the flagship. Each had a "simple eight-inch charge in its own can or tank, to be fired by its own electric primer."[22] After scrounging around the fleet for equipment, Hobson realized that he would have to use batteries to fire the torpedoes individually. He believed using ten torpedoes would compensate for "the innate weakness of the firing arrangements"[23] and the probability that Spanish shellfire would disable at least a few before the moment came to explode them.

Sampson asked for volunteers to man the collier on her one-way journey into the harbor. The fleet surprised him by submitting enough names "to man a hundred *Merrimacs*,"[24] but Hobson needed just seven. He ultimately selected three men each from the *Merrimac* and *New York*, and one from the *Iowa*. They would steer, operate the engines, and explode the torpedoes. Hobson was the only officer.

On board the *Iowa*, Evans surely remembered old Fort Fisher. As on the *Powhatan*, someone flipped a penny to choose among the ship's volunteers. Despite hard years and old scars, "Fighting Bob" could still admire the "poor fellow [who] went forward with the tears streaming out of his eyes because he had lost a chance to have his head shot off."[25] Perhaps, in addition to the naval brigade with its cutlasses and Colts, Evans also remembered Admiral Porter's powder-boat—another plan to end a campaign with a single, spectacular stroke.

Hobson hoped to be ready by midnight on June 1, but preparations were difficult and took longer than expected. It was nearly dawn on June 2 before the *Merrimac* steamed toward the narrow channel with ten torpedoes strapped to her side. At the last moment, Sampson thought better of letting the collier go in broad daylight. He reluctantly signaled her recall and denied Hobson's plea to continue.

After a day of additional preparations and rest for her exhausted crew, the *Merrimac* was ready again that evening. The admiral stood at the *New York*'s gangway, Hobson recalled, "the last to say good-bye, having again a simple word of kindness, a hand-pressure, a look that spoke more than a volume of words."[26]

The fleet went to nighttime stations as her volunteers readied the *Merrimac* for the second run at the Santiago channel. The redundancy that Hobson had built into his plan proved necessary—three of the torpedoes didn't respond to tests, leaving only seven. A nearly full moon rose in a cloudless sky. At 1:30 AM on June 3, Hobson again turned the collier toward the harbor and steamed in "slow speed ahead" from the southwest.[27]

. . .

The ship should have been plainly visible in the moonlight. At 2,000 yards, believing his movements must be obvious, Hobson ordered full speed ahead into the channel.[28] Nothing happened until the *Merrimac* was within 500 yards of the Morro Castle. Then, it wasn't the castle that opened fire, but a little picket boat lying unseen in its shadow.

"If we only had had a rapid-fire gun we could have disposed of the miserable object in ten seconds;" Hobson wrote, "yet there he lay unmolested, firing point-blank at our exposed rudder, so vital to complete success."[29]

The collier continued on as a battery opened up from the western shore. Opposite the Morro, Hobson stopped all engines and ordered the sea connections opened. Suddenly, either a Spanish shell or a combination of damages disabled the steering gear. Hobson dropped the bow anchor as planned, but against the speed of the ship and the surge of the tide he had little hope of controlling the *Merrimac*. The crew began detonating torpedoes. Number 1 went off "promptly and surely." Two others failed, their battery cells wrecked. Rapid-fire guns and machine-gun batteries raked the collier. Torpedo Number 5 went off "with a fine ring," but it was the last. All the other firing mechanisms were damaged.[30]

"With only two exploded torpedoes," Hobson wrote, "we should be some time sinking, and the stern-anchor would be of first importance." The stern anchor was released, also as planned, but the chain was either shot away or broken by the weight of the ship. The *Merrimac* continued down the channel, Hobson wishing in vain "for the warheads to put her down at once!"[31]

With the ship literally being shot to pieces, the constructor and his crew could only keep their heads down and scramble to survive. Moving on the tide, the shattered *Merrimac* was now opposite Estrella Point, just beyond the narrows where Hobson had hoped to sink her. With a roar and a shock, a Spanish mine exploded beneath her. "Lads, they are helping us!" Hobson shouted. Then realizing that the blast was too little, too late, he felt a wave of "indescribable disappointment" sweep over him.[32]

The *Merrimac* grounded briefly on the point under withering Spanish fire. The tide wrenched her off again, straightened her out, "and set us right down the channel toward the part where its width increases." There, the ship struck again, "lowered her head like a faithful animal" and quickly sank, sweeping the crew into the water.[33] Hobson had succeeded in partially obstructing the channel but hadn't blocked it.

Everyone on board was somehow still alive, with only minor wounds among them. Their lifeboat destroyed, the men clung to an overturned raft in the water. They clung, too, to the slim hope that a rescue boat might somehow reach them. Through the rest of the night, Spanish boats and troops along the shore failed to spot them. At daybreak, the crew heard a bugle call in one of the batteries.

"It was pitched out at a high key, and rose and lingered, long drawn out, gentle and tremulous"; Hobson remembered, "it seemed as though an angel might be playing while looking down in tender pity. Could this be a Spanish bugle?"[34]

A large covered launch then appeared from the harbor and steamed toward them. Riflemen on the forecastle aimed at the raft, but Hobson realized they weren't going to fire. He called out to ask if there was an officer in the boat. One appeared and motioned for the riflemen to lower their weapons.

"I struck out for the launch and climbed on board aft with the assistance of the officer, who, hours afterward, we learned was Admiral Cervera himself,"

Hobson wrote.[35] The constructor quietly surrendered, he and his men all becoming prisoners of war.

It briefly appeared on the blockade line that the mission was a success. At first light, according to Captain Clark, "the sunken *Merrimac*, with her smokestack, spars, and upper works showing, seemed to us to be lying directly in the channel."[36] The battleships moved closer to prevent any attempt to board or remove the hulk. When the steam launch appeared nearby, the *Iowa*'s executive officer asked if he should open fire.

Evans uncharacteristically decided to wait and watch the launch's movements. He later wrote thankfully that if the *Iowa* had fired, "two of the most picturesque figures in the Spanish war would have disappeared—Cervera and Hobson."[37]

.   .   .

Later that day, Cervera sent his chief of staff, Capitán de Navío Joaquín de Bustamante y Quevedo, out to the American fleet under a flag of truce. Bustamante carried a personal note to Sampson assuring him that the *Merrimac* crew was safe. Cervera "expressed his warm admiration for the bravery of the men," Sampson remembered, "and the tone of his note was more than polite."[38]

The *New York* signaled the news to the fleet. Ships erupted with such cheering, whistling, and tossing of white hats that to one bluejacket it seemed as if everyone had "suddenly gone daft."[39] Cervera's gesture deeply impressed Sampson's men, who would remember it later when fortunes were reversed.

CHAPTER 17

Blockade

MORE THAN A WEEK after his arrival, Sampson was still uncertain exactly which vessels were bottled in the harbor. The only one positively identified was the *Colón*, although men aloft had glimpsed the masts of at least one other. The hills surrounding Santiago blocked closer observation. As in many wars since, the admiral needed boots on the ground to confirm his sketchy intelligence reports.

The converted yacht *Suwanee* joined the fleet that first week to land arms and supplies for local insurgents west of Santiago. On June 10, Sampson ordered her captain to contact the Cubans and determine which of Cervera's ships were in the harbor. The *Suwanee* skipper decided to dispatch one of his own officers, Lieutenant Victor Blue, to see for himself. Blue set out by mule with a Cuban guide the next day.

On a sunny Sunday morning, June 12, the harbor lay spread like an open map below the lieutenant. Blue spotted two of the *Vizcaya*-class cruisers, plus the *Plutón* and the *Furor*. Both destroyers were under way in the harbor, Blue recalled, while the cruisers were "lying peacefully at anchor with awnings spread; their boats quietly swinging at the booms, and their colors waving in the breeze."[1] Nearer the city were a small gunboat and a number of steamers.

Blue briefly pondered the whereabouts of Cervera's last two ships and whether they had ever reached Santiago. Maneuvering along the hilltops, he spotted the third cruiser and lastly the *Colón*. More than three weeks after its unnoticed arrival, the entire Spanish fleet was finally and definitely located at Santiago de Cuba.

. . .

From the sea, the entrance to Santiago harbor was "almost indistinguishable from the green jungle that rose above it on each side," an American private recalled. "We could see the pinkish ocher of the ancient forts that guarded it. They looked like the toy forts made for children, or like picturesque defenses of the old-time barons."[2]

To bluejackets on the blockade, however, the scene was less exotic. Life on the line assumed an almost domestic routine, with the battleships as the great constant. Lesser ships rotated in and out, and once on station settled down to await the Spaniards. To a gunner on the auxiliary cruiser *Yankee*, the fleet sitting off the entrance resembled "a group of huge gray cats watching a mouse hole."[3]

The blockade usually comprised ten to twelve ships, ranging from battleships to torpedo boats. The day after his arrival, Sampson divided his force into two squadrons, one commanded by him, the other under Schley. (Secretary Long realigned the entire North Atlantic fleet on June 21. It thereafter comprised two large squadrons—the first, under Commodore John C. Watson, operating off northern Cuba, and the second, under Schley, off Santiago. Both men reported directly to Sampson.) Sampson also instituted a new daytime patrol line six miles off the coast.[4] There, the ships steamed slowly back and forth, in column, four or five hundred yards apart. As June progressed, the admiral gradually edged them in closer, until the daytime line was just four miles from shore. The nighttime line was nearer still, only about three miles.

Sampson also introduced what historian David F. Trask has called a "simple but brilliant tactical improvisation"[5]—one that initially unnerved his captains. The tactic was to position one battleship at night just two miles from shore, at a point from which she could aim a searchlight straight up the harbor channel. Smaller ships, launches, and picket boats crept in even closer, each vessel pointing her bow directly toward the entrance. This became the nightly routine within a week. The first battleship on searchlight duty was the *Iowa*.

"The idea of deliberately placing a battle ship within a mile or two of the fastest torpedo boats [destroyers] in the world," Bob Evans noted wryly, "and then turning on a search light to mark her position, was novel at least."[6] When the *Oregon* caught the duty, Charles Clark recalled, "I used to look at the dark forms of my crew sleeping on deck . . . and think what havoc in their ranks a well-directed fire would make."[7]

The duty was stressful, particularly for men at the helm or on the searchlight, especially when swells and tides made maintaining a steady beam difficult. The Spanish batteries never responded with more than Mauser rifle fire, however—perhaps, Evans later quipped, because "they knew there were a lot of search lights in that fleet."[8]

American officers would long debate among themselves whether Cervera's fleet had stood a better chance of escape under cover of darkness or in daylight. According to the Spaniards, this was a moot point. Navigating Santiago's narrow channel at night under the dazzling beam of a searchlight was nearly impossible. "We could not," the admiral's son and flag-lieutenant, Don Angel Cervera, said later. "Your light was maintained continuously, without interruption, shining right up the channel."[9]

As weeks passed, and the likelihood of a surprise Spanish sortie increased, Sampson positioned a second battleship perpendicular to the first. The second didn't shine a light, but unlike the other sentinels pointed her broadside straight up the channel.

. . .

Sampson wasn't content simply to watch his enormous mouse-hole. He also wanted to attack the fortifications that surrounded it. The objective, he later explained, was "to develop the strength of the enemy, and to get ranges and positions which would insure the projectiles doing the most damage."[10] The fleet first bombarded the Spanish batteries on June 6, although with strict orders to avoid hitting the Morro, where Hobson and his crew were now imprisoned. Originally scheduled for June 5, the bombardment was postponed for a day after John Philip of the *Texas*, the most devout Christian among Sampson's captains, had pointed out that the fifth was a Sunday. "[I]f you search all history," he warned, "you will find that whoever fired the first shot on Sunday was defeated."[11]

To Clark on the *Oregon*, the shelling on June 6 seemed a "very one-sided affair. The Spaniards never fired a shot while we were taking position, and if they replied at all during the attack, it was so seldom as to be scarcely noticeable."[12] With echoes of the shelling of old Fort Fisher, the results seemed negligible. Oddly, one of the few casualties was the captain of the *Reina Mercedes*, which was not among the intended targets; the shells simply flew long.[13]

The difficulty, Sampson recalled, was "the elevation at which the enemy's guns were placed—over two hundred feet. If a ship got too near she could not hit at all by reason of the bluff."[14] Naval gunfire was also generally ineffective against earthworks.

The fleet bombarded again ten days later, at the same range, with about the same results. The Spaniards made repairs quickly, in some cases erecting dummy guns to replace weapons that had been dismounted or wrecked. This hoary ploy, still effective today, fooled even Sampson, Evans, and other Civil War veterans, who surely remembered the "Quaker guns" erected by Confederate troops. In postwar assessments, the Navy later discovered that "we had done a great deal more damage than we had supposed."[15]

To maintain the pressure on the Spaniards, Sampson also deployed a unique, yacht-sized vessel classified as a "dynamite-gun cruiser." Aptly named the *Vesuvius*, she had three large pneumatic tubes projecting from her forecastle. These were 15-inch, smoothbore "dynamite guns" that lobbed shells containing as much as 500 pounds of guncotton.[16] Their range was short, however, at most about a mile and a half; since the tubes were fixed and the entire ship had to be aimed at a target, accuracy was nearly impossible.

The sound of these guns was oddly apologetic. The *Vesuvius* "crept in several nights and coughed her three little coughs,"[17] correspondent Goode wrote, but did little except tear up empty hillsides with spectacular explosions. The guns were so difficult and time-consuming to reload that the cruiser fired just one broadside nightly. Concas later reported that the only Spanish casualty from what he called her "peculiar projectiles" was a gunner who had unwisely slept outdoors.[18]

(The only American warship odder than the *Vesuvius* was the armored ram USS *Katahdin*. Designed to sink enemy raiders, she outwardly resembled a submarine and was nicknamed "Old Half-Seas Under." Not fast enough for her intended role, the ram instead guarded harbors from New England to Norfolk during the war and was quickly decommissioned afterward.)[19]

. . .

Somewhat dull after the excitement of the *Merrimac* affair, life on the blockade was hard on men and ships alike. This was particularly true of the ailing fleet commander, who had planned the blockade with little or no help from Washington.[20] Although he constantly expected a Spanish sortie, Sampson wrote, "it would have been a surprise at any time."[21] According to clerk Buenzle, the "burden of suspense and care" fell heavily on Sampson, who again appeared tired and worn. "I wondered as I typed if the old man ever slept."[22]

Mahan later declared that "no more onerous and important duty than the guard off Santiago fell upon any officer of the United States during the hostilities."[23] Correspondent Goode, despite fears of misjudging an officer he obviously admired, came to believe that "if Cervera's ships had escaped beyond hope of capture Sampson would have committed suicide."[24]

As in many other wars, major and minor, before and since, blockade duty off the Cuban coast was long, dull, and unremitting.

"We took coal and food and ammunition on the blockading line," Evans wrote, "and . . . did not leave it until the necessity for a blockade ceased to exist. The infernal place got to look like home to us; we almost knew the sharks and the fishes that swam around us."[25] The blockade, added Wainwright of the *Gloucester*, "from being exciting and interesting, had become tedious. What at first had been a pleasure had become a duty. . . ."[26]

The Navy and fleet, if perhaps not the nation, recognized the great pressures on Sampson. He was ably served by his subordinates, who except for Schley were supportive and loyal. The admiral was especially fortunate in his battle-ship and cruiser skippers, a tightly knit group that had worked together for decades. These men would constitute the deciding factor when the crisis came.

The captains knew each other well. "Jack" Philip of the *Texas* and F. J. "Poppy" Higginson of the *Massachusetts* were lifelong friends who had attended the Naval Academy with Sampson in the Class of 1861. Evans of the *Iowa*, Clark of the *Oregon*, Henry Taylor of the *Indiana*, and Francis Cook of the *Brooklyn* were members of the Class of 1864; Chadwick of the *New York*, who was also Sampson's chief of staff, was just a year behind. Clark and Cook had been Annapolis roommates; Evans and Taylor were related by marriage. Among many other connections, Wainwright of the *Gloucester* was the brother-in-law of Seaton Schroeder, executive officer of the *Massachusetts*.

Sampson's logistics worries also receded somewhat. Marines in mid-June seized and held Guantanamo, just forty miles east of Santiago. This achieved the admiral's main objective (after setting the blockade) of establishing "a har-bor and a base for the operations of the fleet pending a decisive action."[27] Despite continued fighting in the hills, the bay itself was permanently occupied from June 10, offering a safe, calm location for coaling warships.

Crew shortages due to the influx of yachts and liners into the Navy eased as well. Naval cadets from Annapolis quickly expanded the officer corps. (Academy students were called "naval cadets" beginning in 1882. Graduates remained naval cadets for two years, until passing an examination for ensign. The Navy reverted to the traditional "midshipmen" in 1902.) The Class of 1898 graduated early in April, and immediately joined the fleet. The second class fol-lowed in May. With their summer cruise canceled, the lower classes were then given leave but, "[i]ndignant at such treatment, they applied for permission to join the upper classmen."[28] Seventy-five of these underclassmen would make it out to the fleet before the summer ended.

State naval militias likewise filled out the enlisted ranks. Various laws pro-hibited deploying state forces overseas, so federal authorities created a United States Auxiliary Naval Force and asked militiamen to enlist. More than four thousand officers and men did so.[29] The reserves both supplemented regular ships' companies—the *Oregon* alone received sixty from Chicago—and formed entire crews for such auxiliaries as the *Yankee*, *Dixie*, *Prairie*, and *Yosemite*.

One of Sampson's biggest concerns, however, was beyond mortal remedy. As June passed, the admiral increasingly fretted about the weather. Hurricane season in the West Indies was just beginning. With it came the danger that the fleet might be forced out to sea, just the sort of offering from fortune that Cervera hoped for. This risk, as Mahan later pointed out, "was not, perhaps, adequately realized by the people of the United States."[30]

"I again urge earnestly army move with all possible celerity," Sampson cabled to Long on June 17. "Fine weather may end any day."[31] Far less prepared than the Navy for war with Spain, the Army as yet had been nowhere in evidence. Finally, three days after his cable, the first troops arrived off Cuba.

"On the 20th of June the *Wompatuck* appeared," Sampson wrote, "and announced that the army expedition, under the convoy of the *Indiana* and more than a dozen smaller vessels, was fifteen miles to the southwest, where it would await instructions."[32] Journalist Richard Harding Davis, who had accompanied it, later reported, "The largest number of United States troops that ever went down to the sea in ships to invade a foreign country were those that formed the Fifth Army Corps when it sailed for Santiago."[33]

. . .

The hastily assembled corps had sailed from Tampa on thirty-two old transports. Its sixteen thousand troops comprised the bulk of the small regular Army, including African-American "Buffalo Soldiers" from the southwestern forts, plus a number of volunteers. Among the latter was the Navy's old friend and supporter, former assistant secretary Roosevelt. "Teddy" was now lieutenant-colonel of the 1st U.S. Volunteer Cavalry, a regiment then as now best known as the "Rough Riders."

After consulting with Sampson and the Cuban generals, Major-General William R. Shafter landed the Fifth Corps at Daiquirí, in insurgent-controlled territory seventeen miles east of Santiago. The troops started ashore in fifty-two of the fleet's small boats beginning on June 22, supported by Navy shellfire.[34] High surf made the landings hair-raising and hazardous. Army horses and mules simply swam ashore, herded by sailor "wranglers."

Although the landing was unopposed and a second beach was also used at nearby Siboney, getting the troops ashore took three days. Among those commended for performance during the landings was Naval Cadet Thomas C. Hart of the yacht *Vixen*. (He would later lead ABDA, the beleaguered American-

British-Dutch-Australian Command, during World War II.) Most of the Army's supplies were landed by the evening of June 26.

. . .

The landings signaled the beginning of the end for Santiago. Spanish troops were barely holding out against the Cuban insurgents and starvation was imminent. With a corps of American regulars and volunteers in the field, the fall of the city was only a matter of time—perhaps a very short time.

Captain Concas thought the best thing the Spanish fleet could have done to help the city was "the landing of the rapid-fire guns." This was impossible, since the idea of a sortie still "dominated all else in Habana and Madrid."[35] Cervera did land a thousand men under Captain Bustamante to fight in the hills. Even reinforced, Spanish soldiers had little better odds of success at Santiago than did their sailors, if only because the Americans were fresh and decently fed.

Like the American fleet, the Army's Fifth Corps was commanded by aging Civil War veterans. Corpulent Shafter was a former teacher who had begun his military career as a lieutenant in the Michigan infantry; publisher William Randolph Hearst described him as "a sort of human fortress in blue coat and flannel shirt."[36] Among Shafter's commanders was "Fightin' Joe" Wheeler, a former Confederate cavalryman. (Consul-General Fitzhugh Lee, another old rebel cavalry leader, was likewise a major-general of U.S. volunteers.) Adna Chaffee, a Union veteran of Gettysburg and the Indian wars, was also on the scene.

Eager to take Santiago before tropic fevers and conditions decimated his command, Shafter pushed rapidly inland and westward from Daiquirí and Siboney. The corps attacked Santiago's outer defensive lines east of the city on July 1. In costly battles at San Juan Heights and El Caney, it pushed the Spaniards from their trenches on the hilltops dominating the harbor. At San Juan, Roosevelt and his Rough Riders captured Kettle Hill, in the charge that made the former assistant secretary a household name.

About four hundred of Cervera's crewmen took part in the July 1 fight. Bustamante fell while commanding the naval column, mortally wounded by a bullet in the groin. His death on July 19 saddened men in the opposing fleet as well as his own. Admiral Sampson recalled him as a "fine officer and accomplished man" whose courtesy in delivering the note during the *Merrimac* affair "gave us a favorable impression of the Spanish officers."[37]

During the Spaniard's interchange with Sampson, Ship's Writer Buenzle had also found Bustamante "a fine-looking officer, courtly and gracious." The clerk wondered "why we were waging a bitter war of destruction against these men and their nation."[38]

. . .

The fleet shelled Spanish fortifications east of the harbor's entrance to support the Army. The first of several bombardments of Santiago itself came the night of July 1. Firing by using compass bearings from a range of 8,500 yards, the *New York* and *Oregon* lobbed 8-inch shells over the intervening hills—"our first experience in firing at such long range at an invisible target."[39] Soldiers ashore reported the accuracy of the shelling. No lives were lost in the city, according to Goode,[40] and the shelling apparently had little purpose except to maintain pressure on the Spaniards.

With Americans in the hills and shells landing in Santiago, the destruction of Cervera's fleet was clearly imminent. All that was undetermined was the instrument of its demise. For Concas, the choice was stark and simple: "to go out to unavailing death at the entrance of the harbor, or to blow up our ships at the last moment, disembarking the rapid-fire guns and all our forces for the defense of the city."[41]

For a week, Cervera engaged in a three-way tug of war with Madrid and Havana. Authorities in both capitals wanted the fleet to sail, regardless of consequences. The admiral refused to order any such sortie, "for I should consider myself responsible before God and history for the lives sacrificed on the altar of vanity, and not in the true defense of the country."[42]

His was not the final voice, however. Cuban Governor-General Ramón Blanco y Erenas settled the fleet's fate on July 2 when he sent Cervera an order, seconded by the minister of war.[43] "In view of exhausted and serious condition of Santiago . . . your Excellency will reembark landing troops of squadron as fast as possible to go out immediately."[44]

As at the Cape Verdes, Cervera and his captains obeyed the direct order. They unanimously agreed that the fleet should depart the same day, concerned that the insurgents would learn their intentions and quickly warn Sampson. Orders went out recalling the thousand men ashore. The admiral also named Concas his chief of staff in place of Bustamante. The *Vizcaya*'s men were farthest from the harbor, and the last to return to their ship. They arrived exhausted at four o'clock that afternoon.

"For this reason," Concas later wrote, "the admiral decided to suspend the sortie for this day, and allow everybody to rest, since everything was in readiness and no further preparations were necessary."[45]

None of the activity in Cervera's fleet was visible from the blockade line. As night fell, Spanish troops in the hills west and northwest of Santiago abandoned six blockhouses, which were set afire as Cuban insurgents advanced. Some of

Cervera's officers mistakenly regarded the blazes as a signal to the American fleet that the six warships were preparing to sail.[46]

On board the *Iowa*, the officer of the deck called Evans' attention to more smoke, "six columns . . . near the entrance to the harbour which rose straight in the calm evening air." Evans agreed that this smoke indicated that the Spanish fleet had moved out from the city, "but, as they often moved about the harbour, I did not consider it a matter of importance."[47] It made a greater impression on the ship's signal quartermaster, who attached signal 250—"Enemy's ships coming out"—to the halyards, ready to hoist at any time.

Sampson's fleet settled in for another night of watchfulness. There would be changes in the blockade by morning. The *Massachusetts* was leaving overnight for Guantanamo after completing a searchlight watch, her first opportunity for harbor coaling since arriving.[48] Sampson was also preparing to leave in the *New York*, for a morning meeting ashore with General Shafter.

Had he known any of this, Admiral Cervera might have thought that fortune had bestowed upon him two small, improbable gifts. He would have known, as well, that they were far too late to save him.

CHAPTER 18

"God and the Gunners"

EARLY MORNING FOG on July 3 gave way to brilliant sunshine. The land breeze lingered longer than normal. "There was no haze," Bob Evans remembered, "and the blue of the mountains blended with the blue of the sky."[1]

Out on the blockade line, crewmen in their whites prepared for Sunday inspection. The fleet formed a long, fishhook-shaped arc, the bows all pointing toward the harbor entrance. The line from the west to east comprised the *Vixen, Brooklyn, Texas, Iowa, Oregon, Indiana,* and *Gloucester.* The converted liner *Resolute* sat just east of the *Indiana.*[2] Evans thought the rusty, lead-colored warships looked "very business like" as they rolled in a long southeast swell.[3]

The *New York* had left her usual spot between the *Indiana* and *Oregon* at nine o'clock, flying the signal "Disregard motions of commander-in-chief." This simply meant that the others weren't to follow her. Still within sight, the flagship steamed eastward at 8 knots, accompanied by the yacht *Hist* and torpedo boat *Ericsson.*

Admiral Sampson looked oddly out of uniform on the *New York.* Instead of Sunday whites, he wore fatigues, leggings, spurs, and a linen coat for his ride inland from Siboney. Since Shafter was unable to travel due to illness—or to his "great size and weight," according to Lieutenant Staunton[4]—the admiral was going to him. Correspondent Goode thought Sampson was ailing, too, "well-nigh worn out with the tremendous strain of the past month."[5]

The meeting ashore surely weighed on Sampson. His relations with the Army were rocky. He had recommended attacking the outer batteries after the landings, to allow his fleet to clear mines and enter the harbor.[6] Shafter had instead advanced inland on the city. With casualties mounting and a Spanish relief column reportedly marching south from Manzanillo, Shafter had since rethought his strategy. He now wanted Sampson to help the bloodied Fifth Corps by bulling his way into Santiago.

"I urge that you make effort immediately to force the entrance to avoid future losses among my men, which are already very heavy. You can now operate with less loss of life than I can," Shafter stated on July 2. Compounding ignorance with insult, he later added, "I am at a loss to see why the Navy can not work under a destructive fire as well as the Army. My loss yesterday was over five hundred men."[7] (Army casualties were actually much higher.)

Taking battleships up a narrow, mined, and partially blocked channel was an adventure only a landsman could have suggested. Captain Clark of the *Oregon* later observed that it "did not seem good strategy to those who knew that the capture or destruction of Cervera's squadron was the real objective of the Cuba campaign." With empathy for the fears of the corps commander, however, Clark also added that something had to be done, and quickly, "for the yellow fever season was approaching, and that scourge would have mowed down our forces more relentlessly than any human enemy."[8]

Sampson had replied to Shafter with what Goode considered a "calm, masterly letter."[9] After first explaining the hazards of attacking up the channel, he added, "If it is your earnest desire that we should force our entrance, I will at once prepare to undertake it."[10] Sampson also promised to bring forty countermining mines from Guantanamo to begin clearing the entrance. In their conference in the hills behind Siboney, the admiral and the general would try to resolve their differences.

· · ·

Cervera was ready to leave Santiago. The engine-room fires were spread, guns loaded, torpedoes prepared, the crews standing by. Concas had returned earlier from a morning reconnaissance and reported the absence of one of the American battleships. This was the *Massachusetts*, gone with the *Suwanee* and *Vesuvius* to coal at Guantanamo.[11] The admiral had immediately ordered the fleet to weigh anchor. With every anchor now secured, the flagship gave the signal to sortie: "Viva España."

"With the battle flag hoisted," Concas wrote, "the *Infanta María Teresa* advanced ahead of the other cruisers, which for the last time gave the honors due their admiral, saluting him with hurrahs that manifested the spirit of the crews, worthy of a better fate."[12]

Forming the Spanish column behind the *María Teresa* were the *Vizcaya*, *Cristóbal Colón*, and *Almirante Oquendo*, about 800 yards between vessels. Some 1,200 yards behind them came the torpedo-boat destroyer *Furor*, followed by

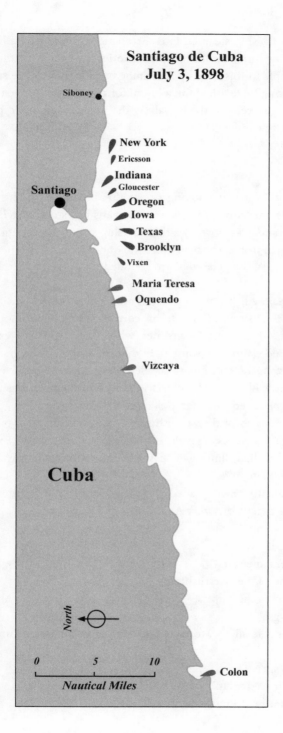

Santiago de Cuba
July 3, 1898

Siboney

New York
Ericsson
Indiana
Gloucester
Oregon
Iowa
Texas
Brooklyn
Vixen

Santiago

Maria Teresa
Oquendo

Vizcaya

Cuba

North

0   5   10

Nautical Miles

Colon

Positions of the
American ships before
the Battle of Santiago,
and final positions of
Spanish ships after the
action. (Map by Tina
Bozzuto)

the *Plutón*.[13] Cervera's flagship steamed into the channel, then in "death-like silence" made the narrow turn near the Spanish batteries.[14]

Concas set an example for his crew by remaining outside the relative safety of the ship's conning tower. He asked the admiral for permission to open fire, which was granted. Bugles relayed the signal. As the notes faded, the captain again turned and spoke to Cervera.

"Poor Spain!" he said.[15]

. . .

In his cabin on the *Iowa*, Evans sat smoking a cigar after breakfast with his son. A naval cadet on the *Massachusetts*, Franck Taylor Evans had stood watch in a picket boat overnight and was now awaiting his ship's return. He, another naval cadet, and five men from their boat were the only *Massachusetts* men off Santiago today. At 9:31 AM, the general alarm sounded. Both Evans men leapt to their feet.

"Papa," Franck exclaimed, "the enemy's ships are coming out!"[16]

Once topside, Bob Evans sent his son to his corresponding division on the *Iowa*. He dispersed the other *Massachusetts* men where they would be useful. Although the *Iowa* would claim with some right that she had fired the first gun and first raised signal 250, the entire fleet seemed to spot the *María Teresa* at nearly the same instant.[17] Bluejackets and officers raced to their stations amid what Clark on the *Oregon* called "the brassy clang of the alarm gongs."[18]

(The *Massachusetts* learned of the Spanish sortie while coaling at 1:55 that afternoon. "Buckets, bags, baskets, shovels, everything were dropped," Executive Officer Schroeder recalled, "lines were cast off, and we backed away from the collier; but it was too late.")[19]

On the *Indiana*, Captain Taylor issued a rapid series of orders that were duplicated more or less exactly on every American warship in sight.

"Sound the general alarm!"

"Clear ship for action!"

"Bugles call to general quarters!"

"Turn on the current of the electric hoists!"

"Steam and pressure on the turrets!"

"Hoist the battle-flags!"

"Lay aloft range-finders in the tops and give us our distance from the Morro!"

"Engines ahead full speed!"

"Be ready with the forced draft!"

"The starboard battery will engage!"

"Set your sights for four thousand yards!"[20]

Seven miles east of the *Iowa*, Sampson stood with Captain Chadwick on the flying bridge of the *New York*. The admiral was dictating a memo to Buenzle when the chief quartermaster spoke from a platform below. "They're coming out, sir!"

"Please give this to George," Sampson said, calmly handing Buenzle a packet of sandwiches his steward had prepared earlier. "I won't need them today."[21] The admiral also remembered a naval cadet who was hoping to accompany him ashore to visit a wounded army captain at Siboney. "Mr. Jones," Sampson said quietly, "I'm afraid you won't see your brother today."[22]

The admiral, Goode reported, then "passed quickly through the rushing, shouting throng that went madly to their battle stations, and gained the bridge."[23] The flagship, *Hist*, and *Ericsson* heeled into their turns and began a pursuit of both the Spanish and American fleets, Sampson wishing, "Oh, that we had wings!"[24]

. . .

Any Southerner in the fleet surely realized the historical coincidence of the date. Thirty-five years earlier, Pickett's Charge on the third and final day of Gettysburg had signaled the "high water mark" of the Confederacy. Union soldiers long remembered the terrible beauty of the rebel formations marching across open fields toward destruction. Similar emotions arose now as Cervera's ships emerged one by one from the channel.

"Their large red-and-yellow ensigns stood out brilliantly against the dark-green background of the Morro and Socapa headlands," Lieutenant Edward Eberle of the *Oregon* recalled, "and their massive black hulls, with great white waves piled under their bows, seemed veritable things of life."[25] Jack Philip on the *Texas* marveled at the ships coming out "as gaily as brides to the altar."[26] Even steely Bob Evans was moved by "the finest spectacle that has probably ever been seen on the water."[27]

Some twelve minutes passed from their first glimpse of the *María Teresa* in the upper channel until the fourth ship, the *Oquendo*, cleared the entrance. "The armored cruisers, as rapidly as they could bring their guns to bear, opened a vigorous fire upon the blockading vessels," Sampson reported, "and emerged from the channel shrouded in the smoke from their guns."[28]

Sampson's standing orders if Cervera tried to escape were to "close and engage as soon as possible, and endeavor to sink his vessels or force them to run ashore in the channel."[29] The fleet quickly got under way, the battleships and cruisers heading toward the entrance, the auxiliaries moving away. The *María*

Teresa, as the lead Spanish ship, withstood all their fire alone for the first ten minutes.[30] Evans wanted to ram or torpedo her, but the Spanish flagship was moving too fast. The *Iowa* exchanged fire with her, the *Vizcaya*, and the *Colón* as they surged past. The *Colón* struck the battleship twice—"two as beautiful shots as I ever saw made by any ship," Evans wrote.[31]

On the *Brooklyn*, near the western edge of the line, Schley had given a Nelsonian command to "go right for them!"[32]

He headed northeast under heavy fire. Schley feared at first that the *María Teresa* and then the *Vizcaya* might ram him. Instead, all four Spanish cruisers turned southwest and then west, keeping near the coast. This left the *Brooklyn* steaming in nearly the opposite direction. Schley could have curled inward to close with Cervera. Instead, he made what became known as the "loop"—a hard starboard turn away from the Spaniards and into the path of his own fleet. Even the Spaniards thought Schley had gone the wrong way. ("The turn was to starboard," Concas wrote, "although it would seem reasonable for it to have made to port.")[33]

The commodore later said that Captain Francis Cook had ordered the turn, and that the maneuver was the correct one. It was invisible to the nearby *Texas*, however, which had turned westward to chase the *María Teresa*. The battleship was so blinded by smoke from her own guns that it seemed to Captain Philip "we might as well have had a blanket tied over our heads."[34] When he last glimpsed her, the *Brooklyn* was rushing northeastward. The cruiser's navigator tried to warn Schley they were cutting across the *Texas'* path. "Let the *Texas* take care of herself," the commodore replied.[35]

(Schley labeled a newspaper account of his colloquy with navigator Lieutenant A. C. Hodgson "one of many fictions"[36] of the battle. Long reported to the president, however, that although its wording might be inexact, the article's substance was "substantially true.")[37]

A lull in the firing and a whiff of breeze cleared the cloud around the battleship. Philip suddenly saw the *Brooklyn* steaming south across his bow, looking "as big as half a dozen *Great Easterns*, and . . . so near that it took our breath away."

"Back both engines hard!" he shouted.[38]

The battleship immediately slowed to avoid the collision. In doing so, she forever shattered her old hoodoo curse; the *Texas* would be unlucky no more. Philip discovered just how fortunate she had suddenly become only moments later as the *Oregon* raced up behind her.

Captain Clark was turning the *Oregon* to port to clear the *Iowa*, which had emerged from a cloud of smoke to starboard. "Look out for the *Texas*!"[39] someone shouted as the battleship suddenly loomed on the *Oregon*'s port bow. Clark could only sheer back toward the *Iowa* and pray that everyone got clear, like jockeys thundering through a crowded turn.

"Captains Philip and Evans, both fine seamen, must have instantly grasped the situation and acted on it, for we did pass between them," Clark wrote, "but by so narrow a margin that I felt that coming to close quarters with the Spaniards would be infinitely preferable to repeating that experience."[40]

If the *Brooklyn* had impaled the *Texas*, "it would probably have been the end of the *Texas* and her half-thousand men," Philip wrote. "Had the *Texas* rammed the *Brooklyn*, it would have been equally disastrous; for the *Texas* was not built for ramming, and she would have doubled up like a hoop."[41] Clark had feared an even greater calamity. For one awful moment, it seemed on the *Oregon* that Schley's cruiser might disable all three battleships simultaneously, "leaving only the *Indiana* and the lightly armed *Brooklyn* to cope with the foe."[42]

Though smiling on the *Texas*, fortune had almost been spectacularly generous to Admiral Cervera. Captain Chadwick of the *New York* later estimated that the *Brooklyn*'s turn had taken her a mile and a half east and a half-mile south, and "carried her for a time out of action and opened the way of escape for the Spanish vessels while bringing the *Texas* to a dead stop for fear of collision."[43]

The three battleships somehow all avoided the errant cruiser and each other to come through unharmed. But on the *New York*, it looked as if Schley's flagship had been crippled and knocked out of the fight. Someone shouted, "The *Brooklyn*'s gone!"[44] Then she completed her unorthodox turn and led the general chase westward.

To Schley, the loop was another tempest in a teapot. He later insisted that the *Brooklyn* was "never nearer than five or six hundred yards" from the *Texas*, which was "never for a moment in the least danger."

Since the *New York* was several miles away, Schley had concluded (with some justification) that he was in tactical command. Oblivious to the chaos in his wake, he looked back to see the *Oregon* bursting through the wall of smoke. "She had what sailors call 'a tremendous bone in her mouth,' and was following the flag, as Clark had seen [my] signals 'Follow the flag' and 'Close up,'" Schley wrote. "This brought a change in the situation, and from that moment the result was in no degree doubtful."[45]

. . .

Sampson's fleet ran westward in a staggered line. Despite the commodore's signal to follow him, Santiago was already what Roosevelt later described as "a captains' fight."[46] Without any real coordination by Schley or Sampson, Captains Evans, Clark, Philip, Taylor, and Wainwright now pursued Cervera's ships like a pack of wolves. One by one, the Spaniards succumbed.

The *Brooklyn* was in the lead with the *Oregon* close behind. Both were nearly abreast of the Spaniards, but the *Oregon* was farther inshore and closer. Behind her came the *Texas*, *Iowa*, and *Indiana*, with the *New York* in the distance. The *Vixen*, *Resolute*, and *Gloucester* had all rightly turned away when the Spaniards broke from the entrance. The *Vixen* now steamed a little ahead of the *Brooklyn*, but much farther out to sea. The *Resolute* was racing east with news of the sortie, while the *Gloucester* had reversed course toward the Spanish destroyers.

Except for the *Furor* and *Plutón*, which emerged last, Cervera's fleet kept together. Evans and Taylor later believed this was the tactic most likely to succeed; Sampson, Clark, Philip, and others, however, suggested that some Spanish ships might have escaped if they had scattered after clearing the entrance. Indeed, the *María Teresa* had initially steered straight for the *Brooklyn*, intending to attack her. Cervera turned west only after Schley had begun his loop, to avoid being rammed by the onrushing *Texas* or *Iowa*.[47]

The first Spanish vessel out, the flagship was also the first heavily damaged. The other cruisers raced ahead as the *María Teresa* now began falling back. Clark came to believe that it was "Cervera's chivalrous idea . . . to cover the retreat of his flying ships and to bear the brunt of the combat."[48] To Sampson, the reason they all continued westward was simpler. "The fact is, they hugged the shore as a possible means of rescue in case of disaster; they did not like to leave the land entirely."[49]

Once the American line formed to seaward, however, the Spaniards could only continue westward. The blue sea off Cuba became a gauntlet strewn with wreckage, the hostile shore on one side, the relentless enemy on the other.

Slowed by boiler repairs begun with Sampson's permission,[50] the *Iowa* was making just 10 knots. Even so, Evans simultaneously engaged the *María Teresa*, the *Vizcaya*, and the *Oquendo*.[51] Although Evans didn't know it, Cervera's flagship was already fatally damaged, hit the same moment the *Oquendo* had emerged from the harbor. Concas later credited the *Iowa* for two 12-inch shells that had caused the damage.

The rounds had exploded on the *María Teresa*'s poop, bursting vital steam pipes to the main pump and engines and starting fires that caused numerous casualties. Concas was on his bridge, trying to determine what was happening, when another explosion seriously wounded him and two officers. The blast seemed to Concas "like the explosion of a magazine or a torpedo." (If the latter, it was one of his own, for the U.S. fleet had fired none.)

"During that furious struggle," Concas recalled, "there was no time nor opportunity to call the executive officer, and therefore the admiral himself took command of the ship, while I was carried to the sick bay."[52]

On the *Brooklyn*, Schley saw the Spanish flagship "wabbling like a bird wounded, and apparently lagging. Smoke was seen issuing from her ports, and, but a few minutes afterwards, from her hatches, in columns mounting straight into the air."[53] With the *María Teresa* on fire fore and aft and rapidly losing headway, Cervera turned her toward the beach. The cruiser grounded at 10:15 AM, just six and a half miles west of the harbor entrance.[54]

. . .

While the American fleet concentrated on the Spanish flagship and Schley's loop disrupted pursuit, the *Vizcaya* and *Colón* had steamed away almost undamaged. Clark raked the dying *María Teresa* as the *Oregon* surged past, although it "went to my heart to do it,"[55] then began firing on the lagging *Oquendo*. He eventually closed to within 800 yards of her.

The *Texas* and *Iowa* also began exchanging fire with the *Oquendo*. A Spanish shell exploded over the *Texas'* forward superstructure, tossing Philip into the air "with my coattails flying out behind me, as if I had been thrown by one of Roosevelt's broncos."[56] Shrapnel from another shell started such a smoky fire that some men thought the *Texas* had blown up.[57] But with the battleships and the *Brooklyn* firing on her, the *Oquendo* sustained much greater damage than she inflicted. Destruction came quickly.

"The ship was a slaughter-pen, everywhere you looked were dead men"; a survivor said, "there was a head here, an arm there; it was impossible to stay at the guns."[58] Evans recalled "the flames bursting out through the shot holes in her sides and leaping up from the deck as high as the military tops."[59]

At about 10:20 AM, with ammunition hoists inoperable, guns out of action, and the ship burning uncontrollably, Captain Lazaga discharged all his torpedoes and turned the *Oquendo* toward shore.[60] Clark's navigator thought the *Oregon* should move in and destroy her. "No, that's a dead cock in the pit," Clark said. "The others can attend to her. We'll push on for the two ahead."[61]

The *Oquendo* raised a white flag as the *Texas* came up fifteen minutes later.[62] She grounded a half-mile from the *María Teresa*.[63] It was a "magnificent, sad sight to see these beautiful ships in their death agonies"; Evans wrote, "but we were doing the work we had been educated for, and we cheered and yelled until our throats were sore."[64]

As the *New York* swept by, the *Oquendo's* main magazine exploded into a fiery mushroom cloud. "How dramatic!" Chadwick said. "How sad it all is!"[65]

Before the day was out, the *Oquendo's* executive officer and 125 other officers and men would be dead.[66] Captain Lazaga would also perish, drowned after the cruiser beached. (Newspapers reports stated that the captain committed suicide. This was disputed by the *Indiana's* chaplain, who examined the body and spoke with the crew.)[67]

. . .

The last of Cervera's ships to emerge were the destroyers. The pair was supposed to come out under the protection of the cruisers and then make a dash for open water. Instead, the *Plutón* and *Furor* appeared 1,200 yards behind the *Oquendo*.

Concas couldn't explain Villaamil's tardiness. He later speculated that the captain might have hoped the American battleships would all pursue the cruisers, and so ignore him. But this overlooked Sampson's auxiliaries, which for the destroyers "were more to be feared than the battle ships themselves."[68]

Lookouts on the *Indiana* saw the pair emerge. Captain Taylor hoisted the signal "Enemy's torpedo-boats coming out." Wainwright on the *Gloucester* read the signal as "Gunboats close in," which he interpreted as an order for him.[69] Evans also saw the signal, and the "two dense spots of black smoke and two long white streaks on the water" that indicated the destroyers' position.[70]

The rapid-fire after batteries of the *Indiana*, *Iowa*, *Oregon*, and *Texas* opened up, while the *Gloucester* made for the pair with a burst of speed. The destroyers fought back. A Marine on the *Oregon* thought one of the Spanish gunners was "one of the bravest men I ever had the pleasure to look upon."[71] Evans marveled that the "gallant little paper shells actually returned the fire of the battleships."[72]

The *Gloucester* was J. P. Morgan's former yacht *Corsair*. She now attacked the destroyers so closely and relentlessly that for some moments the bigger ships didn't see her. Shells from the *Iowa* splashed dangerously close before the battleship abruptly ceased fire. "Both of [the *Gloucester's*] Colt automatic guns were blazing," Evans recalled, "fairly sweeping the decks of the torpedo-boats, and her broadside guns on both sides were firing with mechanical rapidity."[73] Despite conflicting claims from the battleships, the *Gloucester* likely inflicted the greatest damage on both destroyers.

Although under fire from Spanish shore batteries, Wainwright considered the destroyers' automatic Maxim one-pounders the bigger threat. These guns whipped up the sea within twenty yards of the *Gloucester* "as if a hail storm was raging."[74] Then the fire suddenly stopped. The quick little yacht was now making 17 knots and steaming less than 1,200 yards from the destroyers. When the *Plutón* slowed, crippled, Wainwright shifted his fire to the *Furor*.

"We were within six hundred yards of her and every shot appeared to strike."[75] As the *Plutón* ran onto rocks in the surf and blew up, the *Furor* turned to face her tormenter. But the *Furor*, too, was now crippled.

The *New York* rushed past under shellfire from the shore batteries. She lobbed three 4-inch shells at the destroyer, her only opportunity to fire all day. The *Gloucester* raised the signal "Enemy's vessels destroyed."[76] The flagship gave her three cheers and continued westward. The time was just 10:30 AM.

The Spanish shore gunners ceased fire as the *Gloucester* lowered her boats. The *Furor* was afire below-decks and sinking slowly by the stern. Wainwright quickly abandoned any thought of salvaging her. The destroyer sank an hour later after a heavy explosion,[77] 200 yards from shore.[78]

Neither destroyer had made it more than three miles from the harbor entrance.[79] The *Gloucester* captured both ensigns.[80] Captain Villaamil, who might have returned to Spain from the Cape Verdes, was dead, killed on the bridge of the *Furor*, which sank with his body.[81] About a third of his two crews also died.[82] Evans later calculated that the destruction of the *Plutón* and *Furor* had taken eight minutes.

"It was almost wicked," he wrote, "to waste the lives of brave men in such an attempt."[83]

.   .   .

The *Iowa* was steaming closer inshore than the other battleships. A white flag fluttered from the *María Teresa*. American shells were falling around her crew and the *Oquendo*'s as they struggled in the water. Evans raised a signal: "Enemy's ships have surrendered."[84] The *Indiana* and *Gloucester* then ran in to take their surrender.[85] Now only the *Colón* and *Vizcaya* survived.

As the faster *Colón* began pulling ahead, the battleships and the *Brooklyn* concentrated on her slower companion. The *Oregon* soon drew abreast of the *Vizcaya*. Clark fired on Eulate's cruiser continuously from a range of about a mile and a half.[86] The *Iowa*, *Brooklyn*, and *Texas* fired from farther away. The *New York*, too, drew within range; she withheld fire to avoid shooting over the *Iowa*.[87]

On the *Brooklyn*, twenty-five-year-old Chief Yeoman George Ellis was taking ranges on the *Vizcaya* with a stadimeter. His friend Buenzle considered him "one of the most peaceable men in our entire force."[88] Ellis was eight or ten feet from the commodore when a Spanish shell instantly decapitated him.[89] Brains and blood splattered everyone nearby, "and some of it reached me," Schley wrote. "He immediately fell to the deck, of course, and it was a shocking sight to men who had not before seen such things."[90]

Schley wiped gore from his face and coat with a handkerchief. An ensign and a ship's doctor started to slip the corpse overboard but Schley stopped them, saying the chief deserved a Christian burial. A boatswain called for a blanket. Ellis' headless body lay in the lee of the forward turret for the rest of the battle.[91] He would be buried at sunset the following day, July 4, on a hillside overlooking Guantanamo Bay.[92]

The *Vizcaya* meanwhile was "blazing away viciously," Philip remembered, "but the pounding she got from our four ships, more particularly the *Oregon*, was too much for her, and in half an hour she too headed for the beach."[93] The *Vizcaya* now moved "like some sick and wounded thing, seeking a place to die," Clark recalled. The *Oregon* skipper felt none of "the exultation that is supposed to come with victory."[94] Instead, he imagined the faces of Spanish widows and children. Clark found comfort only in the thought that every life taken off Santiago might shorten the war.

Even the *Vixen* closed to fire on the dying cruiser. Shortly after eleven o'clock, the *Vizcaya's* stern flag came down and firing ceased. She was just fifteen miles west of Santiago. Some in the fleet thought Eulate hadn't actually surrendered, that his flag had been shot away. The ship still showed no white flag and her colors flew from the truck. But as the *Texas* steamed past, Jack Philip couldn't bring himself to fire again.

"Flames were shooting from her deck fore and aft," he wrote, "and as her nose touched the beach two tremendous explosions in succession literally shook her to pieces."[95] The *Texas* bluejackets roared over their victory.

"Don't cheer, men," Philip said, gesturing for quiet, "those poor fellows are dying."[96]

(Many accounts read "poor devils," but his friends insisted the devout captain would never utter words so profane. Either way, the remark entered naval history.)[97]

. . .

Now there was one. The *Colón*, "wiliest of all the Spanish vessels," according to Philip, "was making a great race for liberty."[98] To Lieutenant Eberle, an *Oregon* gunnery officer, it was the start of "the grandest chase in naval history."[99] The swift *Colón* was several miles ahead of the fleet and still hugging the shore.[100]

An American officer later wrote that her coal-passers and firemen had been on duty in the trenches outside Santiago without food for a day and a half, then not fed once they reembarked. To compensate for their near starvation, they had received brandy, rendering many of them drunk. Eberle wrote that Spanish officers had shot several men who tried to leave the stifling fire-room. But still the *Colón* pelted on.[101]

The *Iowa* couldn't keep pace, and Evans signaled for permission to pick up survivors. His crew cheered Admiral Sampson as the *New York* surged past at 16 knots. The flagship's bluejackets returned the cheers when Evans answered Sampson's hail with the report, "Not a man hurt aboard the ship!"[102]

The *Brooklyn* continued to lead the chase, but was farthest outside. Next came the *Oregon*, nearer the *Colón* and slowly gaining. The *Texas* was behind, with the *New York* farther back but also gaining. As the *New York* passed the burning *Vizcaya*, crewmen spotted a sailor struggling in the water. "¡Madre de Dios, ayúdame!" the man called. *Mother of God, help me!*

Buenzle and a group of gunners seized the chaplain's pulpit, which hadn't been stowed or jettisoned, and shoved it overboard into the shark-infested sea. A coxswain yelled for the Spaniard to "cling to the cross!" Then the ship swept on, no one seeing whether he reached it.[103] (Sampson also recalled this incident but placed it earlier in the chase. He wrote, perhaps wishfully, that the Spaniard was saved.)[104]

Though she had steamed around South America and served continuously on the blockade since, the *Oregon* kept pace with the fleeing *Colón*. The *Brooklyn*, *Texas*, and *New York* also kept up. "In this chase but few shots were fired on either side," Philip wrote. "It was a test of engines, and not of guns, and we hoped to capture the ship uninjured."[105]

For a time Clark feared the *Colón* might escape, but the Spaniard couldn't maintain her early burst of speed. An hour passed as the Americans slowly gained. Clark spoke with three of his gunnery officers a little after noon; among them was Eberle, who commanded the forward 13-inch turret. Clark decided to risk damaging his ship by elevating a forward gun to maximum elevation and firing once at a range of 9,500 yards. The shot fell short, but caused no harm to the *Oregon*.[106]

The wolves and prey continued west along the mountainous coast. Another hour passed, the *Oregon* periodically firing from her forward turret. At 1:10 PM, 13-inch shells fell close alongside the *Colón*.[107] Naval Cadet William Leahy (later chief of naval operations, then chief of staff for Presidents Roosevelt and Truman in World War II) wrote that the shells then "began to strike ahead and on all sides" of the *Colón*.[108]

The coast ahead jutted seaward, blocking the fleeing cruiser's course. The *Brooklyn* and *Oregon* were outside the *Colón*, the *Texas* and *New York* behind her. "Hemmed in on all three sides there was only the shore to choose," Philip remembered, "and the *Colón* wisely chose it."[109] Untouched by any large shell, she struck her colors and turned for the beach, the crew opening sea valves to scuttle her. She grounded nearly fifty miles from Santiago.[110]

Some men, like Leahy, jumped and yelled and slapped their caps.[111] Others, like Buenzle, wished never to see another war.[112] For everyone, the fight was over. As Evans later wrote, "God and the gunners had had their day."[113]

CHAPTER 19

"Big Enough for All"

WITH THE *Colón* ON THE BEACH, Commodore Schley raised an ebullient if smug signal for the *Oregon*. "Congratulations for the grand victory, thanks for your splendid assistance."[1] He raised another when the *New York* reached the scene. "We have gained a great victory; details will be communicated."[2]

On Sampson's flagship, correspondent Goode thought that Schley's signal, "however well meant, was somewhat superfluous." A megaphone message was also relayed to Admiral Sampson that the commodore claimed "the honor of the capture" of the *Colón*. "This, I believe, was not what the commodore said," Goode later wrote, "but that is the way it was reported to Sampson and understood on the *New York*."[3]

Sampson and Schley were destined always to miscommunicate. The *New York* raised a signal of her own, "Report your casualties." Stung by the apparent slight, Schley unwisely tried again. "This is a great day for the country!"[4] This time, the flagship merely raised a pennant in acknowledgement.

Schley would swallow his pique over these terse signals in his official report to Sampson three days later. "I congratulate you most sincerely upon this great victory to the squadron under your command," he wrote, "and I am glad that I had an opportunity to contribute in the least to a victory that seems big enough for all of us."[5]

. . .

As requested, the *Brooklyn* and other warships now clustered off the coast signaled their casualties—or rather, their lack of them. As at Manila Bay, the losses were astonishingly low: only Chief Ellis killed and a fireman seriously wounded, both on the *Brooklyn*. "It was past all understanding," Goode marveled.[6] Sampson later wrote that many of the Spanish gunners had set their rangefinders for too great a distance, causing their shells to fly over.[7]

Although afloat and intact, Sampson's fleet was also ragged around the edges. The *Brooklyn* had taken twenty hits, most early in the action. The *Texas* had been struck perhaps a dozen times, the Iowa eight or nine, the *Oregon* three, and the *Indiana* twice. Shells intended for the *Brooklyn* had also passed over her, the shrapnel tearing the *Vixen*'s flag. The *Gloucester* was somehow untouched, as was the *New York*.[8] None of the fleet's damage was serious, but bluejackets later delighted in posing beside the battle scars.

Admiral Cervera, in contrast, had lost his entire fleet. Three hundred twenty-three Spaniards were dead or dying, 151 severely wounded—"for there were few slightly wounded," Concas noted.[9] The wounded and more than 1,600 officers and men became prisoners of war. A hundred others had evaded capture and were now making their way slowly back to Santiago afoot from the wrecks of the *María Teresa* and *Oquendo*.[10] (In his history of the war, Captain Chadwick lowered the number of Spanish dead to 264. The number of sailors who eventually reached Santiago he placed at 150.)[11]

. . .

Rescue had begun with the Spanish destroyers and the *Gloucester* as both fleets swept westward and out of view. Wainwright had lowered two boats to pick up survivors from the *Furor*, which then sank off the beach. A third boat headed to the *Plutón*, which was aground in heavy surf that broke over her deck.

"The mortality was not great from our [weapons] fire," a *Gloucester* engineer reported of the *Plutón*, "but large numbers were drowned."[12] Wainwright's boats rushed back and forth like diligent retrievers. Altogether, they picked up forty-five Spaniards from the sea and surf—this out of the two destroyers' combined complement of 128 men.[13]

With nothing more he could do for the destroyers, Wainwright picked up his boats and steamed around the next point. Making for clouds of heavy smoke, the *Gloucester* stood cleared for action in case she found another fight. Instead, the former yacht encountered the nearly adjacent wrecks of the *María Teresa* and the *Oquendo*.

"They were all aflame, and grounded near the beach, and white flags were flying from all parts on the burning vessels," Wainwright recalled. "The Spaniards could be seen crowded on the bows, the point nearest the shore, and many were in the water."[14]

Wainwright again launched his boats. With great effort, his men ran a line from the bow of the *María Teresa* 200 yards to the beach. Wounded men were lowered directly into the boats; uninjured Spaniards climbed out on the line until they could drop into the boats. In three hours, the *Gloucester*'s crew landed 480 officers and men ashore, including the admiral and everyone else alive on the ship.[15] Looking like a drenched tramp, Cervera was then rowed out to the ship.

Wainwright remembered the admiral's kindness toward Hobson. With the crew busy he couldn't "pipe the side," but Wainwright felt privileged to extend his hand and congratulate Cervera for a "heroic fight."[16] Lieutenant Harry Huse, the *Gloucester* executive officer, thought this was "just the right thing to do, and perhaps from that moment dates Admiral Cervera's kindly feeling for this country."[17]

Wainwright said later, "When I saw that gallant gentleman in his wringing wet underclothes, I felt as if I were a culprit." Cervera made a courteous reply and then expressed his concern about the men ashore; according to Wainwright, the admiral "mistrusted Cuban generosity."[18] Although doubtful that the survivors were in danger from insurgent forces, Wainwright sent an armed party ashore for their protection. Huse meanwhile gave Cervera a dry suit of civilian clothes.[19]

The *Gloucester* men also worked to save crewmen still on board the nearby *Oquendo*. The cruiser was aground 300 yards offshore, her bow nearly perpendicular to the beach. She burned so fiercely that her plates glowed and the small-arms ammunition and boilers exploded. Despite the danger, a *Gloucester* boat plucked thirty or forty men from the forecastle, bow, and floating wreckage.[20]

By now the *Indiana* had returned to guard the entrance and assist the *Gloucester*'s relief efforts. She hadn't launched a single boat, however, before the *Resolute* came tearing up to report that a Spanish battleship was about to fall upon the Army transports lying off Siboney and Daiquirí.

Captain Taylor got up steam and called his crew to quarters. The *Indiana* soon spotted the intruder off the coast. Taylor, his executive officer, and his signal officer all agreed she was a Spaniard. The *Indiana* was closing to commence fire at 6,000 yards when the "Spaniard" finally identified herself as the Austrian armored cruiser *Kaiserin und Königin Maria Theresia*. An Austrian lieutenant boarded the *Indiana* in some puzzlement. Informed of the day's events, he blurted, "Then there has been a battle?"[21]

. . .

Farther west along the coast, the *Vizcaya* was aground and burning about 400 yards from shore. Many of her crew were stranded on a submerged sandbar.

From the *Iowa*, Evans saw bullets fired by Cuban insurgents "snipping the water up among them. The sharks, made ravenous by the blood of the wounded, were attacking them from the outside."[22]

The battleship immediately began lowering boats. The *Ericsson* and *Hist*, which Sampson had sent in, soon lowered theirs, too. Evans and others later saluted the fleet's bluejackets for rescuing the Spaniards they had been trying to kill just minutes earlier.

"It was only a short time before the boatloads of dead and wounded began to arrive alongside," Evans recalled, "and then the ghastly, horrible results of our Sunday morning's work were apparent." The *Iowa*'s white quarterdeck was soon stained red. Like the ruined *Oquendo*, she "looked as if she had been used as a slaughter pen."[23]

The battleship picked up 271 officers and men, including 32 wounded, plus 5 bodies. The *Ericsson* rescued about 100 others, and the little *Hist* 166 men.[24]

One of the *Iowa*'s boats also brought out Eulate. The captain had suffered three wounds and wore a bloody handkerchief around his head. Evans had never felt so sorry for anyone. He lowered a chair and received Eulate on deck with full honors. Eulate removed his sword, kissed its hilt, and presented it with a bow to Evans. The *Iowa* skipper instantly returned it, in what Eulate later called "the proudest moment of my life."[25]

Seeing the gesture, Evans wrote, the "brave hearts under the blue shirts appreciated my feelings and they cheered until I was ashamed of myself."[26] He then took Eulate's arm to help him toward his cabin. As they reached the ladder, the Spaniard paused, raised his right hand, and called out over the water.

"Adiós, *Vizcaya*!"

As the words left his lips, "the forward magazine of his late command, as if arranged for the purpose, exploded with magnificent effect."[27] Evans remembered the scene for the rest of his life.[28]

. . .

The *Iowa* began picking up her boats about 1:15 PM[29] after learning from the *Resolute* of the mysterious "Spanish battleship," whose origins were mistakenly confirmed by the *Harvard*. Evans questioned whether such a threat existed "short of the coast of Spain," and if so, why the *Indiana* wasn't "knocking the roof off her." He nonetheless steamed off to investigate.

Upon sighting the stranger, well out to sea, the *Iowa* cleared for action and moved to intercept. The Austrian *Maria* was again slow in identifying herself. Her captain had perhaps wrapped himself in the false security of his red-and-white national flag—"dangerously like" the red-and-gold of Spain, Evans huffed, "for such manoeuvering on that particular day."[30]

(The *Maria Theresia* continued blundering through the fleet until nightfall, seeking Sampson's permission to enter Santiago and evacuate Austrian nationals. The *Brooklyn* finally advised her to remain twenty miles off the coast until daylight. "We will go forty," was the reply.[31] Some of the defenseless Army transports that the cruiser had stampeded didn't stop fleeing until they reached Jamaica.)

The confusion once again resolved, the *Iowa* joined the *Indiana* and *Gloucester* off the harbor entrance. Wainwright landed Cervera and his staff on the *Iowa* and delivered his Spanish prisoners to the *Indiana*, then headed for Siboney with the wounded.

As he had with Eulate, Evans greeted Admiral Cervera with the honors due his rank. The Marine guard was drawn up on the battleship's quarterdeck. The Spaniards stood opposite and the *Iowa* crew looked on from the superstructure and after turrets. Cervera came on board wearing Huse's civilian suit, without a shirt, hat, or shoes. He was nonetheless in Evans' estimation "an admiral every inch of him."

Cervera received the salutes, presentation of arms, and bugle calls, then bowed and offered his hand to Evans. The *Iowa* bluejackets again broke into cheers. "For an instant it seemed to me that Admiral Cervera misunderstood the demonstration"; Evans wrote, "but then he realized its meaning, that it was the tribute of brave men for a brave and gallant foe, and he stood bowing his acknowledgement while the men behind the guns made him understand what they thought of him."[32]

. . .

The *Colón* was beached at Rio Tarquino near the base of a mountain, in "one of the most beautiful spots on the Cuban coast."[33] Surrounded in shades of blue and green, she was sinking at the hands of her own crew. Schley sent Captain Cook to receive the surrender.

"Bravo, Americanos!" Spaniards called down as Cook's boat pulled alongside. "Bravo, Españoles!" the Yankees responded. Most of the cruiser's officers were waiting on deck. "I surrender," Captain Emilio Díaz Moreu told Cook, tears in his eyes. "You are too much for us."[34] Commodore Don José de Paredes y Chacon, Cervera's second-in-command, sobbed bitterly.

As the *Brooklyn* steamed off to confront the *Resolute*'s supposed battleship, Sampson signaled the *Oregon* to take charge of the *Colón* and haul her off the beach. It was past four o'clock before a prize crew reached her. Seawater already stood fifteen feet deep in the engine rooms. The Spanish crew was rounded up and shifted to the *Resolute*. Despite the *Oregon*'s men "working like beavers"[35] to set an anchor and stop the flooding, the *Colón* kept settling.

At 7:30 PM, "she came afloat and came out into deeper water," Captain Chadwick reported. It was soon apparent that the cruiser could never be recovered if she sank there. Brightening the night with a searchlight, the flagship moved in like a tug. With the *New York*'s stem "placed against her quarter, and later, a line being taken from our own bow to hers, the *Colón* was forced ashore."[36] To newspaperman Goode, this maneuver was "the most daring piece of seamanship ever attempted with a modern ship like the costly *New York*."[37]

The effort was in vain, however. At eleven o'clock that night, Lieutenant Eberle wrote, the *Colón* "listed to starboard and turned over on her side, our officers leaving her just in time."[38] Chadwick subsequently reported to Sampson that she sank "in a very moderate depth of water, and it is very probable that she may be saved."[39] Although he wasn't at Rio Tarquino, Concas later wrote that if Sampson, "with a more seamanlike spirit, had ordered the divers to close the valves, he could most certainly have saved" the *Colón*.[40] The admiral, however, reported that the valves had been "treacherously" destroyed after the surrender and couldn't have been closed.[41]

The *Colón* would, in fact, be refloated nearly three months after the scuttling. Following patching and overhauling at Guantanamo, she would start for Norfolk under her own steam, only to be abandoned by the wrecking company in a November gale. She was driven ashore and permanently wrecked on Cat Island in the Bahamas. Chadwick later wrote that the *Colón* should first have been taken by a safer route to Key West. He pointedly added that her abandonment "reflects no credit upon those in charge."[42]

⋅ ⋅ ⋅

Rescue operations continued past sunset. With the prisoners then sent off in the *Resolute*, *Harvard*, and *St. Louis*, the day's second "death-like silence" descended over the exhausted American fleet.[43]

At two o'clock in the morning, the dispatch boat *Dupont* reached Siboney with newsman Goode and Lieutenant Staunton, Sampson's assistant chief of staff. The pair rowed ashore with the text of a cablegram that Staunton had dictated to Buenzle on the *New York*.[44] This official announcement of the victory ran less than a hundred words and bore Sampson's signature. At the last minute and at the suggestion of Schley's flag-lieutenant, also present in the cable shack,

Staunton inserted Ellis' name.[45] A sleepy Army telegrapher then tapped out the message to Washington.

"The fleet under my command offers the nation as a Fourth of July present the whole of Cervera's fleet," it began.[46]

In coming months and years, this phrase would be criticized as a slight to Schley. Sampson's defenders insisted it had only been intended to echo General Sherman's announcement of the fall of Savannah and that the admiral merely signed it. Sampson no doubt "never gave it a thought," Buenzle wrote, "for his mind at the moment was filled with the problem of taking more than a thousand Spanish prisoners on board our ships and transporting them north."[47]

It was the only discordant note at the end of a long and terrible day off Santiago de Cuba. Evans, of all people, was later unexpectedly poetic in praising the *Iowa*'s crew, and by extension every enlisted man and officer in the fleet. "So long as the enemy showed his flag they fought like American seamen"; he reported, "but when the flag came down they were as gentle and tender as American women."[48]

Perhaps in their exhausted silence, men in both fleets also pondered what Lieutenant Huse had realized earlier on the *Gloucester*: Great changes had taken place since breakfast![49]

CHAPTER 20

Aftermath

LATE ON THE NIGHT OF THE BATTLE, the Americans passed along a telegram from Cervera to Governor-General Blanco in Havana. Not much longer than Sampson's cablegram, it began, "In accordance with your Excellency's orders, I went out from Santiago yesterday morning with the whole squadron. . . ."[1]

Unlike his captains, Admiral Sampson had no personal interchange with Cervera. He didn't visit the Spaniard on board the *Iowa*, nor anywhere else later. According to Captain Chadwick, Sampson refrained from "motives of delicacy . . . and wishing to do nothing which might add to the grief of [Cervera's] situation."[2]

The Spanish prisoners were quickly started north on the *St. Louis* and the *Harvard*. In a fatal incident on board the latter, inexperienced soldiers from two volunteer regiments shot and killed five Spaniards in what the guards mistook for a mutiny. The Office of Naval Intelligence later acknowledged that the shooting was "much deplored by our Government and people."[3] Most of the Spanish enlisted men subsequently were imprisoned at Portsmouth, New Hampshire.

Cervera and eighty Spanish officers went to Annapolis, where they spent the balance of war on parole, free to roam the Naval Academy and city. Some attained an unexpected celebrity there. The admiral "walked the streets of Annapolis commanding respect and winning admiration from every one," the *New York Times* reported. He was "all alertness and courtesy to every attention, but always thoughtful, reticent, and almost sorrowful."[4] Once, passing through New York, Cervera was cheered and surrounded by citizens wanting to shake his hand. He appeared "much affected by the genuineness and spontaneity of the feeling manifested."[5]

Flagship *Olympia*, the day after the battle (from Stickney, *War in the Philippines*).

Sunken Spanish gunboat, Cavite (from Stickney, *War in the Philippines*).

USS *Oregon* in wartime gray (from Watterson, *History of the Spanish-American War*).

Flagship *New York* in Cuban waters (from Davis, *The Cuban and Porto Rican Campaigns*).

Spanish cruiser *Vizcaya* (from Graham, *Schley and Santiago*).

Wreck of *Vizcaya*, from a photo (from Goode, *With Sampson*).

Like Cervera, Captain Eulate was formal and reserved at Annapolis, although he brightened for children.[6] The former *Vizcaya* skipper was once heard to lament, "Oh, my beautiful ship!"[7]

. . .

Absent from the battle off Santiago, the *Massachusetts* finally engaged a Spanish warship at midnight on July 5. The decrepit *Reina Mercedes* got under way and steamed into the channel, her mission the reverse of the *Merrimac's*—to block the channel and keep the Americans outside. The *Massachusetts* had the searchlight duty and spotted her. The battleship opened fire, joined by the *Texas*. The *Mercedes* promptly sank, her mission no more successful than Hobson's.[8]

Five and a half days later, on July 11, Sampson's battleships renewed the bombardment of Santiago at the request of General Shafter. The Army signaled the fall of each shell to the fleet.[9] Pressed on all sides, the city fell on July 17. Neither the admiral nor any of his officers was present at the surrender. Although he wired Secretary Long that the slight "may have been a mere oversight," Sampson had clearly exhausted himself and his patience with the Army.

"I do not think the commanding general quite appreciates," Sampson cabled in uncharacteristic pique, "how necessary a part our forces were to the reduction of Santiago and the surrender of its garrison in any case independently of the effect of our shell, which latter was undoubtedly one of the principal causes of the surrender at this time."[10]

. . .

Shafter may not have realized the importance of Sampson's accomplishments off southern Cuba, but most subsequent observers have. The destruction of Cervera's fleet "decided the war," historian David Trask has written.[11] Having reached much the same conclusion, Madrid recalled a naval expedition then steaming to confront Dewey in the Philippines.

Dubbed the Reserve Squadron, the Spanish force comprised the battleship *Pelayo* and armored cruiser *Emperador Carlos V* (both finally, belatedly at sea), two auxiliary cruisers, three destroyers, two armed merchant ships, and two transports with four thousand troops.[12] Having learned from its mistakes, Madrid also sent two colliers.

The squadron had left Spain on June 16 and headed east across the Mediterranean under Vice Admiral Don Manuel de la Cámara y Livermoore. If he possessed greater fighting qualities than Montojo, and if the *Pelayo* and *Carlos V* weren't merely seagoing Potemkin villages, Cámara posed a considerable threat to Dewey's Asiatic Squadron. The military situation created by Cámara's movement, strategist Mahan later wrote, was "to my apprehension the most important and instructive of the war."[13]

Mahan suspected that the expedition was actually an elaborate bluff by Madrid. If so, it was a good one. Cámara had transited the Suez Canal before news from Santiago reached him in the Red Sea. With Cervera destroyed, Madrid feared that Washington might now send a strong force to threaten the largely undefended coasts of Spain. Secretary Long, in fact, was preparing to do just that with a new Eastern Squadron (including the *Oregon* and *Massachusetts*) under Commodore Watson.

With few other options, Madrid ordered Cámara's return to Cartagena on July 7 with "all possible speed."[14] Spain could now only look on as the United States began nibbling at her scattered empire.

The cruiser *Charleston* had already seized Guam, in the Ladrone (Mariana) Islands, on June 20 without firing a shot. An army under General Nelson A. Miles then invaded Puerto Rico in late July, aided by the ubiquitous *Gloucester*. Troops were marching on San Juan when halted by news of a peace settlement. Peace protocols were signed on August 12, with a conference on the future of the Philippines set for Paris later in the year. Events in the islands, however, immediately outstripped diplomacy.

General Wesley Merritt had gradually accumulated an army outside Manila. On August 13, before news of the peace protocols arrived, the city capitulated following a sham battle between Spanish and American troops. The Filipino insurgents who had been cooperating with Dewey were excluded from this face-saving pantomime. Amid the tears of Spanish women and scowls of Spanish soldiers, Dewey's flag-lieutenant, Thomas M. Brumby, raised the *Olympia*'s largest American flag over the city.

"It was a most dramatic scene," Brumby wrote to his sister. "An empire had changed hands."[15]

· · ·

The leader of the Philippines independence movement was young Emilio Aguinaldo y Famy, whom the cutter *McCulloch* had fetched from exile in Hong Kong sixteen days after the battle at Manila Bay. Dewey "put him ashore in Cavite, gave him a great deal of ammunition and a few cannon, and he started to work," newsman Stickney later reported. "His campaign was wonderful and Admiral Dewey was greatly pleased."[16]

Aguinaldo soon declared the Philippines' independence from Spain and moved against the Spaniards across Luzon. Assistant Engineer Beach of the *Bal-*

timore wasn't alone in admiring him. "Under that intrepid and remarkably successful leader," Beach later wrote, "the Filipinos defeated the Spaniards everywhere in the archipelago, except for Manila and Cavite, the two places clearly taken by American forces."[17]

Aguinaldo's government wasn't recognized by the United States, however, and he grew disenchanted with Washington. Other, more powerful interests determined the islands' future. "The truth is I didn't want the Philippines and when they came to us as a gift from the gods, I did not know what to do about them," President McKinley said later.[18] He ultimately decided to keep the islands. In the Treaty of Paris, signed on December 10, the United States assumed permanent control of the Philippines, for which it paid Spain $20 million.

Ignored in the agreement—"they did not belong to the union," in Beach's acid phrase[19]—Aguinaldo and his forces turned against America. Washington had failed to foresee that without careful forethought and planning, peace might quickly spiral into violence.

The Philippine Insurrection was dark, bloody, and divisive, perhaps the ugliest projection of American power until the Vietnam War more than sixty years later. "A more hopeless, gallant, ignorant war was never waged by any people," Beach wrote. "Of course they were conquered. Their strongholds were taken by American troops. Their armies were smashed. Their great leader, Aguinaldo, was captured."[20]

The United States suffered 7,000 casualties before the conflict ended in 1902. The insurgents lost 20,000 killed; ten times as many civilians died from war-related causes.[21] From this terrible base, American-Filipino relations gradually improved over subsequent decades. Small insurgencies were never truly stamped out, however, and a terrorist-connected group survives today in Muslim-dominated Mindanao.

The Philippines became a commonwealth with an elected government in 1935. After invasion and brutal occupation by Japanese troops during World War II, and liberation by American armed forces under Douglas MacArthur, the islands became an independent nation on July 4, 1946.

.   .   .

Under the Paris treaty, the United States also retained Guam and Puerto Rico; both are still American territories today. Even more important, Madrid granted independence to Cuba, as America had demanded at the start of the war.

American relations with the Cubans were better than with the Filipinos, but nonetheless strained. The Platt Amendment, passed by the U.S. Senate in 1901 and written into the Cuban constitution, gave America the right to intervene in

Cuban affairs, a hobble on Cuban autonomy that didn't end until 1934. The United States also gained rights to build military bases on the island. "Thus Cuba had become a client American state," an American historian has written.[22]

An American military government ruled the island until independence in 1902, then again from 1906 to 1909. Cuban administrations before and after were generally the unsavory sort that most Americans wouldn't have voted into office themselves; the 1902–34 era has sometimes been called the Plattist Republic.

Cuban-American relations remained complicated and unbalanced until Fidel Castro overthrew dictator Fulgencio Batista y Zaldivar in 1959—after which they grew infinitely worse. They have yet to improve in any meaningful way.

The United States still maintains a naval base in Cuba, for which it has a permanent lease. From its initial use as a coaling station, and later as an outpost against Cold War communism, Guantanamo Bay assumed a new, prominent custodial role in the twenty-first-century war on terrorism.

. . .

In its ill-advised and avoidable war with America, Spain gained nothing except international sympathy and $20 million. Having lost great swathes of its empire, it then sold off bits of what little remained.

Guam with its fine harbor was the jewel of the Ladrones. With that southernmost island in American hands, Spain sold the rest of the chain to Germany. The Kaiser added these islands to his ill-conceived Pacific empire in New Guinea, the Bismarck Archipelago, and the Marshalls. Madrid also sold him the Caroline and Palau islands. Wilhelm II didn't long retain these strategically valuable groups, however—to the ultimate detriment of the United States.

When Germany went to war in 1914, Great Britain had a naval alliance with Japan. Although not bound to enter the war, Tokyo used the opportunity to attack and seize the German colony at Tsingtao, China. Although later forced by international pressure to relinquish Tsingtao, Japan retained the Spanish-turned-German islands it also had seized early in the war.

In the first days of World War II, the United States quickly lost Guam to nearby Japanese forces. It then fought bitter Pacific campaigns not only to regain it, but to conquer all the island groups that had once belonged to Spain and Germany.

. . .

After the Spanish War, the American Navy studied both what it had done well and what it hadn't. Although seemingly at odds with two smashing victories, the weakness most readily apparent was in gunnery. The accuracy of naval fire was much lower than first advertised.

The poor performance shouldn't have been surprising. Lieutenant Sims had reported from Paris before the war that gun-pointers in several European navies were better trained than the Americans. "We would now be thrashed hands down by an English, French, German, and possibly Russian ship," he concluded.[23] Lieutenant Fiske subsequently observed firsthand at Manila Bay that gunnery skills indeed seemed lacking.

Postwar analyses proved both men correct. Fewer than 2.5 percent of American shells fired in Manila Bay hit a target. In the waters off Santiago, where distances were longer and the targets more maneuverable, the figure was less than 1.3 percent.

The Navy won both battles by filling the skies with metal projectiles, like the clouds of British arrows over Agincourt. Dewey's crews fired almost six thousand shells of all calibers at Manila Bay. Sampson's count approached ten thousand shells off Santiago.[24] Some were bound to hit something. While such figures were discouraging, historian Trask considered it unlikely that "any navy could have done much better at the time."[25]

The Americans at least had held regular gunnery practice. It hardly diminished the performance of such men as Fiske on the *Petrel* or Wainwright on the *Gloucester* to note that they were fortunate in engaging a navy whose gunners had rarely fired their weapons for any reason at all. Except for the *Colón*'s two passing shots at the *Iowa*, Spanish proficiency was atrocious.

One force that clearly could have outperformed the Americans was the Royal Navy. Britain's (and therefore the world's) foremost gunnery expert was Captain Sir Percy Scott, a protégé of Admiral Sir John Arbuthnot "Jacky" Fisher. Scott wanted British gunners "trained to hit the target, and hit it often, at ever greater ranges, in all kinds of weather and sea conditions."[26]

After the Spanish War, Sims learned Scott's gunnery theories and methods from the man himself in Hong Kong. Sims then vigorously advocated their adoption by the American Navy. Like Scott, he backed adoption of a sturdy telescope-sight invented by Fiske, which for years had been grossly underappreciated by Evans and others in his own Navy. Also like Scott, Sims supported "spotting," the task that Fiske had performed aloft on the *Petrel* at Manila Bay.

Supported by Theodore Roosevelt, now the American president, Sims introduced Scott's innovations to the Navy. Elected vice president in 1900, Roosevelt entered the White House after McKinley's assassination the following year. Sims twice circumvented the chain of command, in 1901 and 1902, by writing to the president directly—"a most improper proceeding from the point of view of officialdom," according to Fiske. Roosevelt nonetheless applauded his zeal. Sims was appointed to the new post of Inspector of Target Practice. Sims then brought about "an actual revolution in our methods of target practice, and in the matters of construction of ordnance apparatus as applied to naval gunnery," Fiske wrote years later.[27]

The Navy also learned the value of having sufficient coaling stations, colliers, and supply vessels to support extended operations. At the least, it would never relinquish the valuable base at Guantanamo Bay.

"If ever there was a 'logistics war,' hostilities between Spain and the United States provided the ultimate proving grounds," a Navy supply expert has written.[28] Many lessons learned in that logistics war paid dividends less than twenty years later when America entered the Great War in Europe.

. . .

The Navy tackled its gunnery and logistics problems internally and successfully. The dirty linen over whether Sampson or Schley deserved more credit for the victory at Santiago, however, flapped wildly about in public.

The admiral and the commodore each had supporters and detractors in the ugly public debate that played out largely in the newspapers. A published poem asked, "Was It Sampson or Was It Schley?"[29] As the more colorful and approachable figure, Schley was at first viewed more favorably. A moving picture produced by the Edison Manufacturing Company depicted the commodore on his bridge under fire, while Sampson was shown taking tea with well-to-do ladies.

Tellingly, there was little controversy within the Navy itself. Almost to a man, his captains and officers saluted Sampson for the victory. As Evans stated, "The credit for the blockade, for the arrangement of the ships at the opening of the fight, and for the first movements forward into the fight must of course belong to Admiral Sampson, whose orders we were putting into effect."[30] To Schley's credit, the commodore cabled Secretary Long a week after the battle, "Feel some mortification that the newspaper accounts of July 6th have attributed victory of July 3d almost entirely to me."[31]

The "unhappy controversy," Long wrote, arose from political and partisan interests, and raged more in the press and public discussion than in the Navy. The rancor nonetheless diminished both Sampson and Schley in the public's eyes. Looking back after his term as secretary, Long called it "the only incident of any moment that mars the otherwise universally applauded record of the navy during the Spanish War."[32]

The single controversy aside, the Navy rode an almost unprecedented wave of popularity and support. All of the commanding officers in the two battles and many of their officers and engineers were advanced two to ten numbers on the Navy list, almost ensuring promotion. (Admiral Sampson declined to make any recommendation about Schley, who was advanced six numbers.) More than a few men also gained fame, which they enhanced by writing books and memoirs. Grand public arches and monuments were erected for Dewey, although not for Sampson.

With the value of a robust fleet no longer in question, Congress in 1899 and 1900 authorized six new battleships and six armored cruisers.[33] By the summer of 1901, sixty ships of all types were under construction.[34] After assuming the presidency that fall, Roosevelt declared that none of his policies was more important than naval expansion.[35]

Thanks to this flurry of naval shipbuilding, Roosevelt sent his celebrated "Great White Fleet" of sixteen battleships on a fourteen-month world cruise that began in December 1907—this while the Panama Canal, which Roosevelt also championed, was still under construction. The cruise proved, among other things, that the Atlantic Fleet could deploy into the Pacific to counter any emergency.

Increasingly, the likely source of such a threat seemed to be Japan. The Navy maintained and improved its new bases at Subic Bay, Cavite, and Corregidor, and began a massive expansion of its coaling facility at Pearl Harbor. The outlines of the Navy's stance during World War II thus took shape before World War I had even begun.

. . .

The decisive battles at Manila Bay and Santiago were not the only naval actions of the Spanish War in 1898. Numerous smaller actions were fought in the West Indies. "Most encounters were only skirmishes resulting in few if any casualties," writes a modern naval historian. "A few actions were intense,"[36] such as those involving the *Marblehead* and *Nashville* at Cienfuegos, the *Winslow*, *Wilmington*, and *Hudson* at Cardenas, and the *Saint Paul* at San Juan. But Manila and Santiago were the pivots upon which the war turned.

The Spanish War secured the continued growth of the American Navy. Dewey was the war's greatest naval hero, but Sampson had shouldered the greater burdens. Sampson's success at Santiago nonetheless lacked the sheen of Dewey's at Manila Bay, which goes far in explaining why his enormous contributions are largely overlooked today. The news from the Philippines had come suddenly, unexpectedly. If war can be likened to sports without trivializing its price or effects, Dewey's Asiatic Squadron destroyed, literally, an opponent that was widely (and mistakenly) considered its equal, if not an outright favorite.

Victory for the North Atlantic fleet, in contrast, was not only expected, but perhaps for some too long in arriving. Sampson's success was also dimmed by the subsequent controversy with Schley. Americans prefer their heroes to smile and link arms (as indeed Sampson and Schley had done at celebrations in New York, before controversy forever divided them).[37]

In 1898, Americans also loved the aggressiveness of George Dewey, who providently remained on the far side of the world for more than a year, removed from intense public scrutiny. Then, too, unlike with the colorless Montojo, Americans felt great sympathy for Cervera, Eulate, and their Spaniards, who had met disaster with courage and dignity.

Poor Sampson! In war, as in sports, it's not always easy to appreciate a champion. So it is that George Dewey is remembered a hundred years on, while the name William T. Sampson is largely unrecognized.

History is not always generous.

EPILOGUE

GEORGE DEWEY (1837–1917) was promoted to rear-admiral, commended by Congress, and later advanced to admiral of the navy, a rank created especially for him. He remarried and remained in the Navy well beyond normal retirement age.

DON PATRICIO MONTOJO Y PASARÓN (1839–1917) returned to Spain and was court-martialed for his performance at Manila Bay. Admiral Dewey submitted written testimony in his defense. Briefly imprisoned, Montojo was later absolved but discharged from the navy.

WILLIAM T. SAMPSON (1840–1902) was promoted permanently to rear-admiral and died soon after retiring. "Few men have deserved so well of their country," wrote his former clerk, Fred Buenzle, "and few have received less honor where honor was due."[1]

DON PASCUAL CERVERA Y TOPETE (1839–1909) returned to a cold reception in Spain. Public sentiment warmed after publication of his letters; Cervera was then promoted to vice-admiral and later named a senator. In noting his death at age seventy, the New York Times eulogized him as an "amiable, courteous and really courageous man."

WINFIELD S. SCHLEY (1839–1909) was promoted to rear-admiral, but did not receive prestigious assignments. In 1901, he requested an inquiry into his conduct at Santiago de Cuba. Schley retired before the board issued its findings, which were largely unfavorable to him.

DON VÍCTOR M. CONCAS Y PALAU (1845–1916) returned to Spain and wrote a bitter examination of the political decisions that sent Cervera's fleet to the West Indies. He rose to vice admiral, then became minister of marine and later a state counselor.

Many of Dewey's and Sampson's officers gained promotions and a measure of fame. But the rigors of wartime command compounded the hardships of lifetimes spent at sea; postwar retirements and mortality were consequently high.

CHARLES V. GRIDLEY (1844–98) of the *Olympia* died of his illness before reaching home, at Kobe, Japan, a month after the battle.

EDWARD P. WOOD (1848–99) of the *Petrel* died in Washington a year and a half later, of typhoid fever.

JOHN PHILIP (1840–1900) of the *Texas*, promoted to rear-admiral, died suddenly of heart trouble the following summer.

CHARLES E. CLARK (1843–1922) left the *Oregon* in poor health after Santiago. He recovered, and retired in 1905 as a rear-admiral.

NEHEMIAH M. DYER (1839–1910) of the *Baltimore* likewise lost his health and was sent home after the surrender of Manila. Before leaving the ship, he tearfully apologized to his crew for his harshness.

. . .

Several of the junior officers in the Manila and Santiago campaigns achieved notable success after the war.

RICHMOND P. HOBSON (1870–1937) became such a popular hero that smitten women often asked if they might kiss him. He instead handed out small candies dubbed "kisses." Hobson resigned from the Navy in 1903 and later served four terms in Congress. In 1933, he received the Medal of Honor for his exploits with the *Merrimac*. His seven enlisted crewmen received the medal as well.

BRADLEY ALLEN FISKE (1854–1942) became one of the Navy's great inventors, writers, and reformers. Among his many supporters was Congressman Hobson. Fiske was also an early proponent of air power. He retired a rear-admiral in 1916.

WILLIAM S. SIMS (1858–1936) continued his support of technological advances in the Navy. During World War I, as temporary admiral, he commanded U.S. naval forces in European waters. After the war, he was promoted to admiral on the retired list.

THOMAS M. BRUMBY (1855–99), Dewey's flag-lieutenant at Manila, died in Washington six days after Wood, also of typhoid fever. His nephew FRANK H. BRUMBY (1874–1950), an ensign on the *New York* at Santiago, was commandant of the Fifth Naval District at Norfolk before retiring as an admiral.

FRED J. BUENZLE (1873–1946), with support from President Theodore Roosevelt (1858–1919) and others, successfully sued American businesses that discriminated against uniformed servicemen. He retired a chief yeoman, his hearing permanently affected by gunfire during the Spanish War.

·   ·   ·

ROBLEY D. EVANS (1847–1912) remained on active duty despite decades of injuries. He commanded the Great White Fleet as a rear-admiral, but illness prevented him from completing its historic voyage. His monument in Arlington National Cemetery bears the inscription "The Path of Duty Was the Way to Glory."

DON ANTONIO EULATE Y FERY (1845–1932) was at Admiral Cervera's deathbed eleven years after Santiago. He was a retired vice-admiral at his own death twenty-three years later. His daughter sent word of his passing to Evans' son, retired Captain Franck Taylor Evans of New York City.

Comparative Squadron Strength, Manila Bay

American Squadron, Commodore George Dewey

Ship	Type	Displace-ment (tons)	Main battery	Secondary battery (rapid-fire)	Torpedo tubes	Commanding officer
Olympia	Protected cruiser	5,870	4 8" 10 5"	21	6	Capt. C. V. Gridley
Baltimore	Protected cruiser	4,413	4 8" 6 6"	8	—	Capt. N. M. Dyer
Boston	Protected cruiser	3,000	2 8" 6 6"	6	—	Capt. F. Wildes
Raleigh	Protected cruiser	3,213	1 6" 10 5"	12	2	Capt. J. B. Coghlan
Concord	Gunboat	1,710	6 6"	6	—	Cdr. A. Walker
Petrel	Gunboat	892	4 6"	3	—	Cdr. E. P. Wood
McCulloch[a]	Revenue cutter	1,280	4 3"	—	—	Capt. D. B. Hodgsdon

[a] Not engaged.

Spanish Squadron, Rear-Admiral Don Patricio Montojo y Pasarón

Ship	Type	Displace-ment (tons)	Main battery	Secondary battery (rapid-fire)	Torpedo tubes	Commanding officer
Reina Cristina	Unprotected cruiser	3,520	6 6.2"	13	5	Capt. L. Cadarso
Castilla	Unprotected cruiser	3,260	4 5" 2 4.7"	14	2	Capt. A. Algado
Isla de Cuba	Protected cruiser	1,045	4 4.7"	4	2	Cdr. I. Sidrach
Isla de Luzon	Protected cruiser	1,045	4 4.7"	4	2	Cdr. I. L. Human
Don Antonio de Ulloa	Unprotected cruiser	1,160	4 4.7"	6	—	Cdr. E. Robión
Don Juan de Austria	Unprotected cruiser	1,159	4 4.7"	8	2	Cdr. I. de la Concha
Marqués del Duero	Gunboat	500	1 6.2" 2 4.7"	—	—	Lt. S. M. de Guerra
General Lezo[a,b]	Gunboat	520	2 4.7"	2	1	Lt. R. Benavente
Velasco[a,b]	Unprotected cruiser	1,150	3 5.9"	4	—	—
El Correo[a]	Gunboat	560	3 4.7"	3	1	—
Argos[a]	Survey vessel	508	1 3.5"	—	—	—

[a] Not engaged.
[b] Battery said to be ashore.
Source: Dewey, *Autobiography*

Comparative Fleet Strength, Santiago de Cuba

American Fleet, Rear-Admiral William T. Sampson
(Commodore Winfield S. Schley, Second Squadron)

Ship	Type	Displace-ment (tons)	Main battery	Secondary battery (rapid-fire)	Torpedo tubes	Commanding officer
Texas	Battleship	6,315	2 12" 6 6"	22	6	Capt. J. W. Philip
Indiana	Battleship	10,288	4 13" 8 8"	30	7	Capt. H. C. Taylor
Massachusetts[a]	Battleship	10,288	4 13" 8 8"	30	7	Capt. F. J. Higginson
Oregon	Battleship	10,288	4 13" 8 8"	30	7	Capt. C. E. Clark
Iowa	Battleship	11,340	4 12" 8 8"	32	6	Capt. R. D. Evans
New York	Armored cruiser	8,200	6 8"	24	6	Capt. F. E. Chadwick
Brooklyn	Armored cruiser	9,215	8 8"	28	5	Capt. F. A. Cook
Gloucester	Converted yacht	786	4 6-pdr.	—	—	Lt.-Cdr. R. Wainwright
Hist	Converted yacht	494	1 3-pdr.	4	—	Lt. L. Young
Ericsson	Torpedo boat	120	4 1-pdr.	—	3	Lt. N. R. Usher

[a] Not engaged.

Spanish Fleet, Rear-Admiral Don Pascual Cervera y Topete
(Captain Don Fernando Villaamil Fernandez-Cueto, Destroyer Flotilla)

Ship	Type	Displace-ment (tons)	Main battery	Secondary battery (rapid-fire)	Torpedo tubes	Commanding officer
Cristóbal Colón	Armored cruiser	6,840	0 10" 10 6"	16	5	Capt. E. Díaz Moreu
Infanta María Teresa	Armored cruiser	7,000	2 11" 10 5.5"	14	8	Capt. V. M. Concas y Palau
Almirante Oquendo	Armored cruiser	7,000	2 11" 10 5.5"	16	8	Capt. J. Lazaga
Vizcaya	Armored cruiser	7,000	2 11" 10 5.5"	16	8	Capt. A. Eulate
Plutón	Destroyer	420	2 14-pdr.	4	2	Lt.-Cdr. P. Vázquez
Furor	Destroyer	380	2 14-pdr.	4	2	Lt.-Cdr. D. Carliez
Terror[a]	Destroyer	380	2 14-pdr.	4	2	Lt.-Cdr. J. de la Rocha

[a] Not engaged.

Sources: Goode, *Sampson*; Concas, *Squadron*; *DANFS*; Spanish American War Centennial Web site.

NOTES

Manila and Santiago draws heavily on autobiographies and memoirs from principal commanders. Shorter eyewitness accounts, including several by these same officers, are found in *Century Illustrated Monthly* and the U.S. Naval Institute *Proceedings*. The *Century* series is generally accepted as accurate, but various captains and especially Admiral Sampson may have had help writing the articles published under their names. Correspondents attached to the fleet also supplied valuable insight, although the partisan nature of daily journalism in 1898 should be kept in mind. Some historians question details of Captain Evans' *Sailor's Log*. Could he actually have recognized the rebel commander at Fort Fisher? Did he really retain his revolver in the hospital? "Fighting Bob" was an accomplished raconteur. If perhaps he embellished what hardly needed it, the primary facts are indisputable and remarkable.

Abbreviations Used

ADMC: *Admiral Dewey and the Manila Campaign*, Sargent

AFSW: "The Atlantic Fleet in the Spanish War," Sampson

AGD: *Autobiography of George Dewey*

BA: *Bluejacket: An Autobiography*, Buenzle

DANFS: *Dictionary of American Naval Fighting Ships*

FFY: *Forty-five Years under the Flag*, Schley

FYN: *My Fifty Years in the Navy*, Clark

MRA: *From Midshipman to Rear-Admiral*, Fiske

NAN: *The New American Navy*, Long

NOWS: *Naval Operations of the War with Spain*

NYT: *New York Times*

RUSP: *The Relations of the United States and Spain*, Chadwick

SAC: *The Squadron of Admiral Cervera*, Concas

SL: *A Sailor's Log*, R. Evans

STW: *With Sampson through the War*, Goode

TAS: "The 'Texas' at Santiago," Philip

VAC: *Views of Admiral Cervera*, Cervera

WP: *War in the Philippines and Life and Glorious Deeds of Admiral Dewey*, Stickney

WWS: *The War with Spain in 1898*, Trask

PART ONE: THIRTY-THREE YEARS (1865–98)

Chapter 1: Fort Fisher

1. Description of Fort Fisher and portions of the battle are based on Rod Gragg, *Confederate Goliath: The Battle of Fort Fisher*, 13–15, 110–117, 142–167.
2. Dewey's role in the battle is based on *AGD*, 122–137.
3. Winston Churchill, *Review of Reviews*, in Murat Halstead, *Life and Achievements of Admiral Dewey*, 182.
4. *AGD*, 108.
5. Ibid., 128.
6. Ibid., 133.
7. Evans' role in the battle is based on *SL*, 95–112.
8. Ibid., 41.
9. Ibid., 53, 57–58, 61–62.
10. Ibid., 87.
11. Ibid., 99.
12. Edgar Stanton Maclay, *Reminiscences of the Old Navy*, 311.
13. *SL*, 100.
14. Ibid., 100.
15. *AGD*, 135–136.
16. *SL*, 102.
17. Ibid., 104.
18. *WP*, 149.
19. *SL*, 108–112.

Chapter 2: The Doldrums

1. *SL*, 115.
2. Ibid., 116.
3. Ibid., 118.
4. Ibid., 120.
5. Ibid., 121–122.
6. Ibid., 121.
7. Richard W. Turk, "Robley D. Evans: Master of Pugnacity," in James Bradford, *Admirals of the New Steel Navy*, 73.
8. *AGD*, 142.
9. Ibid., 145.
10. Laurin Healy and Luis Kutner, *The Admiral*, 4.
11. Edward L. Beach Jr., "The U.S. Navy's Remarkable Transformation," *Sea Power*, January 2000, 6.
12. *DANFS*, 3:776.
13. Kenneth J. Hagan, *This People's Navy: The Making of American Sea Power*, 176.
14. *AGD*, 163.
15. Ibid., 150.
16. *SL*, 185–186.
17. *FYN*, 110.
18. *AGD*, 145.
19. *FYN*, 110.
20. *AGD*, 154, 162.
21. Ronald Spector, *Admiral of the New Empire: The Life and Career of George Dewey*, 22.
22. Jack Sweetman, introduction to *FYN*, xv.
23. Alfred T. Mahan, *From Sail to Steam: Recollections of Naval Life*, 197.

Chapter 3: The Commodore

1. *AGD*, 154, 157.
2. Ibid., 157.
3. Michael Blow, *A Ship to Remember: The Maine and the Spanish-American War*, 217.
4. Richard S. West Jr., *Admirals of American Empire: The Combined Story of George Dewey, Alfred Thayer Mahan, Winfield Scott Schley, and William Thomas Sampson*, 136.
5. Theodore Roosevelt, *Theodore Roosevelt: An Autobiography*, 207.
6. *ADMC*, 3.
7. *DANFS*, *The National Cyclopaedia of American Biography*, and other sources.
8. *AGD*, 167.
9. West, *Admirals*, 138.
10. Roosevelt, *Autobiography*, 213.
11. *NAN*, 2:174.
12. G. J. A. O'Toole, *The Spanish War: An American Epic—1898*, 102.
13. *AGD*, 168.
14. Blow, *A Ship to Remember*, 363.
15. Vernon Williams, "George Dewey: Admiral of the Navy," in Bradford's *Admirals*, 222–252.
16. Roosevelt, *Autobiography*, 212.
17. *AGD*, 169.

18. William Draper Lewis, *The Life of Theodore Roosevelt*, 131.

19. *ADMC*, 6.

20. *AGD*, 173–174.

21. Adelbert Dewey, *The Life and Letters of Admiral Dewey*, 411.

22. *WP*, 160–161.

23. *AGD*, 176.

24. Ibid., 170.

25. Roosevelt, *Autobiography*, 208.

26. *ADMC*, 4.

27. *AGD*, 170–172.

28. Healy and Kutner, *Admiral*, 3.

29. Maxwell P. Schoenfeld, *Charles Vernon Gridley: A Naval Career*, 104.

30. Ibid., 76.

31. *AGD*, 175.

32. *ADMC*, 8.

33. *AGD*, 176–177.

34. Maclay, *A History of the United States Navy: From 1775 to 1901*, 148.

35. *AGD*, 178.

Chapter 4: The *Maine*

1. Charles D. Sigsbee, "My Story of the Maine," *Cosmopolitan*, 53 (1912): 376.

2. *NYT*, February 21, 1898.

3. Sigsbee, "Personal Narrative of the 'Maine,'" *Century Illustrated Monthly*, 57 (1898–99). 252.

4. Jack Sweetman, *The U.S. Naval Academy: An Illustrated History*, 67.

5. Sigsbee, "Story," 377.

6. James Rankin Young, *History of Our War with Spain*, 59.

7. *NYT*, February 18, 1898.

8. Sigsbee, "Narrative," 76.

9. Ibid., 377.

10. Sigsbee, "Narrative," 252–254.

11. *NOWS*, 11–14.

12. Sigsbee, "Story," 376.

13. Ibid., 378.

14. Sigsbee, "Narrative," 255.

15. *BA*, 23, 306.

16. *NYT*, February 19, 1898.

17. Sigsbee, "Narrative," 253.

18. Stan Cohen, *Images of the Spanish-American War: April–August 1898*, 41–42.

19. *NYT*, February 22, 1898.

20. *NYT*, February 25, 1898.

21. Ibid.

22. *NYT*, February 26, 1898.

23. Sigsbee, "Narrative," 376.

Chapter 5: Inquiry

1. *AGD*, 139.

2. Peggy and Harold Samuels, Remembering the Maine, 157.

3. *MRA*, 199.

4. *STW*, 5–6.

5. *NYT*, February 19, 1898.

6. H. G. Rickover, *How the Battleship Maine Was Destroyed*, 45.

7. *NYT*, February 23, 1898.

8. *NYT*, September 14, 1881.

9. *NOWS*, 17.

10. *AFSW*, 913.

11. Rickover, *Battleship Maine*, 86.

12. H. W. Wilson, *The Downfall of Spain: Naval History of the Spanish-American War*, 29–37.

13. Rickover, *Battleship Maine*, 91.

14. Ibid., 55.

15. Ibid., 94.

16. Ibid., 4, 75.

17. Mahan, *Sail to Steam*, 3.

18. Sigsbee, "Narrative," 252.

PART TWO: MANILA

Chapter 6: Hong Kong

1. *NOWS*, 65.

2. *DANFS*, 4:296.

3. *WP*, 23–24.

4. *AGD*, 180.

5. Ibid., 186.

6. *ADMC*, 15.

7. *AGD*, 187–192.

8. Ibid., 185.

9. Ibid., 181.

10. Ibid., 182–185.

11. *MRA*, 240.

12. *AGD*, 188.

13. Louis Stanley Young and Henry Davenport Northrop, *Life and Heroic Deeds of*

Admiral Dewey, Including Battles in the Philippines, 146.

14. John Barrett, *Admiral George Dewey: A Sketch of the Man*, 80.
15. Ibid., 82.
16. Spector, *Admiral*, 52.
17. *AGD*, 192.
18. West, *Admirals*, 200.
19. Thomas J. Vivian, *With Dewey at Manila and the Fall of Santiago*, 10.
20. *WP*, 25.
21. *AGD*, 188.
22. *WP*, 25–26.
23. Maclay, *History*, 149.
24. Schoenfeld, *Gridley*, 89.
25. *AGD*, 194.
26. Ibid.
27. *ADMC*, 20.
28. John M. Ellicott, "The Naval Battle of Manila," United States Naval Institute *Proceedings*, 26 (1900): 490.
29. Ellicott, "Under a Gallant Captain at Manila in '98," United States Naval Institute *Proceedings*, 69 (1943): 35.
30. Hagan, *People's Navy*, 214.
31. *RUSP*, 1:156.
32. *New York Herald*, April 22, 1898.
33. Barrett, *Admiral George Dewey*, 68.
34. *ADMC*, 96.
35. Ibid., 20.
36. *AGD*, 190.
37. Spector, *Admiral*, 2.
38. *AGD*, 195.
39. Schoenfeld, *Gridley*, 89.
40. Ellicott, "Naval Battle," 491.
41. George A. Loud, Charles P. Kindleberger, and Joel C. Evans, "The Battle of Manila Bay: The Destruction of the Spanish Fleet Described by Eye-Witnesses," *Century Illustrated Monthly*, 56 (1898): 627.
42. Ibid., 612.
43. Spector, *Admiral*, 51.
44. *MRA*, 241.
45. *AGD*, 195.
46. Vivian, *With Dewey*, 11.
47. *AGD*, 195.
48. Ibid.
49. Ibid., 196.

Chapter 7: Cruisers

1. *DANFS*, 8:87.
2. Arthur Hawkey, *Black Night off Finisterre: The Tragic Tale of an Early British Ironclad*, 47.
3. Robert K. Massie, *Dreadnought: Britain, Germany, and the Coming of the Great War*, xix–xx.
4. Elting E. Morison, *Admiral Sims and the Modern American Navy*, 57.
5. *RUSP*, 1:28.
6. Wilson, *Downfall*, 50.
7. Young and Northrop, *Life*, 140.
8 *ADMC*, 27.
9. *AGD*, 203, 294–295.
10. *ADMC*, 26.
11. Wilson, *Downfall*, 65–69.
12. *AGD*, 203.
13. José Poncet, "Admiral Patricio Montojo y Pasarón," The Spanish-American War Centennial Web site.
14. *ADMC*, 46.
15. *MRA*, 49.
16. Seaton Schroeder, *A Half Century of Naval Service*, 65.

Chapter 8: "God of Victories"

1. *WP*, 48–53.
2. Halstead, *Life*, 336.
3. Chester Hearn, *Admiral David Glasgow Farragut: The Civil War Years*, 50.
4. Ibid., 42.
5. *AGD*, 50.
6. Loud, Kindleberger, and Evans, "Battle," 620.
7. *AGD*, 204.
8. Loud, Kindleberger, and Evans, "Battle," 620.
9. Edward L. Beach Sr., "Manila Bay in 1898," United States Naval Institute *Proceedings*, 46 (1920): 589.
10. Ellicott, "Naval Battle," 495.
11. Schoenfeld, *Gridley*, 91.
12. Ellicott, "Gallant Captain," 36.
13. *WP*, 27–30.
14. *AGD*, 230.

15. Ellicott, "Gallant Captain," 33.
16. Cyrus Townsend Brady, *Under Tops'ls and Tents*, 11–13.
17. Beach Sr. and Jr., *From Annapolis to Scapa Flow: The Autobiography of Edward L. Beach Sr.*, 85–86.
18. *AGD*, 204–205.
19. Ibid., 205.
20. Ellicott, "Naval Battle," 498.
21. Carlos Gilman Calkins, "Historical and Professional Notes on the Naval Campaign of Manila Bay in 1898," United States Naval Institute *Proceedings*, 25 (1899): 269.
22. *ADMC*, 32.
23. A. Dewey, *Life*, 277–282.
24. Calkins, "Notes," 270.
25. *AGD*, 202.
26. Ellicott, "Naval Battle," 498.
27. Ibid.
28. *MRA*, 242.

Chapter 9: Magistrate and Monk

1. *WP*, 35.
2. Ellicott, "Naval Battle," 499.
3. Barrett, *Admiral George Dewey*, 138.
4. *MRA*, 246.
5. *AGD*, 198.
6. Ellicott, "Naval Battle," 493.
7. *AGD*, 199.
8. *ADMC*, 15.
9. Ellicott, "Corregidor in 1898," United States Naval Institute *Proceedings*, 68 (1942): 499.
10. Calkins, "Notes," 291.
11. *AGD*, 208.
12. Ibid., 206.
13. Ibid., 210.
14. Vivian, *With Dewey*, 33.
15. *WP*, 36.
16. Henry Watterson, *History of the Spanish-American War: Embracing a Complete Review of Our Relations with Spain*, 119.
17. *AGD*, 210.
18. Beach, "Manila Bay," 589.
19. Ellicott, "The Defenses of Manila Bay," United States Naval Institute *Proceedings*, 26 (1900): 283.

20. *MRA*, 243.
21. Ibid.
22. Ellicott, "Gallant Captain," 38.
23. Ellicott, "Naval Battle," 500.
24. *MRA*, 245.
25. Calkins, "Notes," 269.
26. Ellicott, "Defenses," 283.
27. Ellicott, "Corregidor," 641.
28. Ellicott, "Gallant Captain," 38.
29. A. Dewey, *Life*, 428.

Chapter 10: "Perfect Line of Battle"

1. Loud, Kindleberger, and Evans, "Battle," 621.
2. Fiske, "Why We Won at Manila," *Century Illustrated Monthly*, 57 (1898–99): 128.
3. Ellicott, "Naval Battle," 501.
4. Beach, "Manila Bay," 590.
5. Beach Sr. and Jr., *From Annapolis*, 88–90.
6. Ellicott, "Gallant Captain," 37.
7. *WP*, 59.
8. *AGD*, 211.
9. Ibid., 302.
10. *MRA*, 250.
11. *WP*, 41.
12. *AGD*, 215.
13. *WP*, 59.
14. *MRA*, 247.
15. *AGD*, 212.
16. Ibid., 213.
17. Fiske, "Why We Won," 129.
18. Ellicott, "Naval Battle," 502.
19. Ibid.
20. Loud, Kindleberger, and Evans, "Battle," 615.
21. *WP*, 42.
22. *AGD*, 214.
23. Young, *History*, 138.
24. Blow, *A Ship to Remember*, 225.
25. *National Cyclopaedia*, 9:7.
26. *AGD*, 214.
27. Loud, Kindleberger, and Evans, "Battle," 621.
28. Fiske, "Why We Won," 129.
29. *WP*, 53.
30. Ibid.
31. Calkins, "Notes," 276–277.

32. *AGD*, 304.
33. Ibid., 221.
34. Ibid., 216–217.
35. *MRA*, 249.
36. Ellicott, "Gallant Captain," 40.
37. Halstead, *Life*, 361.
38. Fiske, "Why We Won," 132.
39. Calkins, "Notes," 275.
40. Ibid., 281.
41. *AGD*, 216.
42. Ibid., 305.
43. Ibid., 305.
44. Loud, Kindleberger, and Evans, "Battle," 625.
45. Beach, "Manila Bay," 593.
46. Ibid.
47. *AGD*, 217.
48. Ibid., 305.
49. Ibid., 305–306.
50. Young and Northrop, *Life*, 145.
51. *AGD*, 218.
52. Ibid.
53. *MRA*, 250–251.
54. *AGD*, 219.
55. Calkins, "Notes," 283.
56. *MRA*, 250.
57. Ellicott, "Gallant Captain," 41.
58. *AGD*, 219.
59. Ellicott, "Naval Battle," 504.
60. Loud, Kindleberger, and Evans, "Battle," 617.
61. Ellicott, "Gallant Captain," 38.
62. Beach Sr. and Jr., *From Annapolis*, 82.
63. Loud, Kindleberger, and Evans, "Battle," 617.
64. *WP*, 54.
65. Schoenfeld, *Gridley*, 94.
66. *AGD*, 306.
67. Ellicott, "Gallant Captain," 44.
68. *AGD*, 221.
69. Ibid.
70. *MRA*, 252–253.
71. *AGD*, 306.
72. Ellicott, "Naval Battle," 510.
73. Ellicott, "Gallant Captain," 44.
74. Ibid.
75. *MRA*, 253.
76. Ibid.

77. *AGD*, 222.
78. Ibid.
79. Ibid., 306–307.
80. Ibid., 224.
81. Ibid., 225.
82. Dion Williams, "The Battle of Manila Bay," United States Naval Institute *Proceedings*, 54 (1928): 351.
83. Loud, Kindleberger, and Evans, "Battle," 623.
84. *AGD*, 217.
85. *MRA*, 257.
86. *AGD*, 232.
87. *MRA*, 263.
88. *ADMC*, 44–45.
89. Ibid., 44.

PART 3: SANTIAGO

Chapter 11: "Fighting Bob"

1. Harold D. Langley, "Winfield Scott Schley: The Confident Commander," in Bradford's *Admirals*, 192.
2. *FFY*, 222.
3. Ibid., 223.
4. *SL*, 276.
5. Ibid., 277.
6. Ibid., 276.
7. Joyce S. Goldberg, *The Baltimore Affair*, ix.
8. Ibid., 91.
9. *SL*, 297.
10. Ibid., 303.
11. Ibid., 311.
12. Goldberg, *Baltimore Affair*, 92.
13. *SL*, 310.
14. Turk, "Robley D. Evans," in Bradford's *Admirals*, 82.
15. *SL*, 312–313.
16. *FFY*, 236.
17. Ibid., 240.
18. Ibid., 258.
19. Ibid., 260.
20. Turk, "Robley D. Evans," in Bradford's *Admirals*, 83.
21. *SL*, 391.
22. Ibid., 396.
23. Ibid.

24. Ibid., 407.

25. Ibid., 409.

26. Ibid., 410.

27. Ibid., 422.

28. Ibid., 423.

29. Ibid., 424.

Chapter 12: Cervera

1. *NAN*, 1:206.

2. Joseph Stringham, *The Story of the U.S.S. "Yosemite" in 1898*, 46.

3. *NAN*, 1:207–208.

4. Roosevelt, *Autobiography*, 216.

5. Ibid., 217.

6. AFSW, 889.

7. *NAN*, 1:203.

8. Ibid., 205.

9. Mahan, *Lessons of the War with Spain and Other Articles*, 98.

10. SAC, 18.

11. Carlo D'Este, *Eisenhower: A Soldier's Life*, 319–320.

12. FFY, 287.

13. Manuel Cervera, Wayne A. Lydick, and Angel L. Cervera, "Admiral D. Pascual Cervera," The Spanish-American War Centennial Web site.

14. Harpur Allen Gosnell, "The Squadron of Admiral Cervera: An Account of the Insurmountable Handicaps Imposed upon a Noble Body of Men," United States Naval Institute *Proceedings*, 54 (1928): 651.

15. VAC, 7.

16. Ibid., 8.

17. Ibid., 9.

18. Ibid., 16.

19. Wilson, *Downfall*, vi.

20. John Alden, *The American Steel Navy: A Photographic History of the U.S. Navy from the Introduction of the Steel Hull in 1883 to the Cruise of the Great White Fleet, 1907–1909*, 149.

21. *NOWS*, 28.

22. SAC, 23.

23. *NAN*, 1:237.

24. VAC, 23.

25. SAC, 29.

26. Ibid., 32.

27. VAC, 24.

28. SAC, 33.

29. Mahan, *Lessons*, 93.

Chapter 13: Battleships

1. Richard Harding Davis, *The Cuban and Porto Rican Campaigns*, 2.

2. STW, 29.

3. *NOWS*, 174.

4. Ibid.

5. STW, 25.

6. SL, 427–428.

7. Ibid., 425–426.

8. *NOWS*, 171.

9. Ibid.

10. Mahan, *Lessons*, 185–186.

11. DANFS, 3:750.

12. Frank M. Bennett, *The Monitor and the Navy Under Steam*, 257.

13. Schroeder, *Half Century*, 211.

14. Wilson, *Downfall*, 43.

15. Ibid., 44.

16. Alden, *American Steel Navy*, 65.

17. Wilson, *Downfall*, 46.

18. Martin Gilbert, *Churchill and America*, 15.

19. *NYT*, September 2, 1898.

20. FYN, 140.

21. S. A. Staunton, "The Naval Campaign of 1898 in the West Indies," *Harper's New Monthly Magazine*, 98 (1899): 176.

22. SL, 428.

23. SAC, 23.

24. *NOWS*, 28.

25. *NAN*, 1:224.

26. Wilson, *Downfall*, 58–60.

27. VAC, 7.

28. Wilson, *Downfall*, 62.

29. VAC, 23–24.

30. *NAN*, 1:86.

31. Frank J. Allston, "A Centennial Perspective: Logistics Comes of Age in the Spanish-American War," *The Navy Supply Corps Newsletter*, part 1 (March/April 1998).

32. Gosnell, "Squadron," 654.

33. *NAN*, 1:225.

34. VAC, 19.

35. *RUSP*, 1:39.

36. *NAN*, 1:225.

37. *VAC*, 23.

38. *SAC*, 42.

39. Allston, "Centennial Perspective," part 1.

40. Mahan, *Lessons*, 75–76.

41. *NAN*, 1:238.

Chapter 14: The Crossing

1. AFSW, 888–889.

2. Ibid., 890.

3. *SL*, 438.

4. AFSW, 891.

5. Staunton, "Naval Campaign," 180.

6. *WWS*, 119.

7. AFSW, 889.

8. Allston, "Centennial Perspective," part 2 (May/June 1998).

9. *SAC*, 43.

10. Mahan, *Lessons*, 79.

11. AFSW, 887.

12. Beach Sr. and Jr., *From Annapolis*, 94, 103.

13. *NOWS*, 361, 363.

14. *FYN*, 146.

15. AFSW, 887.

16. *FYN*, 146.

17. Ibid., 147.

18. *FYN*, 148.

19. Joshua Slocum, "Sailing Alone Around the World," *Century Illustrated Monthly*, 59 (1899): 595.

20. Lino Lopez-Cotarelo, "Capitan de Navio Fernando Villaamil," The Spanish-American War Centennial Web site.

21. *SAC*, 44.

22. Ibid., 45.

23. Gosnell, "Squadron," 653.

24. Ibid.

25. *SAC*, 51.

26. *WWS*, 117.

27. *SAC*, 49.

28. Ibid., 47.

29. Ibid., 47.

30. Ibid., 50–51.

1. AFSW, 894.

2. *SL*, 445.

3. *FFY*, 261–262.

4. *BA*, 312.

5. Ibid., 318.

6. Beach Jr., *The United States Navy, 200 Years*, 365.

7. *NOWS*, 394.

8. *NAN*, 1:213.

9. *WWS*, 116.

10. Bennett, *Monitor*, 316.

11. *STW*, 115.

12. *FFY*, 265.

13. *SL*, 446.

14. *FFY*, 268.

15. *SL*, 447.

16. Ibid.

17. John R. Spears, *Our Navy in the War with Spain*, 227.

18. Ibid., 228.

19. *SL*, 448.

20. Staunton, "Naval Campaign," 181.

21. *WWS*, 124.

22. *NOWS*, 395.

23. Ibid., 397.

24. Mahan, *Lessons*, 177.

25. *NAN*, 1:276.

26. *NOWS*, 399.

27. *SL*, 448.

28. Ibid.

29. *SAC*, 57.

30. *NAN*, 1:276.

31. *FFY*, 265.

32. *SL*, 449.

33. Ibid., 450.

34. Ibid.

35. *FFY*, 282.

36. *SL*, 451.

37. Ibid., 452.

38. *SAC*, 59.

39. *NOWS*, 54.

40. *STW*, 129.

41. Ibid., 143.

42. AFSW, 900.

43. *SL*, 452.

Chapter 15: Cienfuegos

Chapter 16: The *Merrimac*

1. *SAC*, 52–53.
2. *STW*, 136.
3. *SAC*, 54.
4. *VAC*, 9.
5. Staunton, "Naval Campaign," 182.
6. AFSW, 897.
7. *SAC*, 55.
8. *STW*, 136.
9. *SAC*, 57.
10. AFSW, 898.
11. Ibid., 897–898.
12. Ibid., 899.
13. *BA*, 321.
14. *Dictionary of American Biography*, 9 (part 2, supplement 2): 308.
15. Staunton, "Naval Campaign,"183.
16. AFSW, 899.
17. *NOWS*, 437.
18. Richmond Pearson Hobson, *The Sinking of the "Merrimac*," 75.
19. *FFY*, 287.
20. Hobson, *Sinking*, 31.
21. Ibid., 14.
22. Ibid., 15.
23. Ibid., 20.
24. AFSW, 899.
25. *SL*, 453.
26. Hobson, *Sinking*, 76.
27. Ibid., 88.
28. Ibid., 90.
29. Ibid., 92.
30. Ibid., 96.
31. Ibid., 97.
32. Ibid., 102.
33. Ibid., 111–112.
34. Ibid., 120.
35. Ibid., 123.
36. *FYN*, 153.
37. *SL*, 456.
38. AFSW, 900.
39. Russell Doubleday, *A Gunner Aboard the "Yankee": From the Diary of Number Five of the After Port Gun*, 104.

Chapter 17: Blockade

1. Victor Blue, "The Sighting of Cervera's Ships," United States Naval Institute *Proceedings*, 25 (1899): 591.
2. Charles Post, *The Little War of Private Post*, 106.
3. Doubleday, *Gunner*, 164.
4. AFSW, 901.
5. *WWS*, 261.
6. *SL*, 459.
7. *FYN*, 154.
8. *SL*, 460.
9. Harry P. Huse, "On the 'Gloucester' After the Battle," *Century Illustrated Monthly*, 58 (1899): 116.
10. AFSW, 902.
11. Maclay, *Life and Adventures of "Jack" Philip*, 88.
12. *FYN*, 155.
13. *NOWS*, 565.
14. AFSW, 902.
15. Ibid.
16. Alden, *American Steel Navy*, 47.
17. *STW*, 171.
18. *SAC*, 60.
19. *DANFS*, 3:602–603.
20. Mahan, *Lessons*, 181.
21. AFSW, 906.
22. *BA*, 326–327.
23. Mahan, *Lessons*, 182.
24. *STW*, 196–197.
25. *SL*, 454.
26. Richard Wainwright, "The 'Gloucester' at Santiago," *Century Illustrated Monthly*, 58 (1899): 77.
27. AFSW, 903.
28. Sweetman, *Naval Academy*, 138.
29. Wilson, *Downfall*, 71.
30. Mahan, *Lessons*, 184.
31. *WWS*, 141.
32. AFSW, 903.
33. Davis, *Cuban*, 86–89.
34. *STW*, 181.
35. *SAC*, 60.
36. O'Toole, *Spanish War*, 286.
37. AFSW, 900.
38. *BA*, 323–324.

39. AFSW, 906.
40. STW, 189.
41. SAC, 60.
42. WWS, 258.
43. SAC, 62.
44. WWS, 260.
45. SAC, 70.
46. FFY, 297.
47. SL, 461.
48. Schroeder, *Half Century*, 225.

Chapter 18: "God and the Gunners"

1. Evans, "The 'Iowa' at Santiago," *Century Illustrated Monthly*, 58 (1899): 50.
2. NOWS, 535.
3. Evans, "The 'Iowa' at Santiago," 50.
4. Staunton, "Naval Campaign," 185.
5. STW, 194.
6. RUSP, 2:22
7. NOWS, 504.
8. FYN, 156.
9. STW, 191.
10. NOWS, 504.
11. Staunton, "Naval Campaign," 187.
12. SAC, 73.
13. NOWS, 507, 569.
14. SAC, 73.
15. Ibid., 74.
16. Evans, "The 'Iowa' at Santiago," 50.
17. SL, 463.
18. FYN, 156.
19. Schroeder, *Half Century*, 224.
20. Henry C. Taylor, "The 'Indiana' at Santiago," *Century Illustrated Monthly*, 58 (1899): 65.
21. BA, 327.
22. STW, 196.
23. Ibid.
24. AFSW, 907.
25. Edward W. Eberle, "The 'Oregon's' Great Voyage," *Century Illustrated Monthly*, 57 (1898): 105.
26. TAS, 90.
27. Evans, "The 'Iowa' at Santiago," 53.
28. NOWS, 507.
29. Ibid., 511.
30. SAC, 74.

31. SL, 465.
32. FFY, 301.
33. SAC, 74.
34. TAS, 91.
35. Maclay, *History*, 3:363.
36. FFY, 302.
37. NAN, 2:192.
38. TAS, 91.
39. FYN, 157.
40. Ibid.
41. TAS, 91.
42. FYN, 157.
43. RUSP, 2:137.
44. STW, 200.
45. FFY, 302–303.
46. NAN, 2:208.
47. SAC, 74.
48. FYN, 158.
49. AFSW, 911.
50. Maclay, *History*, 3:357.
51. Evans, "The 'Iowa' at Santiago," 53.
52. SAC, 75–76.
53. FFY, 303.
54. NOWS, 508.
55. FYN, 158.
56. TAS, 92.
57. Ibid., 93.
58. RUSP, 2:179.
59. SL, 466.
60. STW, 224.
61. FYN, 158.
62. TAS, 93.
63. RUSP, 2:142.
64. SL, 466.
65. BA, 332.
66. SAC, 83.
67. William Cassard, "Rescuing the Enemy," *Century Illustrated Monthly*, 58 (1899): 117.
68. SAC, 77.
69. Taylor, "The 'Indiana' at Santiago," 68.
70. SL, 467.
71. FYN, 176.
72. Evans, "The 'Iowa' at Santiago," 55.
73. Ibid., 56.
74. Wainwright, "The 'Gloucester' at Santiago," 80.
75. Ibid.
76. Ibid., 81.

77. *NOWS*, 542.

78. Wainwright, "The 'Gloucester' at Santiago," 80.

79. *NOWS*, 591.

80. Ibid., 542.

81. Lopez-Cotarelo, "Villaamil."

82. *SAC*, 77.

83. Evans, "The 'Iowa' at Santiago," 56.

84. *SL*, 467–468.

85. *TAS*, 93.

86. Ibid., 94.

87. *SL*, 467.

88. *BA*, 336.

89. *FFY*, 305.

90. George Edward Graham, *Schley and Santiago*, 419.

91. Ibid., 330.

92. *FFY*, 321.

93. *TAS*, 94.

94. *FYN*, 159.

95. *TAS*, 94.

96. Maclay, *Life*, 104.

97. Ibid., 6.

98. *TAS*, 94.

99. Eberle, "The 'Oregon' at Santiago," *Century Illustrated Monthly*, 58 (1899): 108.

100. *FYN*, 159.

101. Eberle, "The 'Oregon' at Santiago," 110–111.

102. Evans, "The 'Iowa' at Santiago," 57.

103. *BA*, 333–334.

104. AFSW, 907.

105. *TAS*, 94.

106. *FYN*, 159.

107. Ibid.

108. Henry H. Adams, *Witness to Power: The Life of Fleet Admiral William D. Leahy*, 17.

109. *TAS*, 94.

110. *NOWS*, 590, 509, 523.

111. Adams, *Witness*, 17.

112. *BA*, 333.

113. *SL*, 468.

Chapter 19: "Big Enough for All"

1. *NOWS*, 526.

2. *FFY*, 310.

3. *STW*, 205–206.

4. *FFY*, 310.

5. *NOWS*, 519.

6. *STW*, 206.

7. Ibid., 229.

8. *NOWS*, 517–546.

9. *SAC*, 83.

10. Ibid., 102.

11. *RUSP*, 2:176–177.

12. Wainwright, "The 'Gloucester' at Santiago," 82.

13. *NOWS*, 542.

14. Wainwright, "The 'Gloucester' at Santiago," 82.

15. Ibid., 83.

16. Ibid., 84.

17. Huse, "On the 'Gloucester,'" 115.

18. Wainwright, "The 'Gloucester' at Santiago," 83–84.

19. Huse, "On the 'Gloucester,'" 115.

20. Wainwright, "The 'Gloucester' at Santiago," 84.

21. Taylor, "The 'Indiana' at Santiago," 73.

22. Evans, "The 'Iowa' at Santiago," 58.

23. *SL*, 469.

24. *NOWS*, 538–546.

25. *Hero Tales of the American Soldier and Sailor as Told by the Heroes Themselves and Their Comrades: The Story of Our Great Wars*, 265.

26. *SL*, 470.

27. Ibid.

28. Evans, "The 'Iowa' at Santiago," 61.

29. *NOWS*, 554.

30. *SL*, 471–473.

31. Francis A. Cook, "The 'Brooklyn' at Santiago," *Century Illustrated Monthly*, 58 (1899): 100.

32. *SL*, 475–477.

33. *FYN*, 160.

34. Cook, "The 'Brooklyn' at Santiago," 99.

35. Eberle, "The 'Oregon' at Santiago," 110.

36. *NOWS*, 521.

37. *STW*, 210.

38. Eberle, "The 'Oregon' at Santiago," 111.

39. *NOWS*, 521.

40. *SAC*, 80.

41. *NOWS*, 509.

42. *RUSP*, 2:180.

43. *SL*, 475.

44. *BA*, 334.
45. *STW*, 211.
46. *NOWS*, 505.
47. *BA*, 335.
48. *NOWS*, 539.
49. Huse, "On the 'Gloucester,'" 115.

Chapter 20: Aftermath

1. *FFY*, 315.
2. *RUSP*, 2:189.
3. *SAC*, 107.
4. *NYT*, August 21, 1898.
5. *NYT*, August 18, 1898.
6. *NYT*, August 21, 1898.
7. Alden Hatch, *Heroes of Annapolis*, 194.
8. *NOWS*, 557–558.
9. Ibid., 623.
10. Ibid., 628.
11. Trask, "Spanish-American War."
12. Allston, "Centennial Perspective," part 3 (July/August 1998).
13. *WWS*, 277.
14. Allston, "Centennial Perspective," part 3 (July/August 1998).
15. Thomas Mason Brumby, "The Fall of Manila, August 13, 1898," United States Naval Institute *Proceedings*, 86 (1960): 93.
16. *WP*, 278.
17. Beach Sr. and Jr., *From Annapolis*, 96.
18. O'Toole, *Spanish War*, 386.
19. Beach Sr. and Jr., *From Annapolis*, 97.
20. Ibid.
21. O'Toole, *Spanish War*, 395.
22. Ibid., 399.
23. E. Morison, *Admiral Sims*, 50.
24. *RUSP*, 1:203–204; 2:177.
25. *WWS*, 265.
26. Massie, *Dreadnought*, 400.
27. *MRA*, 347.
28. Allston, "Centennial Perspective," part 1 (March/April 1998).
29. *Hero Tales*, 177.
30. *NAN*, 2:201.
31. *FFY*, 335.
32. *NAN*, 2:44–45.
33. Allston, "Centennial Perspective," part 3 (July/August 1998).
34. Hagan, *People's Navy*, 232.
35. James R. Reckner, *Teddy Roosevelt's Great White Fleet*, 4.
36. Mark L. Hayes, "War Plans and Preparations and Their Impact on U.S. Naval Operations in the Spanish-American War," Naval Historical Center Web site.
37. Langley, "Winfield Scott Schley," in Bradford's *Admirals*, 205.

Epilogue

1. *BA*, 337.

Abbot, Willis. *Blue Jackets of '98: A History of the Spanish-American War*. New York, 1904.

Adams, Henry H. *Witness to Power: The Life of Fleet Admiral William D. Leahy*. Annapolis, 1985.

Alden, Carroll, and Ralph Earle. *Makers of Naval Tradition*. New York, 1942.

Alden, John. *The American Steel Navy: A Photographic History of the U.S. Navy from the Introduction of the Steel Hull in 1883 to the Cruise of the Great White Fleet, 1907–1909*. Annapolis, 1989.

Alger, R. A. *The Spanish-American War*. New York, 1901.

Allston, Frank J. "A Centennial Perspective: Logistics Comes of Age in the Spanish-American War." *The Navy Supply Corps Newsletter*, 3 parts (March/April, May/June, and July/August, 1998). http://www.navsup.navy.mil/npi/lintest/index1.htm. Accessed January 8, 2004.

American National Biography. New York, 1999.

Anderson, Bern. *By Sea and By River: The Naval History of the Civil War*. Reprint, New York, 1989.

Barrett, John. *Admiral George Dewey: A Sketch of the Man*. New York, 1899.

Beach, Edward L., Jr. *The United States Navy, 200 Years*. New York, 1986.

———, "The U.S. Navy's Remarkable Transformation." *Sea Power*, January 2000, 5–7.

Beach, Edward L., Sr. "Manila Bay in 1898." United States Naval Institute *Proceedings* 46 (1920), 587–602.

Beach, Edward L. Sr., with Edward L. Beach

Jr. *From Annapolis to Scapa Flow: The Autobiography of Edward L. Beach Sr*. Annapolis, 2003.

Bennett, Frank M. *The Monitor and the Navy Under Steam*. New York, 1900.

Berner, Brad K. *The Spanish-American War: A Historical Dictionary*. Lanham, 1998.

Blow, Michael. *A Ship to Remember: The Maine and the Spanish-American War*. New York, 1992.

Blue, Victor. "The Sighting of Cervera's Ships." United States Naval Institute *Proceedings* 25 (1899): 585–592.

Boatner, Mark. *The Civil War Dictionary*. New York, 1991.

Bradford, James, ed. *Admirals of the New Steel Navy*. Annapolis, 1990.

Brady, Cyrus Townsend. *Under Tops'ls and Tents*. New York, 1901.

Brands, H. W. *T. R.: The Last Romantic*. New York, 1997.

Brown, Joseph H. *The Correspondents' War: Journalists in the Spanish-American War*. New York, 1967.

Brumby, Thomas Mason. "The Fall of Manila, August 13, 1898." United States Naval Institute *Proceedings* 86 (1960): 88–93.

Buenzle, Fred. *Bluejacket: An Autobiography*. Reprint, Annapolis, 1986.

Calkins, Carlos Gilman. "Historical and Professional Notes on the Naval Campaign of Manila Bay in 1898." United States Naval Institute *Proceedings* 25 (1899): 267–321.

Campo, Juan del. "The Peruvian Navy: The XIX Century Maritime Campaigns—

1866: The 'Dos de Mayo' Combat." Maritime Campaigns of the Peruvian Navy. http://members.lycos.co.uk/Juan39/PERUVIAN_MARITIME_CAMPAIGNS.html.

Canney, Donald L. *Lincoln's Navy: The Ships, Men and Organization, 1861–1865.* Annapolis, 1998.

Cassard, William. "Rescuing the Enemy." *Century Illustrated Monthly* 58 (1899): 116–118.

Cassard, William, ed. *The Battleship Indiana and Her Part in the Spanish-American War.* New York, 1898.

Cervera, Manuel, Wayne A. Lydick, and Angel L. Cervera. "Admiral D. Pascual Cervera." The Spanish-American War Centennial Web site. http://spanamwar.com/cervera.htm.

Cervera y Topete, Pascual. *Views of Admiral Cervera Regarding the Spanish Navy in the Late War.* Washington, 1898.

Chadwick, French E. "The 'New York' at Santiago," *Century Illustrated Monthly* 58 (1899): 111–114.

———. *The Relations of the United States and Spain: The Spanish American War.* 2 vols. New York, 1911.

Chatterton, E. Keble. *Battles by Sea.* New York, 1925.

Clark, Charles E. *My Fifty Years in the Navy.* Reprint, Annapolis, 1984.

———. "Note on Cervera's Strategy." *Century Illustrated Monthly* 58 (1899): 103.

Clark, George, et al. *A Short History of the United States Navy.* Philadelphia, 1939.

Cohen, Stan. *Images of the Spanish-American War: April–August 1898.* Missoula, 1997.

Concas y Palau, Víctor M. *The Squadron of Admiral Cervera.* Washington, 1900.

Cook, Francis A. "The 'Brooklyn' at Santiago." *Century Illustrated Monthly* 58 (1899): 95–102.

Cooling, Benjamin Franklin. *USS Olympia: Herald of Empire.* Annapolis, 2000.

Coontz, Robert E. *From the Mississippi to the Sea.* Philadelphia, 1930.

Crawford, Michael J., Mark L. Hayes, and Michael D. Sessions. *The Spanish-American War: Historical Overview and Select Bibliography.* Washington, 1998.

Crucible of Empire: The Spanish-American War. PBS Home Video DVD, 1999.

Davis, Richard Harding. *The Cuban and Porto Rican Campaigns.* New York, 1898.

deKay, James Tertius. *Monitor: The Story of the Legendary Civil War Ironclad and the Man Whose Invention Changed The Course of History.* New York, 1997.

D'Este, Carlo. *Eisenhower: A Soldier's Life.* New York, 2002.

Dewey, Adelbert. *The Life and Letters of Admiral Dewey.* Akron, 1899.

Dewey, George. *Autobiography of George Dewey, Admiral of the Navy.* New York, 1913.

Dictionary of American Biography. New York, 1928–1937.

Dictionary of American Naval Fighting Ships. 8 vols. Washington, 1959–1981.

Dierks, Jack Cameron. *A Leap to Arms: The Cuban Campaign of 1898.* Philadelphia, 1970.

Dieuaide, T. M. "A Historic Scene on the 'Texas.'" *Century Illustrated Monthly* 58 (1899): 118.

Doubleday, Russell. *A Gunner Aboard the "Yankee": From the Diary of Number Five of the After Port Gun.* New York, 1898.

Eberle, Edward W. "The 'Oregon' at Santiago." *Century Illustrated Monthly* 58 (1899): 104–111.

———. "The 'Oregon's' Great Voyage." *Century Illustrated Monthly* 57 (1898): 912–924.

Ellicott, John M. "Corregidor in 1898." United States Naval Institute *Proceedings* 68 (1942): 639–641.

———. "The Defenses of Manila Bay." United States Naval Institute *Proceedings* 26 (1900): 279–285.

———. "Effect of Gun-Fire, Battle of Manila Bay, May 1, 1898." United States Naval Institute *Proceedings* 25 (1899): 323–334.

———. "The Naval Battle of Manila." United States Naval Institute *Proceedings* 26 (1900): 489–512.

———. "Under a Gallant Captain at Manila in '98." United States Naval Institute *Proceedings* 69 (1943): 33–44.

Evans, Robley. "The 'Iowa' at Santiago." *Century Illustrated Monthly* 58 (1899): 50–62.

———. *A Sailor's Log: Recollections of Forty Years of Naval Life.* Reprint, Annapolis, 1994.

Everett, Marshall, ed. *Exciting Experiences in our Wars with Spain and the Filipinos.* Chicago, 1900.

Falk, Edwin A. *Fighting Bob Evans.* New York, 1931.

Feuer, A. B. *The Spanish-American War at Sea: Naval Action in the Atlantic.* Westport, 1995.

Fiske, Bradley. *From Midshipman to Rear-Admiral.* New York, 1919.

———. "Why We Won at Manila." *Century Illustrated Monthly* 57 (1898–99): 127–135.

Fowler, William M., Jr. *Under Two Flags: The American Navy in the Civil War.* New York, 1990.

García, Antonio Carrasco. *En Guerra con Estados Unidos: Cuba 1898.* Madrid, 1998.

Gilbert, Martin. *Churchill and America.* New York, 2005.

Goldberg, Joyce S. *The Baltimore Affair.* Lincoln, 1986.

Goode, W. A. M. *With Sampson through the War.* New York, 1899.

Gosnell, Harpur Allen. "The Squadron of Admiral Cervera: An Account of the Insurmountable Handicaps Imposed upon a Noble Body of Men." United States Naval Institute *Proceedings* 54 (1928): 651–657.

Gragg, Rod. *Confederate Goliath: The Battle of Fort Fisher.* New York, 1992.

Graham, George Edward. *Schley and Santiago.* Chicago, 1902.

Greater America. New York, 1898.

Green, Nathan. *The War with Spain and Story of Spain and Cuba.* Baltimore, 1899.

Hagan, Kenneth J. *This People's Navy: The Making of American Sea Power.* New York, 1991.

Hale, John Richard. "Santiago: Don't Cheer, Boys. Those Poor Devils Are Dying!" In *Fire When Ready, Gridley: Great Naval Stories from Manila Bay to Vietnam,* edited by William Honan, 18–30. New York, 1993.

Halstead, Murat. *Life and Achievements of Admiral Dewey.* Chicago, 1899.

Harris, Richard. "'You May Fire When You Are Ready, Gridley.'" *American History* 32 (1998). http://www.historynet.com/.

Hatch, Alden. *Heroes of Annapolis.* New York, 1945.

Hawkey, Arthur. *Black Night off Finisterre: The Tragic Tale of an Early British Ironclad.* Annapolis, 1999.

Haydock, Michael D. "'This Means War!'" *American History* 32 (1998): 42–53.

Hayes, Mark L. "War Plans and Preparations and Their Impact on U.S. Naval Operations in the Spanish-American War." *Selected Naval Documents: Spanish-American War.* Naval Historical Center, 1998. http://www.history.navy.mil/wars/spanam.htm.

Healy, Laurin and Luis Kutner. *The Admiral.* New York, 1944.

Hearn, Chester. *Admiral David Glasgow Farragut: The Civil War Years.* Annapolis, 1998.

Hero Tales of the American Soldier and Sailor as Told by the Heroes Themselves and Their Comrades: The Story of Our Great Wars. Philadelphia, 1899.

Hobson, Richmond Pearson. *The Sinking of the "Merrimac": A Personal Narrative.* New York, 1899.

Howarth, Stephen. *To Shining Sea: A History of the United States Navy, 1775–1991.* New York, 1991.

Huse, Harry P. "On the 'Gloucester' After the Battle." *Century Illustrated Monthly* 58 (1899): 115–116.

Jane, Fred T., ed. *Jane's All the World's Fighting Ships 1898: A Reprint of the First Annual Issue of All the World's Fighting Ships.* New York, 1969.

Johnson, Robert U., and Clarence C. Buel, eds. *Battles and Leaders of the Civil War.* 4 vols. Reprint, Secaucus, NJ, 1982.

Kennedy, Paul M. *The Rise and Fall of British Naval Mastery.* New York, 1976.

Leutze, James. *A Different Kind of Victory: A Biography of Admiral Thomas C. Hart.* 1985.

Lewis, William Draper. *The Life of Theodore Roosevelt.* New York, 1919.

Log of the U.S. Gunboat Gloucester. Annapolis, 1899.

Long, John D. *The New American Navy.* 2 vols. New York, 1903.

Lopez-Cotarelo, Lino. "Capitan de Navio Fernando Villaamil." The Spanish-American War Centennial Web site. http:// spanamwar .com/Vilamil.htm.

Loud, George A., Charles P. Kindleberger, and Joel C. Evans. "The Battle of Manila Bay: The Destruction of the Spanish Fleet Described by Eye-Witnesses." *Century Illustrated Monthly* 56 (1898): 611–627.

Maclay, Edgar Stanton. *A History of the United States Navy: From 1775 to 1901.* Vol. 3. New York, 1901.

———. *Life and Adventures of "Jack" Philip.* New York, 1900.

———. *Reminiscences of the Old Navy.* New York, 1898.

Mahan, Alfred T. *From Sail to Steam: Recollections of Naval Life.* New York, 1907.

———. *Lessons of the War with Spain and Other Articles.* Boston, 1899.

Massie, Robert K. *Dreadnought: Britain, Germany, and the Coming of the Great War.* New York, 1991.

Matthews, Franklin. *With the Battle Fleet.* New York, 1909.

Morison, Elting E. *Admiral Sims and the Modern American Navy.* Boston, 1942.

Morison, Samuel Eliot. *The Two-Ocean War: A Short History of the United States Navy in the Second World War.* Boston, 1963.

Morris, Jan. *Fisher's Face: Or, Getting to Know the Admiral.* New York, 1995.

Murphy, Ed, as told to Sam M. Hawkins. "We Remembered the *Maine.*" United States Naval Institute *Proceedings* 70 (1944): 55–61.

Musicant, Ivan. *Empire by Default: The Spanish-American War and the Dawn of the American Century.* New York, 1998.

The National Cyclopaedia of American Biography. New York, 1907.

National Park Service Spanish-American War Centennial Web page. http://www.cr .nps.gov/history/1spamwar.htm. Accessed May 1, 1998.

Naval Operations of the War with Spain: Appendix to the Report of the Chief of the Bureau of Navigation, 1898. Washington, 1898.

O'Toole, G. J. A. *The Spanish War: An American Epic—1898.* New York, 1984.

Philip, John W. "The 'Texas' at Santiago." *Century Illustrated Monthly* 58 (1899): 87–94.

Photographic History of the Spanish-American War. Baltimore, 1899.

Poncet, José. "Admiral Patricio Montojo y Pasarón." The Spanish-American War Centennial Web site. http:// spanamwar.com/montojo.htm.

Porter, David Dixon. *Incidents and Anecdotes of the Civil War.* New York, 1885.

Post, Charles. *The Little War of Private Post.* Boston, 1960.

Reckner, James R. *Teddy Roosevelt's Great White Fleet.* Annapolis, 1988.

Rickover, H. G. *How the Battleship Maine Was Destroyed, With a New Foreword by Francis Duncan, Dana M. Wegner, Ib S. Hansen, and Robert S. Price.* Annapolis, 1995.

Robinson, Charles M., III. *Hurricane of Fire: The Union Assault on Fort Fisher.* Annapolis, 1998.

Roosevelt, Theodore. *Theodore Roosevelt: An Autobiography.* New York, 1920.

Russell, Walter. "An Artist with Admiral Sampson's Fleet." *Century Illustrated Monthly* 56 (1898): 573–577.

Sampson, William T. "The Atlantic Fleet in the Spanish War." *Century Illustrated Monthly* 57 (1898–99): 886–913.

Samuels, Peggy and Harold. *Remembering the Maine.* Washington, 1995.Sargent, Nathan. *Admiral Dewey and the Manila Campaign.* Washington, 1947.

Schley, Winfield Scott. *Forty-five Years Under the Flag.* New York, 1904.

Schoenfeld, Maxwell P. *Charles Vernon Gridley: A Naval Career.* Erie, 1983.

Schroeder, Seaton. *A Half Century of Naval Service.* New York, 1922.

Selected Naval Documents: Spanish-American War. Naval Historical Center. http://www.history.navy.mil/docs/spanam/spanam.htm. Accessed June 28, 2003.

Sigsbee, Charles D. "My Story of the Maine." *Cosmopolitan* 53 (1912): 148–383.

———. "Personal Narrative of the 'Maine.'" *Century Illustrated Monthly* 57 (1898–99): 74–97, 241–263, 373–394.

Simpson, Richard Brumby. *The Brumby Family In America: Ancestry and Descendants of Thomas Brumby and Wife Susannah Greening.* n.d.

Slocum, Joshua. "Sailing Alone Around the World." *Century Illustrated Monthly* 59 (1899): 589–595.

The Spanish American War: Birth of a Super Power. History Channel DVD, 2005.

Spanish-American War Centennial Web site. http://www.spanamwar.com/.

Spears, John R. *Our Navy in the War with Spain.* New York, 1898.

Spector, Ronald. *Admiral of the New Empire: The Life and Career of George Dewey.* Baton Rouge, 1974.

Staunton, S. A. "The Naval Campaign of 1898 in the West Indies." *Harper's New Monthly Magazine* 98 (1899): 175–193.

Stickney, Joseph. *War in the Philippines and Life and Glorious Deeds of Admiral Dewey.* Chicago, 1899.

Stringham, Joseph. *The Story of the U.S.S. "Yosemite" in 1898.* Detroit, 1929.

Sullivan, Mark. *Our Times, 1900–1925: The Turn of the Century.* New York, 1926.

Sweetman, Jack. *The U.S. Naval Academy: An Illustrated History.* Annapolis, 1979.

Taylor, Henry C. "The 'Indiana' at Santiago." *Century Illustrated Monthly* 58 (1899): 62–75.

Tisdale, G. *Three Years Behind the Guns: The True Chronicles of a "Diddy-Box."* New York, 1908.

Trask, David. "The Spanish-American War." Hispanic Division, Library of Congress. www.loc.gov/rr/hispanic/1898/trask.html.

———. *The War with Spain in 1898.* New York, 1981.

Unsolved History: Death of the USS Maine. Discovery Channel DVD, 2003.

Vivian, Thomas J., ed. *With Dewey at Manila and the Fall of Santiago.* New York, 1898.

Wainwright, Richard. "The 'Gloucester' at Santiago." *Century Illustrated Monthly* 58 (1899): 77–86.

Warner, Oliver. *The British Navy: A Concise History.* London, 1975.

"War Time Snap Shots." *Munsey's* 19, no. 6 (1898): 746–760.

Watterson, Henry. *History of the Spanish-American War: Embracing a Complete Review of Our Relations with Spain.* Cleveland, 1898.

Webster's American Military Biographies. Springfield, 1978.

West, Richard S., Jr. *Admirals of American Empire: The Combined Story of George Dewey, Alfred Thayer Mahan, Winfield Scott Schley, and William Thomas Sampson.* Indianapolis, 1948.

White, W. L. *They Were Expendable.* New York, 1942.

Who Was Who in America: Vol. 1, 1897–1942. Chicago, 1942.

Williams, Dion. "The Battle of Manila Bay." United States Naval Institute *Proceedings* 54 (1928): 345–359.

Williams, Henry L. *Taking Manila or In the Philippines with Dewey: Giving the Life and Exploits of Admiral George Dewey, U.S.N.* New York, 1899.

Wilson, H. W. *The Downfall of Spain: Naval History of the Spanish-American War.* Reprint, New York, 1971.

Wilson, Rufus R. "Our Fighting Navy." *Munsey's* 19, no. 4 (1898): 485–503.

Wood, E. P. "The Battle of Manila Bay." *Century Illustrated Monthly* 57 (1898–99): 957–958.

The World of 1898: The Spanish-American War. Hispanic Division, Library of Congress. http://www.loc.gov/rr/hispanic/1898/.

Young, James, and J. Hampton Moore. *Reminiscences and Thrilling Stories of the War by Returned Heroes.* Philadelphia, 1899.

Young, James Rankin. *History of Our War with Spain.* New York, 1898.

Young, Louis Stanley, and Henry Davenport Northrop. *Life and Heroic Deeds of Admiral Dewey, Including Battles in the Philippines.* Toronto, 1899.

INDEX

ABOUT THE AUTHOR

JIM LEEKE attended journalism school at Ohio State University after serving in the U.S. Navy during the Vietnam War. He wrote for newspapers and national magazines as a police reporter, lifestyle columnist, sportswriter, and business and technology writer. Now active in communications and advertising, he is the author or editor of several books.